792·1

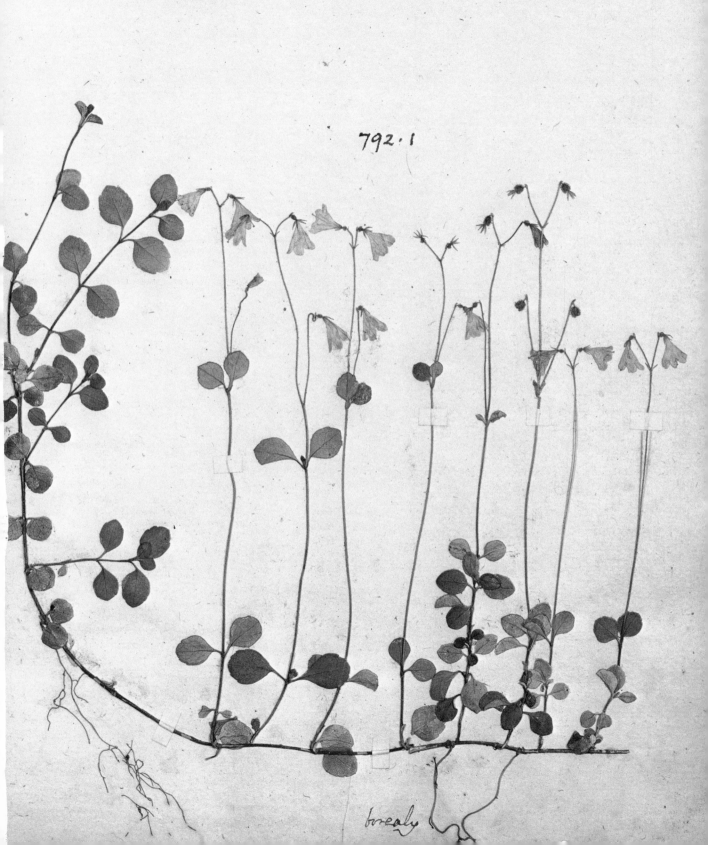

borealis

The Compleat Naturalist

A Life of Linnaeus

Wilfrid Blunt

with the assistance of William T. Stearn

A Studio Book
The Viking Press, New York

Published in 1971 by The Viking Press Inc.
625 Madison Avenue, New York, NY 10022

SBN: 670–23396–x
Library of Congress catalog card number: 78–147393

Type set in Poliphilus by Jarrold & Sons Limited, Norwich, England
Color and jacket origination and printing by Westerham Press, Westerham, England
Book printed and bound by Jarrold & Sons Limited, Norwich, England

This book was designed and produced by
George Rainbird Limited
Marble Arch House, 44 Edgware Road
London W2

House editor: Caroline Lightburn
Designer: Pauline Harrison
Indexer: Sandra Raphael

To Ruth

CONTENTS

COLOR PLATES

ACKNOWLEDGMENTS: I acknowledge with deep gratitude the great help I have received in the writing of this book from two of the leading authorities on Linnaeus: Dr William T. Stearn of the Natural History Museum, London, and Dr Carl-Otto von Sydow, editor of the Swedish Linné Society's Journal. Both were kind enough to read my typescript with the greatest thoroughness and to provide me with invaluable criticism and suggestions. Dr von Sydow was also so good as to act as my cicerone when I was in Uppsala, and to extend the same courtesy to our photographer, Mr G. H. Roberton, on a later occasion. To Dr Stearn, who has made a lifelong study of Linnaeus, I am further indebted for an Appendix on Linnaean classification, nomenclature, and method, a list of the principal works of Linnaeus published during his lifetime, and a list of some sources of further information. I count it a great honour that he agreed to sacrifice part of a much needed holiday in order to make the time necessary for this task. My book is primarily for the general reader, but Dr Stearn's contribution will make it of value to the specialist.

I am also very indebted to many friends who have assisted me in various ways. To Mr G. H. Roberton for his skilful photography both in this country and in Sweden; to Lady Wenham, Dr Mary Clarke, Mrs Robert Cohen, and Mr Paul Britten Austen for help with translation from the Swedish, and to Mr Francis Thompson for elucidating some Latin; to Mr Hugh Pagan for advice on numismatical matters; to Miss Sandra Raphael, Miss Alice Coats, Mrs Arthur Harrison and Dr Frans Stafleu for stimulating suggestions and other kindnesses; to Mr Adam Helms for help and hospitality when I visited Stockholm and for the generous gift of a number of most useful books; to the staff of the Bibliothèque Centrale of the Muséum National d'Histoire Naturelle, Paris, for allowing me to study the *vélins* in their collection and to reproduce two of them; to Mary, Duchess of Roxburghe, for permission to reproduce the drawing of Linnaeus in her possession; to my patient and efficient typist, Miss Charmian Young; to Mrs Caroline Lightburn and the staff of George Rainbird Limited for all the care they have taken over the production of this book; and last but far from least to Mr T. O'Grady and Mr Gavin Bridson of the Linnean Society, London, who did so much to facilitate my work in the Library of the Society and the collections which the English were so fortunate as to purchase from Linnaeus's widow in 1784.

Prologue

very so-called 'educated' man and woman can be expected to have at least some idea of what Rembrandt and Michelangelo, Bach and Chopin, stand for: what they contributed to the enrichment of the civilized world; for these men created in media which are internationally comprehensible. But those who create in *words* are, inevitably, severely handicapped. 'Traduttore, traditore' – 'translators are traitors' – as the Italians say. The poets suffer most, the scientists perhaps least, by translation; but all suffer to some degree in the process. Moreover there remains a wealth of essential material which is still available only in the language in which it was written, and in this respect the scientists fare very badly.

But this is not the only handicap under which scientists of whatever nationality suffer. An Englishman (if I may take an Englishman as an example) who considered himself educated would feel embarrassed at having to admit that he had never read *Lycidas*, never been to the National Gallery, never heard a Mozart opera; yet probably he would be totally unashamed to confess that he knew nothing of logarithms, relativity, or Boyle's law. In fact, many 'cultured' people actually pride themselves on their ignorance of science, while many a young scientist takes an equal pride in being a philistine and is often quite unaware that he cannot express himself coherently and grammatically in his own language. This gulf which yawns between the sciences and the arts is much to be deplored.

Where we in England are concerned, Linnaeus suffers under every conceivable disadvantage. He was a scientist. He wrote in Swedish or in a Latin which was vivid and personal rather than grammatical – often, indeed, in a mixture of the two. Relatively little of what he wrote has been translated into English or French, and not a great deal even into German; and what has been translated is for the most part far from easy to obtain. It is therefore hardly surprising that today few people outside Sweden know much, even anything at all, of the man or his work. Ask a reasonably well read Englishman what he can tell you about Linnaeus, and you are unlikely to receive a very informative answer. Ask when he lived, and you may well be told that it was 'in classical times', the Latin termination of his name being misleading; ask his nationality, and the chances are that the answer will be wrong. Many people will, however, probably associate his name with plants, and possibly even with the classifica- tion and naming of plants. But you will be lucky if you get more information than that.

It is, indeed, far more surprising that there was not always this ignorance. But in England in the early part of the nineteenth century every child was made to improve his or her mind (in other words, kill time) by collecting, painting and pressing wild flowers and identifying them according to the Linnaean system. Books for the young praised the great Swede who had arranged and named the flowers, and some, such as Mrs Jane Marcet's *Conversations on Botany* (1817), were in dialogue form:

EDWARD: You said something about a very industrious man, who had examined a great many plants.
MOTHER: Yes: – we were speaking of Linnaeus, a celebrated botanist, who did so much to increase our knowledge of the works of nature, that he was called the Father of Natural History. . . .
EDWARD: When I have examined a plant, mamma, how am I to find out its name?
MOTHER: Before you can do so, you must learn how the vegetables that are known have been arranged; and I will explain to you, as clearly as I can, the system of Linnaeus. . . .

And this she proceeds to do, sparing poor Edward nothing.

But today, when industrial development kills wild flowers and television kills time, and when the Linnaean sexual system has been superseded, Linnaeus himself is largely forgotten – except in Sweden, where he is considered as a great national figure, as important as is Shakespeare to the English, Dante to the Italians, or Goethe to the Germans. To the Swedes, Linnaeus appears as a benign old naturalist, married to a commonplace and domineering wife, for ever walking through flowery meadows with a band of devoted pupils at his side, with larks ever singing and the sun ever shining. To the non-Swede who chances to be acquainted with him he presents a very different picture, probably that of a tiresome, dryasdust, conceited old pedant – 'nothing more than a living lexicon of self-invented words' (as one of his German contemporaries called him) – who played havoc with plant names.

Neither image is wholly false; but neither is complete, and the truth is an amalgam of the two. The greatness of Linnaeus cannot be denied. He found the three kingdoms of Nature in chaos, and performed the almost superhuman task of producing order out of that chaos – even though that order is not very attractive to the layman. He was not, however, just a dry scientist who believed that an animal was of no interest until it had been pickled in alcohol, a flower of no significance until it was dead and buried in the cupboards of a herbarium; he adored Nature in all her manifestations; and above all, he never lost his sense of wonder.

Sachs, in his *History of Botany*, wrote of Linnaeus that he was content 'to know all his species exactly by name' and 'never made a single important discovery throwing light on the nature of the vegetable or animal kingdom'. The judgment is severe, but it is not unjust. However, what Linnaeus elected to do he did supremely well, and the task that he set himself was admirably described by Dr William T. Stearn when lecturing at Wisconsin in 1969:

For better or for worse, Linnaeus dominated eighteenth-century biology. This was not because he was a great original thinker; it was because he was a tremendously hard worker who devoted his time and his talents to an immense task which met the needs of the age – and the essential need of the age was the encyclopaedia. In the eighteenth century the great encyclopaedias of the world came into existence. . . .

This was no coincidence, he continued; it was the consequence of the accumulation of facts and ideas which stemmed from the overseas expansion of the British, Dutch and French peoples, and also of the creative activity of the seventeenth century:

Linnaeus was really the great biological encyclopaedist. The preparation of an encyclopaedia calls for qualities which he possessed in very great measure: extensive though not necessarily profound scholarship; clear and concise expression; great industry and mental tenacity; the gift for methodical organization and the co-ordination of facts, and the awareness of their relevance to current ideas. . . . It was the good fortune of Linnaeus that his talents so precisely met the needs of the times, and it was the good fortune of other people that they had Linnaeus to do this job for them. His essential task was to provide the means of identifying and naming all the organisms then known. . . . Linnaeus lived at a time, possibly the very last time, when a person of his capability could accomplish it single-handed – provided that he was willing to pay the price.

The price for Linnaeus was a heavy one; he paid it, and the world has been in his debt ever since.

PART I

The years of struggle
1707–1735

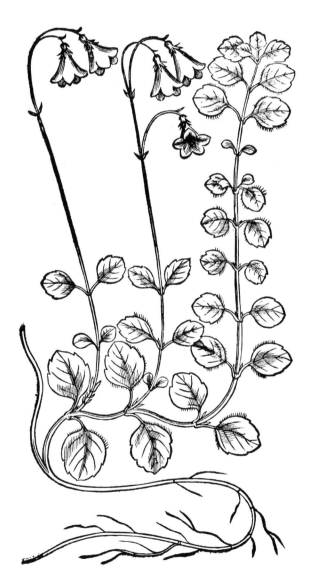

First Swedish illustration of *Linnaea borealis,* a woodcut published by Rudbeck the Younger in *Acta Literaria Sueciae,* 1720–4.

I.

Childhood

Linnaeus's father.

The year 1707 saw the young and valiant King of Sweden, Karl XII, at the height of his popularity. In the Great Northern War, in which not long after his accession to the throne in 1697 he had recklessly plunged his country, his armies had defeated the Danes, the Russians, the Saxons and the Poles; no one could then have predicted his crushing defeat at the hands of the Russians at Poltava two years later, or that within little more than a decade the Swedish Empire would have been overrun and Sweden have ceased to be a great Power. It was therefore very natural that when, on 23 May (New Style) 1707, Christina Linnaea, the young wife of a Lutheran curate, Nils Ingemarsson Linnaeus, gave birth to her first child, the boy should have been christened Carl.

Nils Linnaeus was a Smålander, and the natives of this southern province of Sweden were renowned for their energy and their tenacity. 'Put a Smålander on a rock,' ran the saying, 'and he will feed himself; give him a goat and he will grow rich.' Nils's ancestors had been peasants, priests, or farmers for many generations. His father, Ingemar Bengtsson, was a well-to-do farmer, and, as was the custom in Sweden, Nils had at first borne a patronymic, Ingemarsson;[1] but on enrolling at the University he had been obliged to add a surname of his choice. Now there had stood for many years, at Jonsboda on land belonging to his family, a large and venerated lime tree (Swedish *lind*, Latin *tilia*), and tradition had it that this tree had provided the names Lindelius and Tiliander, 'Lime-man', for other members of the family in similar circumstances. Nils followed the example set by his predecessors, choosing *lin* (the Smålandic form of *lind*) to create the name 'Linnaeus'.

In 1704 Nils Linnaeus was ordained priest and in due course appointed Curate of Stenbrohult, a village in Småland on the shores of Lake Möckeln. At first he lodged at the Rectory, where he was soon to be found courting the Rector's eldest daughter, Christina Brodersonia, and in March 1706 the two were married; the bridegroom was thirty-one, the bride seventeen. A year later, in the Curate's house – a simple, turf-roofed homestead which Nils had just built at Råshult about a mile from the Rectory – their first son, Carl, was born, after a difficult delivery, 'at one o'clock in the morning [wrote Linnaeus later], between the month of growing and the month of flowering, when the cuckoo was announcing the imminence of summer, when the trees were in leaf but

[1] Son of Ingemar; cf. Johnson, Fitz-herbert, Macdonald, etc.

14

before the season of blossom'. His hair in infancy was said to have been 'as white as snow, but it became brown when he grew up'.

Christina had hoped for a girl, but her husband's undisguised happiness at having a son and heir soon overcame her disappointment. She was later to have three daughters, and a further son, Samuel, who ultimately succeeded his father as Rector of Stenbrohult and who was the author of a 'short but reliable' manual on bee-keeping, earning him the nickname of 'Bi-kung' – the King of the Bees.

A year after the birth of his first grandson, Pastor Brodersonius died. And so, almost immediately, did his chosen successor, with the happy result for Nils that, having pulled the right strings in the right quarters, he found himself appointed Rector of Stenbrohult. In June 1709 the young couple and their two-year-old son moved from the Curate's house into the less cramped quarters of the Rectory.

Samuel Linnaeus, writing many years later, has left us some particulars of his father and mother and of their early days in the Rectory; since he was not born until 1718 he was of course dependent for his information upon what he learned from others. Carl too, in his Autobiography,[1] supplements the picture. Nils was, it seems, a simple, upright man who knew little of the wickedness of the world and shunned its vanities. He was conscientious in his parish duties, thrifty, and so tenderhearted that 'if he saw anyone suffering or in want he would burst into tears'. He was also, perhaps, what today would be called a 'hearty' clergyman, 'always friendly, jolly, happy and extremely amusing'. A portrait of him in old age suggests that he can never have been other than very plain, his mouth, in particular, being of almost simian ugliness; yet Samuel describes him as 'good looking, with brown curly hair, a high forehead, and brown eyes', adding that he spoke clearly in spite of having lost all his teeth.

Christina Linnaea was an intelligent and vivacious girl, energetic, a good housekeeper, and very devout. We see her in a portrait in which she is wearing her wedding-dress, but which may perhaps have been painted at a rather later date. She looks attractive (but who would not, in such a dress?), though the rather naive painter, who had little understanding of the laws of perspective, has failed sadly over the drawing of the nose.

Nils and Christina lived contentedly together until her death in 1733; thus Carl's childhood was a happy one, and it was always with pleasure that he returned home. Stenbrohult must certainly in those days have been a pleasant spot; Carl calls it

Linnaeus's mother.

> one of the most beautiful places in all Sweden, for it lies on the shores of the big lake of Möckeln, on an inlet more than a mile and a half long....[2] The church is surrounded on all sides by flat arable land, except to the west where it is lapped by the clear waters of the lake. Away to the south are lovely beech woods, to the north the high mountain ridge of Taxås, and westwards across the lake the Möckeln promontory. To the north-east are pine woods, to the south-east charming meadows and leafy trees....

These meadows, he thought, were more like gardens, so full were they of flowers: 'When one sits there in the summer and listens to the cuckoo and the song of all the other birds, the chirping and humming of the insects; when one looks at the shining, gaily coloured flowers; one is completely stunned by the incredible resourcefulness of the Creator.'

[1] There are a number of autobiographical fragments, to which I refer collectively as his Autobiography. In them he writes throughout in the third person, referring to himself as 'Linnaeus' and so achieving a nice objectivity.

[2] Linnaeus writes 'a quarter of a mile'. The Swedish mile is rather more than six and a half English miles, and for convenience I give distances throughout in English miles.

15

Råshult, Linnaeus's birthplace, engraved by Akrell.

Nils Linnaeus was a keen horticulturist and something of a botanist. He had done what he could to make a garden during his short spell at Råshult; it contained a number of uncommon plants, some brought from Germany by an uncle, Sven Tiliander, in whose house Nils had spent a part of his boyhood. Christina, who till now had hardly seen a garden, was deeply impressed. A curious and slightly absurd feature of the design, apparently one that was then fashionable, was a raised circular bed, an imitation of a dining-room table, which was planted with flowers to represent the dishes and surrounded by shrubs which stood for the guests. In view of Carl's future career, it is perhaps significant that Christina, during her first pregnancy, would sit for hours at a time admiring this floral *tour de force*. But Stenbrohult afforded Nils greater scope; he transferred many plants there from Råshult, and before long the Rectory garden was acknowledged the finest in the neighbourhood.

'As soon as the child was old enough to take notice of anything [wrote Samuel], his father . . . began to decorate his cradle with flowers, and a year later he would often carry his little son out into the garden or to the meadows, put him down on the ground and give him a flower to play with.' Whenever he was tetchy or tiresome, a flower put in his hand immediately made him reasonable. In the words of Mrs Florence Caddy, 'Carl was nursed in beauty, fragrance and pure delights. His toys were flowers.'[1]

When the boy was about four years old his father took him and some of his friends on a picnic to the Möckeln promontory. It was a lovely summer's day, and towards evening the Rector, to improve the shining hour and entertain his guests, delivered himself of a little botanical homily, 'explaining how every flower had its name, adding various interesting facts about plant life and showing them the roots of succisa [scabious], tormentilla, orchises and other plants'. The child was fascinated, and from that moment was always pestering his father to tell him the names of the wild flowers that he brought home from the meadows. 'But he was still only a child, and often forgot them; so one day his father spoke sharply,

[1] *Through the Fields with Linnaeus* (2 vols, Longmans, 1887) – one of several sentimental biographies of charming absurdity which have been overlooked or scorned by recent biographers of Linnaeus.

16

saying that he would not tell him any more names if he continued to forget them. After that, the boy gave his whole mind to remembering them, so that he might not be deprived of his greatest pleasure.' This passion for *names* remained with him till the end of his life.

'Whenever the father planted and cultivated the gay parterre,' wrote Stoever in his biography of Linnaeus, 'he was sure of finding CHARLEY skipping by his side, to share the pleasant toil, and to water the beds'; he was, as Dr Boerman put it, very much 'Daddy's boy'. Then he was given his own little snippet of garden to tend, and finally a more substantial patch – one large enough to be dignified with the name of 'Carl's garden'. He had, as he later said, acquired 'an unquenchable love of flowers' along with his mother's milk; already he saw where his destiny was leading him.

When the boy was seven it was considered time for him to have a tutor. The choice fell upon Johan Telander, the twenty-year-old son of a local yeoman; 'a morose and ill-tempered man [Carl wrote] who was better calculated to extinguish a child's talents than to develop them'. Carl, it was generally agreed, was intelligent enough; but it proved difficult to keep him to his books when tuition was so disagreeable and when the garden perpetually called, and harder still when his father, eager to foster this interest in natural history, took his side. Christina supported Johan, and it was probably as a result of their combined pleading that, two years later, Nils agreed that Carl should be sent to the Lower Grammar School at Växjö, a country town about thirty miles to the north-east of Stenbrohult.

The boy was unhappy at school, where 'brutal teachers used such brutal methods to give their pupils a taste for learning, that it made the boys' hair stand

Växjö in 1708, from *Suecica Antiqua et Hodierna*.

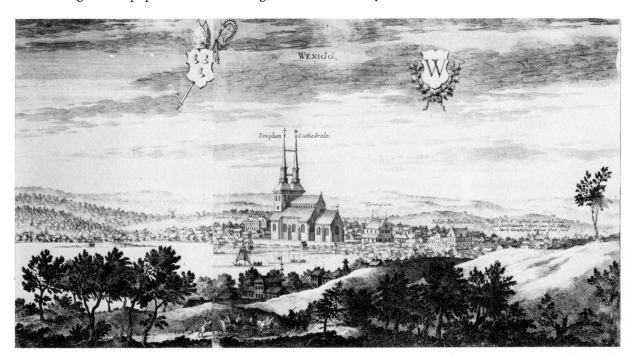

on end'. Things improved, however, when he came into contact with an intelligent and sympathetic young High School scholar, Gabriel Höök, who was in fact many years later to become his brother-in-law. But even Höök could not persuade Carl to work, and when, as he moved up the school, he came to have more freedom, he was always playing truant in the summer months and going off into the countryside to look for plants. The boys nicknamed him 'the little botanist'.

By the age of fifteen Carl had, however, succeeded in reaching the top form, which was taught by the Rector (headmaster) of the Lower School, Daniel Lannerus. This man was a close friend of Nils Linnaeus, and something of a botanist. He gave Carl the run of his garden and the privilege of his company out of school; he also introduced him to Dr Johan Rothman, the State Doctor for the province and one of the senior masters at the Växjö Gymnasium (High School), where he lectured on logic and physics.

Rothman took an immediate fancy to Carl and was to play a vital role in the boy's development; he not only furthered his botanical studies (all doctors at that time were botanists too), he also aroused his interest in medicine. In the holidays Carl was soon amusing himself by 'playing the doctor' to his brother and sisters, taking their pulses or making a lancet out of wood and pretending to bleed them. He had managed to get hold of one or two old-fashioned botanical and zoological books from his father's library, and with their help he concocted herbal mixtures to treat their imaginary ailments. Now for the first time he began to wonder whether he might not one day make a career in medicine.

In 1724 he passed, though with no great distinction, into the Gymnasium. Here the curriculum was designed to fit the needs of boys intended for the priesthood; the emphasis was upon Greek, Hebrew, theology, metaphysics and oratory – subjects in which he was little gifted and even less interested. Apparently he shone at physics and mathematics (though to judge from his later travel books, simple addition was never his forte), and became fluent in spoken Latin if never very sound on the syntax. This worried him little for, as he used to say, he 'would rather receive three cuffs from Priscian [the Latin grammarian] than one from Nature'. But his parents, and his pious mother in particular, had always taken it for granted that he would be ordained; it was the old, familiar story: the tacit assumption of parents that a boy would be willing and eager to follow in his father's footsteps. Carl, however, was becoming each day more convinced that this was impossible for him.

The months passed. He was now nineteen and within a year of exchanging the Gymnasium for a university; but still he lacked the courage to tell his parents what he knew must hurt and disappoint them. However, the matter was soon to settle itself. Nils, who had recently been ill, decided to visit Växjö on a double errand: to consult Dr Rothman professionally, and to learn at first hand how his son was getting on. We do not know what Rothman's medical verdict was, but what Nils heard from his son's teachers came as a shock; they unanimously declared that he would never become a scholar. He was fitted only for manual work. He might make a carpenter or a tailor perhaps, but never a priest.

Carl realized what a terrible blow this news must be to his father, who had

18

Corona Solis, foliis amplioribus laciniatis. Inst. rei Herb. 490

N. Reb. p.

Rudbeckia laciniata. (*Lin:*)

América sept:

scraped and saved to give his elder son a good education and who would now feel that all his sacrifices had been in vain. Rothman, however, thought otherwise. He told Nils that in his opinion Carl, though ill suited for the priesthood, might have a distinguished and profitable career in medicine. He was ready, he said, to take the young man without payment into his own house and to coach him in botany and physiology for the year that remained to him at the Gymnasium. Nils gratefully accepted this kind offer; but it was some months before he could bring himself to tell his wife what Rothman had said, and when he finally told her she was heartbroken. It was in fact the eight-year-old Samuel who suffered most immediately and most directly from his brother's apostasy; from that moment botany became for Christina a dirty word, and the boy, who always enjoyed working in the garden, was strictly forbidden to meddle with flowers in the future. Perhaps it was now that he transferred his attention to bees.

Meanwhile, all was going very well with Carl at Växjö. Rothman treated him like a son, showed him that botany was a serious study and not just an agreeable hobby, taught him to classify his plants according to Tournefort's system[1] and – most valuable of all – made known to him the contents of Vaillant's essay on the sexuality of plants.[2] The summer holidays were spent identifying and classifying all the plants that grew around Stenbrohult.

In August 1727 Carl, now in his twenty-first year, went to Lund to be enrolled at the University where his father had also matriculated. As was the custom, he had provided himself with a testimonial from the Headmaster of the Gymnasium, Nils Krok, to be handed over on his arrival to the Rector of the University. Krok wrote:

> As Nature by the timely transplantation of plants hastens their happy and early development and thus provides a pleasing display, so too the Muses sometimes agreeably choose to offer to particularly talented youths a change of seat of learning in order that they may be able the more speedily to transmute the sweet nectar of their studies into blood and substance. To this end the Muses of the University call to themselves from our Gymnasium Carl Linnaeus, an exceptionally gifted young man of good family; and so that he may be the more welcome, and able at once to place himself under their gracious protection, he requests a testimonial of his conduct and industry. I therefore hereby certify that he has conducted himself in a pious, upright and honourable manner, has worked diligently, and has kept himself from evil company. Therefore, Rector Magnificus, I commend into your hands, to your protection, favour and kindness, this exemplary youth. . . .

From Carl's point of view it was a pity that this testimonial could not have been written by Rothman or by Höök. What Krok had said was friendly enough; but the document, though stressing his pupil's industry and potential talent, was pointedly silent on the subject of knowledge actually acquired. In fact, Carl tells us that Höök, who had now become a master of philosophy at Lund, thought it best to suppress it, and agreed personally to present him to the Rector as his private pupil.

'*Corvus glandarius*' (jay), by Olof Rudbeck the Younger.

[1] Joseph Pitton de Tournefort (1656–1708), French botanist, who formulated a system for the classification of plants by a consideration of the shape of the corolla (petals).

[2] Tournefort's pupil, Sébastien Vaillant, French botanist and author of *Sermo de Structura Florum* (*Discourse on the Structure of Flowers*), published in 1718. Linnaeus did not actually see this essay until later.

2.

Lund

The town of Lund is situated in Scania (Skåne), the flat and pastoral southernmost province of Sweden, one that has always been closely associated with Denmark and which in fact became Swedish territory only in 1658; as the crow flies it is less than thirty miles from Copenhagen. It is an ancient city, having (according to tradition) been founded early in the eleventh century by Canute – King of England, Denmark and Norway – and named by him *Londinum Gothorum*, 'the London of the Goths'; probably it was in fact even older, for by the twelfth century it had already become the largest town in Scandinavia. Its University, however, was only sixty years old at the time of Carl's arrival there.

Those who visit this clean and attractive old town today may find it difficult, in spite of the Kulturen (an open-air historical museum which includes examples of old southern Swedish buildings), to picture it as it was on that August day in 1727 when Linnaeus – as we may now call him – first passed through its ancient city gates. It was no longer the big town that it had once been, and except in the immediate neighbourhood of its grey Romanesque cathedral consisted principally of 'narrow passages overgrown with grass where swine and geese waddled up and down'.[1] These alleys were bogs in the winter months, and foul and stinking all the year round. Karl XII, not a squeamish man, had commented unfavourably on them when he had been there ten years earlier, and an official report mentions 'the dead cats and dogs, together with other carcases', that no one troubled to clear away. Lund, which had suffered in the war, had in fact touched its nadir; twenty years later Linnaeus was able to write that it had improved out of all recognition since his student days.

One of the reasons for Linnaeus's choice of Lund had been that a member of his family, Professor Humerus, was Dean of Lund Cathedral. 'When Carl arrived at the town gates of Lund [wrote Samuel], all the bells were tolling. He asked a bystander why this was, and was told, "For Professor Humerus".' It was a bad start; but worse was to follow, for Linnaeus soon discovered that instruction in the medical and botanical faculties was hopelessly inadequate. Now that his potential benefactor was dead, Lund appeared to have little to offer. There was no professor of botany, and in the medical faculty no one but Dr Johan von Döbeln – a learned man but old and idle now and disillusioned by his failure,

[1] Knut Hagberg, *Carl Linnaeus* (1939); English translation by Alan Blair (Cape, 1952).

year after year, to get enough money to buy the equipment necessary to keep up to date. *Faute de mieux*, however, Linnaeus began attending his lectures.

Perhaps he already had doubts as to whether he would stay the course at Lund, for he did not follow the usual custom of joining one of the twelve 'Nations'. These were students' clubs, each with its own club-room, and a student was expected to become a member of the nation of his own part of the country – for Linnaeus, the Småland. And possibly he was also reluctant to expose himself to the gross bullying and the 'fagging' to which all freshmen, in spite of a royal decree forbidding these 'diabolical' practices, were still subjected.

But throughout his life Linnaeus was often to fall on his feet. Höök had persuaded Dr Kilian Stobaeus, a distinguished local doctor and keen student of natural history, to take the young man as a lodger. At first, admittedly, it did not look as though the arrangement would work well, for Stobaeus was little impressed by the rather scruffy youth who 'neither in appearance, dress, nor habits had anything to recommend him more than an ordinary stranger who wished to devote himself to the study of medicine'. Nor can Linnaeus have been immediately attracted to Stobaeus, whom he describes as 'sickly, a constant victim of hypochondria, back-ache and migraine, blind in one eye and lame in one foot'; but he at once recognized Stobaeus's brilliance and tried to ingratiate himself with his host by attending his course of lectures on conchology. He also spent many enjoyable hours in the Doctor's cabinet of minerals, shells, birds and pressed plants, and was fascinated to observe the way in which the herbarium specimens were mounted; but what he really wanted was access to Stobaeus's books, and the library was always kept locked.

Stobaeus, in constant demand as the best doctor in Lund and also much occupied with University affairs, was badly overworked. One day when he was exceptionally busy and when, presumably, his secretary was not at hand, he asked Linnaeus to deal with some correspondence which he had no time to answer himself. Here was Linnaeus's chance – and he missed it; the letters he drafted were found to be so ill written that they could not be sent. Whether it was the orthography or the calligraphy that was at fault is not clear. Pulteney describes Linnaeus's handwriting as 'remarkable for its legibility and elegance'. At times it certainly was; but at other times it could be as ugly and as illegible as that of most medical men.

In a quite unexpected way Linnaeus finally found favour with Stobaeus, and the young man describes the circumstances in his Autobiography. The Doctor also had living with him at this time a German medical student named David Koulas, whom he employed as a secretary but treated as a son, who was allowed to make use of his fine library. Linnaeus soon made friends with the German, and struck a bargain with him that was mutually advantageous: Koulas was surreptitiously to borrow books from Stobaeus's library so that Linnaeus could study them by night, and in return Linnaeus was to give Koulas tuition in physiology.

Now Stobaeus also had in his house his mother – an old lady who suffered from insomnia and who, as was only natural in a town where almost all the buildings were of wood, had a great dread of fire. In her sleepless hours she noticed that there was a light in Linnaeus's room, and thinking that he must go to sleep with his candle still burning she asked her son to investigate:

A couple of days later at two o'clock in the morning, when Linnaeus was busily studying Stobaeus's books, the Doctor, in a very bad temper, crept silently up the stairs, expecting to find Linnaeus asleep. Seeing that he was not, he asked him why he did not sleep at night, like everyone else. Then he came to the table, on which a large pile of his own books were lying open. He asked for an explanation, and Linnaeus had to tell him the whole story. Stobaeus ordered him to go to bed at once and sleep by night like all reasonable people. But next morning he summoned him and questioned him further about the books, after which he gave him the library key and told him that he could borrow whatever he pleased.

According to Linnaeus, from this moment there was a sudden and dramatic change in his relationship with Stobaeus. The Doctor now realized that what he had taken for a very ordinary and rather unattractive student was in fact a young man deserving of every encouragement. He gave him not only the run of his books but also free board at his own table and free admission to his lectures. He took him with him on his rounds. Soon he even went so far as to hint that, since he had no children of his own, he might perhaps make Linnaeus his heir. Linnaeus was deeply grateful to Stobaeus 'to whom [he wrote later] I am indebted, so long as I live, for the love he bore me, and that he loved me, not as a pupil, but as if I were a son'.

When season and weather were favourable, Linnaeus made a number of plant-hunting forays in the neighbourhood of Lund, taking with him one or two students whom he had infected with his own enthusiasm. He noticed with interest how different was the Scanian flora from that of Småland. Geology was

Uppsala, 1770, engraved by Akrell.

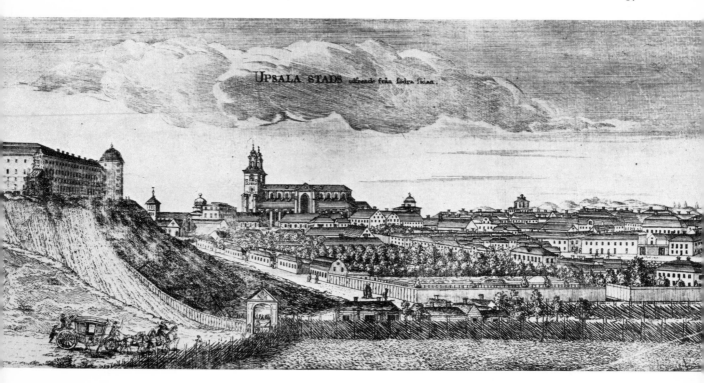

24

also included, and a favourite hunting-ground was Fågelsång, about five miles from Lund, which offered both a hill of pyrites and a valley of uncommon plants.

To the study of the botany and geology of Scania an unhappy circumstance was now to add a very painful introduction to its fauna. On 26 May 1728 the party went as usual to Fågelsång and, it being a hot day, Linnaeus took off his coat and waistcoat. Suddenly he felt something biting or stinging his right arm. He thought little of it at the time, but blood-poisoning set in and the arm swelled alarmingly. Stobaeus, who took a very grave view of the matter, did all in his power but effected no improvement; then he was obliged to go away, leaving his patient in the care of a surgeon named Schnell. It seemed to Schnell that, conventional treatment having failed, the time had come to try a drastic remedy: he therefore made 'a great incision from the elbow to the armpit', after which Linnaeus turned the corner and rapidly recovered. Linnaeus gave much thought to the identification of his assailant, ultimately blaming – though probably erroneously – a small, hair-like worm on which he later took his revenge by naming it *Furia infernalis*; it was probably a horse-fly.

He recovered in time to spend his summer vacation with his family at Stenbrohult, where he worked tirelessly at botany, geology and zoology. His father was now reconciled to his son's becoming a doctor, but Christina still clung with pathetic obstinacy to a hope that a year at Lund might have turned his thoughts to ordination; however, when she saw he did nothing but glue plants to paper she had to admit that the battle was lost.

Then Rothman came over from Växjö to hear how his former pupil was getting on. What Linnaeus told him of Lund made him believe that Uppsala University would provide a better course for a medical student. Nils agreed to the change being made, and on 23 August 1728 Carl Linnaeus set out on the 400-mile journey to Uppsala. In his wallet there jingled cheerfully a hundred silver dalers[1] – his parents' final gift to him, he wrote; in the future he would have to fend for himself.

[1] A relatively small sum: a silver daler (= 3 copper dalers) was worth about 1s. 5d. in English money of the day. I cannot see that, with sterling so unstable, anything is to be gained by attempting to give, here and elsewhere, modern equivalents.

3.

Uppsala

The little university town of Uppsala, situated about forty miles to the north of Stockholm, might perhaps be described as the Cambridge of Sweden, though it cannot boast an equal architectural splendour. The placid, reed-fringed Fyris, overhung with willows and maples, is its Cam. The old town stands on rising ground on the west bank of the river and is dominated by the ponderous unfinished *Slott* (Castle), built by Gustavus Vasa in the middle of the sixteenth century, and by its big and lofty red-brick Gothic Cathedral which was designed by one of the assistant architects of Notre-Dame in Paris. The University, the first in Sweden, was founded in 1477 and has today a high reputation for scholarship.

Rothman had graduated at Uppsala, but his recommendation of that University to a young medical student would seem to suggest that he had lost touch with it in recent years. For if conditions at Lund were bad, those at Uppsala were little better. There were at this time two professors of great distinction in the medical faculty at Uppsala, Olof Rudbeck the Younger and Lars Roberg, who divided the field of medicine between them, Rudbeck making himself responsible for anatomy, botany, zoology and pharmacology, and Roberg for theoretical and practical medicine, surgery, physiology and chemistry. On paper the syllabus appeared satisfactory enough; in practice it proved a mockery. Let us look in turn at each of the two men who were jointly responsible for a faculty in the senior and most famous University in Sweden – men whose reputation had been the cause of Rothman's recommendation.

Olof Rudbeck the Younger – but no longer young: he was in his sixty-ninth year and so in those days a very old man – was the son of a yet more distinguished father. The elder Olof Rudbeck (1630–1702), an all-round scientist and a man of the widest culture, is remembered as a discoverer of the lymphatic system, the founder of the Uppsala Botanic Garden, the author of the provocative *Atlantican* – a book in which he patriotically attempted to establish that Plato's Atlantis was Sweden and its capital Uppsala – and the compiler, with the assistance of his son, of the *Campus Elysii*. This monumental botanical work – a survey of all the then known plants together with many thousands of woodcuts designed to illustrate it – and most of his and his son's notes and other material, had been almost entirely lost in the disastrous fire which in 1702 destroyed three-

Olof Rudbeck the Elder.

Left: title-page of Olof Rudbeck the Elder's *Atlantican* (1675–89).

quarters of Uppsala. The elder Rudbeck, shattered by the blow, died a few months later.

In 1695 the younger Rudbeck, already a widely travelled man, had made an important scientific expedition to Lapland. On his return he had worked for some years on the material he had brought back, almost the whole of which (but for a fragment already published) had also been destroyed in the fire. (Of the twelve projected volumes, only two perfect copies of the first and several of the second survive.) After this double disaster he understandably found that his heart was no longer in natural history, though he was obliged to continue to earn his living by teaching it; instead he turned to his chief hobby, philology, and henceforward devoted to the writing of a gigantic *Thesaurus* (lexicon) of

27

The Uppsala fire, 1702 (contemporary illustration).

European and Asiatic languages much of the time and energy that should have gone into his University lectures. Finally, in recognition of his own and his father's work and of the great loss they had sustained, he was given permission to discontinue public lecturing so that he might complete the *Thesaurus*; his lectures were taken over by his son-in-law, Dr Petrus Martin, until the latter's death in 1727. Martin was replaced by Nils Rosén, Rudbeck's assistant, of whom we shall hear more; but Rosén was abroad at the time, and he in turn was temporarily replaced by the conceited and wholly incompetent Elias Preutz. In other words, so far as anatomy, botany, zoology and pharmacology were concerned, such instruction as was available at Uppsala was virtually worthless.

Then Roberg. He too was undoubtedly extremely able; but he was now an idle, disappointed, disillusioned, avaricious old man of sixty-five, no longer interested in much beyond making money – which he found easier to do by the private coaching of rich students than by public lecturing. And Linnaeus could afford to attend those private lectures only by half-starving himself and going about in rags. Surprisingly, he and Roberg appear to have taken a great liking to one another; but it never seems to have occurred to the old miser to offer him board or hospitality. This help was, however, soon to come from another source.

Admittedly Roberg had some excuse for being a disappointed man, though none for being a mean one. The University Hospital, the centre of much of his work, was ill endowed, and all his efforts, in the days when he was still young and eager, to raise money to run it properly had failed. He had even tried letting out a part of the building as a tavern; but noise and scandal had soon led to the resignation of the whole hospital staff and finally to the tavern's closure. So the time came when Roberg lost heart and interest; as Gibbon wrote of an English university professor, he 'well remembered that he had a salary to receive, and only forgot that he had a duty to perform'.

28

There was no clinical teaching at Uppsala at that time. There was no chemical laboratory and rarely a lecture on chemistry. Anatomy was feebly pursued in a shack, and there were no dissections. The Botanic Garden was a wreck, with 'hardly two hundred species and not more than a hundred plants of any interest'. Where zoology was concerned things were even worse; Roberg's museum contained a 'dragon' and a two-headed snake, but little else had been rescued from the flames. Thus Linnaeus had arrived at a moment when medicine at Uppsala had become a farce; the miracle was that during his time there he managed to achieve so much.

If the teachers at Uppsala, especially those in the medical faculty, were ineffective, it must be admitted that the taught did not in general provide them with very promising material. The most graphic description of Uppsala undergraduates in the eighteenth century is to be found in the *Travels* of Dr E. D. Clarke, a Cambridge don who had wandered all over Europe. Though he wrote of conditions at the end of the century, they were probably much the same – perhaps indeed even worse – during Linnaeus's student days.

Clarke would certainly not have agreed with Uppsala being likened to Cambridge; even Oxford, he felt, was by comparison almost a civilized place. Indeed 'it is not easy to conceive anything more foreign to all our notions of the dignity and splendour of a national seminary for education, than in the real state of things in *Upsala*. Perhaps there may be something to compare with it in the Universities of *Scotland*; but even in the last there is nothing so low as in *Sweden*.' Of the undergraduates he wrote that they had 'rather the appearance of so many labouring artificers, and might have been mistaken for a company of workmen in a manufactory'; it was impossible, he added, 'to consider them as gentlemen':

> Let the Reader figure to himself a few dirty-looking lackeys out of place, lounging about in slouched white hats, with a loose surtout thrown over their shoulders, one arm of which hangs empty and dangling by their side, and long military boots rising above the knees; their hair uncut, uncombed, and undressed, hanging as long in front as in the rear, but parted over the middle of the forehead, so as to fall in long unsightly tresses about the eyes, cheeks, and ears; giving to the whole figure the appearance not unlike the effigies which the rabble in England dress up to represent *Guy Fawkes* upon the Fifth of *November*.

In fact we need only to look around us today in order to picture the appearance of a typical Uppsala undergraduate of that time. Clarke continues:

> Everyone studies what, and when, he pleases: of course, very little real application to learning takes place among them. Soon after midday, they resort in numbers, '*à la cave*', as it is termed; that is to say, to a public cellar for drinking. . . . In these cellars they remain, not only the whole of the rest of the day, but until long after midnight, and sometimes all night. Their revels too, or rather brawls, are not unfrequently attended by blows. . . .

Clarke visited one of these cellars, where he found 'about twenty of the students enveloped by thick fumes of tobacco-smoke; some of whom were sleeping upon

Olof Rudbeck the Younger, by J. Streng, 1732.

Lars Roberg, by Paul Dahlman.

chairs, and others upon a bench', in a heat 'almost equal to that of a vapour bath'. He was told that after a bout of drinking they proved themselves adepts in the gentle art of professor-baiting:

> Sometimes they all sally forth; and woe betide the unpopular Professor who may happen to be in their way, when the *convives* quit their sudatories! They have two different watch-words; one of which controuls or animates their fury upon these occasions. If the Professor be a favourite, the cry of '*vivat!*' is heard, and he is suffered to proceed without molestation; but if otherwise, a shout of '*pereat!*' is the signal for attack; when the Professor either makes his escape as rapidly as he can, or is very roughly handled.

Clarke attended a lecture by the Professor of Botany, Linnaeus's pupil Thunberg, at which the audience consisted of 'only half-a-dozen slovenly boys . . . the eldest of whom could not be more than fourteen years of age'. He estimated the total number of students at about 300. In the fifties and sixties of the eighteenth century conditions were better and numbers much larger; and for this temporary improvement Linnaeus's long spell as professor at Uppsala was, as we shall see, largely responsible.

During Linnaeus's first term at Uppsala University Rudbeck found himself obliged, much against his will, to deliver several public lectures on birds; but he got no further than the fowl. Three more, on birds of prey, followed in the spring, all illustrated by the handing round of some impressive water-colour drawings which he had made many years earlier. Roberg too gave in the spring four lectures on Aristotle and a course in medicine; Linnaeus, during the whole of his time at Uppsala, was never able to hear a single lecture, public or private, on botany. Of his first term at Uppsala he tells us only the following:

> When Linnaeus came to Uppsala his money was soon finished, nor was there any opportunity of his earning some more by coaching, as students often did, because medicine was at that time looked upon as an inferior subject. He had to borrow to buy food and could not even pay to have his shoes soled, being obliged to lay paper in them and go barefoot [*sic*]. He would gladly have returned to Stobaeus who had treated him so kindly, but he could not afford the journey. Besides, Dr Stobaeus would have been extremely angry to meet again the youth for whom he had taken such a fancy and who had deserted him without even asking his advice.

Linnaeus mentions in a letter 'the precious and delightful cabinet of curios' which he saw in December 1728 in the University Library, and the famous collection of dried plants, made by Joachim Burser a century earlier, which was to be of great importance to him later when preparing his *Species Plantarum*.[1] But though his scientific interests covered the whole realm of Nature, he was, like so many scientists, largely blind to the visual arts except where they served to provide a record of natural objects, and deaf to man-made music. Flowers and birdsong were thrilling; architecture, painting, and sculpture meant little to him aesthetically, and most of his own drawings are pathetically feeble. Nowhere, so far as I am aware, does he mention Uppsala's magnificent Gothic Cathedral, or refer more than casually to the remarkable relics of Sweden's pagan kings at

[1] For the English translations of the titles of Linnaeus's works see page 251.

30

Gamla (Old) Uppsala, a couple of miles to the north of the modern town; he did, however, examine and attempt to read such runic inscriptions as came his way.

It was the same throughout his whole life. In Holland, where he was to spend three years, he never noticed Rembrandt or Frans Hals. Still more strangely he never mentioned the great flower painters Jan van Huysum and Rachel Ruysch, both of whom were still alive and working in Amsterdam. It was said of Linnaeus, 'God created, Linnaeus set in order'; but what *man* created, Linnaeus largely ignored, except where his archaeological, ethnographical, or practical interests were aroused. Perhaps, however, it was just as well that he had these blind spots: a tenth part of the task he was to set himself would have been a life-time's work for any ordinary man (as he frequently said). Moreover, he did possess what is none too common in scientists: literary talent of a very personal kind.

In December 1728, at the end of his first term, Linnaeus was awarded a minor scholarship. The financial rewards were slight; but he decided to spend this little windfall, not on the food and clothing that he so much needed, but on a visit in January to Stockholm. The particular object of this journey was to be present at a dissection, something which he had had no opportunity of witnessing in Uppsala; the corpse was that of a woman whose hanging had been postponed to a moment convenient for the College of Medicine. A second demonstration, which he also attended, followed in February.

The winter was severe. To Linnaeus, who all his life dreaded the cold and who could now hardly afford the bare necessities of food, fuel and clothing, these were difficult days. But with the spring, indeed almost before the spring, came two encounters which warmed at least his heart. He had not been long at Uppsala before he had heard mention on every hand of the name of Peter Artedi. All declared him to be the most brilliant medical student in the University, and Linnaeus was eager to meet him. But Artedi, who came from Ångermanland, had been summoned home because of the illness of his father, after whose death he had remained to put his affairs in order; it was therefore not until March 1729 that he returned to Uppsala. Linnaeus, writing nine years later, recalls his first meeting with Artedi, who was two years his senior:

> I saw before me a tall, slim young man with long black hair, whose features reminded me of John Ray's.[1] He gave me the impression of being modest and not over-hasty in forming an opinion, yet at the same time he seemed alert, determined and mature – a man of old-fashioned integrity and honour. I was delighted to find that we immediately started talking about stones, plants and animals, and I was much touched at his confiding in me, at our very first meeting and with great frankness, so many of his observations in the field of science. I wanted his friendship; and not only did he give it to me, but he also promised me his help whenever I needed it – a promise that he faithfully kept. This sacred friendship grew steadily during our seven years in Uppsala. He was my dearest, my most intimate friend.

Besides their enthusiasm, the two young men had this in common: both were 'sons of the manse' and destined for ordination, and both had disappointed

John Ray, engraved after a painting by W. Faithorne, 1688, from *Stirpium Europaearum . . . sylloge*, 1694.

[1] John Ray (1628–1705), English naturalist who made a great contribution to plant classification. Linnaeus would have known the engraving of him on the title-page of his *Stirpium Europaearum . . . sylloge* (London, 1694), a copy of which he possessed. No portrait of Artedi survives.

31

their parents by abandoning theology for medicine. But in appearance and in temperament, Linnaeus tells us, they were very different, 'Artedi being tall, earnest and deliberate whereas Linnaeus was short and broadly-built, impetuous, ardent'. Mrs Caddy, romantic always, assures us that 'both were handsome in feature, improved by the beauty of expression caused by the habitual admiration of God's works'; but another friend of Artedi describes him as 'rather plain'. Mrs Caddy adds that they 'loved like David and Jonathan'. Certainly it was a sudden, deep, and lasting friendship which was formed that March day at Uppsala; it was, however, an attraction based on common interests and opposite temperaments: each was the perfect foil to the other, each stimulated the other. There are no grounds whatever for supposing that there was a sentimental relationship between them.

Artedi's principal interest at this time was chemistry (including alchemy), but he was also a botanist and a zoologist; it was therefore inevitable that from time to time there should be a certain amount of friendly rivalry between the two clever young men. When one of them discovered something, he began by keeping it to himself; but before three days had passed he could not resist boasting about it to the other. In the end they decided to divide between them some of those fields of study where their interests overlapped. Artedi took the Amphibia, reptiles, Batrachia, and fish, Linnaeus the birds and insects; both worked on mammals and mineralogy; and though Linnaeus made a corner in botany, he agreed to leave to Artedi the Umbelliferae (the family which includes the hemlock, cow parsley, etc.) 'as he wanted to work out a new method of classifying them'. This, said Linnaeus, aroused in himself a desire to do the same for plants in general. He already knew something of Vaillant's work, but he had recently come across a review of his *Sermo de Structura Florum*; 'it greatly pleased him, because he began to realize the role played by the stamens and pistils of flowers, and what the essential parts of a flower were'.

Artedi and Linnaeus now made a pact: if one of them should die, 'the other would regard it as a sacred duty to give to the world what observations might be left behind by him who was gone'. Eight years later this melancholy task fell to Linnaeus.

In addition to Rudbeck and Roberg there was another local naturalist whom Linnaeus must have hoped one day to meet: Dr Olof Celsius (1670–1756), Professor of Theology, a Dean of the Cathedral and an uncle of the astronomer Anders Celsius, the reputed inventor of the centigrade thermometer.

During the first few months of Linnaeus's time at Uppsala Dean Celsius had been in Stockholm attending a series of conferences in connection with the revision of ecclesiastical law. But the fame of this enthusiastic amateur botanist and of his remarkable library and garden would of course have aroused Linnaeus's curiosity, and he describes how in the spring of 1729 chance brought the two men together:

Linnaeus was sitting one day in the neglected Botanic Garden when an elderly clergyman came up to him and asked him what he was looking at, whether he knew about plants and had studied botany, where he came from, and how long he had been at Uppsala. He asked the names of a number of plants, which Linnaeus gave

Statue of the young Linnaeus, by Carl Eldh (1873–1954), in the Old Botanic Garden, Uppsala.

according to Tournefort's system. Finally he asked him how many plants he had collected and pressed. When Linnaeus told him that he had more than six hundred native wild flowers, he invited the young man to come back with him to his house. . . .

It was only now that Linnaeus discovered that he had been talking to Olof Celsius. He was sent home to fetch his own collection, with which Celsius was duly impressed. But the Dean had not failed to notice that this talented young student looked poor and hungry; he therefore, like Stobaeus at Lund, offered him a room in his house, two meals a day at his table, and the run of his library. Once again Linnaeus was in luck.

Linnaeus was able to repay in part this kindness. Celsius had two botanical projects in hand: a book, *Hierobotanicon*, dealing with plants mentioned in the Bible, and the compilation of a flora of Uppland, the province of which Uppsala was the capital. Linnaeus lent a hand with the *Hierobotanicon*, a dry work which was eventually published in two volumes (1745, 1747), put Celsius's Uppland specimens in order, and accompanied him on a number of local botanical forays. It was a mutually profitable alliance, and Linnaeus later marked his gratitude to his benefactor by naming the genus *Celsia* in his honour.

Very likely it was on Celsius's recommendation that in June 1729 Linnaeus

The young Linnaeus, by Louis Prosper Roux, 1847.

33

was awarded a Royal Scholarship (second class) in the medical faculty, which in December was advanced to a first class. About this time the University Librarian, Georg Wallin, led a disputation, *De Nuptiis Arborum* ('Concerning the Nuptials of Trees'). It was the custom of the University for dissertations, usually written in large part by the professors of the students who proposed them, to be 'opposed' by other students having the same interests, and subsequently printed at the expense of the proposer. This particular disputation was something very much in Linnaeus's line, for the sexuality of plants was a subject that had been in his mind ever since Växjö days. But for some unknown reason he was not present; he therefore decided, when he had read it, to put his views in writing and to present his thesis – *Præludia Sponsaliarum Plantarum* – to Dean Celsius in lieu of the verses which students customarily addressed to their professors on New Year's Day.

> I am no poet [he tells Celsius in his foreword], but something, however, of a botanist; I therefore offer to you this fruit from the little crop that God has granted me. . . . In these few pages I treat of the great analogy which is to be found between plants and animals, in that they both increase their families in the same way. I beg you graciously to accept this humble gift. . . .

Linnaeus, who wrote his paper in Swedish and not in Latin, not only shows great erudition by apt quotation from the works of many botanists both past and present; he also makes it plain that, in spite of his modest denial, he was at all events a poet in prose. His style, as Hagberg says, is something quite new and quite unexpected in the Age of the Baroque and the Rococo: 'Its simple fresh-ness reminds one most of the thirteenth-century English folk song "Sumer is icumen in, Lhude sing cuccu!" It is quite spontaneous. . . . There is the same melody in the *Carmina burana*, the medieval spring songs of the wandering scholars.' The dissertation opens:

> In spring, when the bright sun comes nearer to our zenith, he awakens in all bodies the life that has lain stifled during the chill winter. See how all creatures become lively and gay, who through the winter were dull and sluggish! See how every bird, all the long winter silent, bursts into song! See how all the insects come forth from their hiding-places where they have lain half dead, how all the plants push through the soil, how all the trees which in winter were dormant now break into leaf! Why, even into man himself new life seems to enter. . . .
>
> Words cannot express the joy that the sun brings to all living things. Now the black-cock and the capercailzie begin to frolic, the fish to sport. Every animal feels the sexual urge. Yes, Love comes even to the plants. Males and females, even the hermaphrodites, hold their nuptials (which is the subject that I now propose to discuss), showing by their sexual organs which are males, which females, which hermaphrodites. . . .
>
> The actual petals of a flower contribute nothing to generation, serving only as the bridal bed which the great Creator has so gloriously prepared, adorned with such precious bed-curtains, and perfumed with so many sweet scents in order that the bridegroom and bride may therein celebrate their nuptials with the greater solemnity. When the bed has thus been made ready, then is the time for the bridegroom to embrace his beloved bride and surrender himself to her. . . .

Olof Celsius the Elder, after an engraving by J. Gillberg, and below, *Celsia cretica*, from the *Botanical Magazine*, 1806.

34

Linnaeus's own sketch for the title-
page of *Præludia Sponsaliarum Plantarum*, 1729, and the actual page.

And he proceeds to describe the functions of stamens and pistils in pollination
(the sexual act). If the anthers are removed (castration), fertilization does not
take place. Pollen is the sperm, seeds are the ova, and so on. Sex in the date
palm (every date palm is either male or female) was known to the ancients
though it remained for Camerarius to prove the sexuality of plants experi-
mentally (1694); but problems still remained to be solved: how, for example,
did the pollen reach the ova? What Linnaeus had written was, however, not
only something almost completely novel in Sweden, where Vaillant's pioneer
work, which he dutifully acknowledges, had as yet made hardly any impact; it
was also highly provocative. For it was a dangerous step to equate the sex life of
plants, with all its implications of polygamy, polyandry and incest, with that of
animals; and later his 'sexual system', as expounded in his *Systema Naturae*, was
to earn for Linnaeus the strong disapproval of the strait-laced.

But Celsius, impressed and flattered, was delighted with his protégé's thesis.
He showed it to Rudbeck, who expressed himself eager to know personally the
young man of whom he was constantly hearing such favourable reports. Copies
of the text, soon circulating among the students, caused something of a stir; and
probably it was Rudbeck who saw that one of these came into the hands of the
Uppsala Royal Society of Science, whose members wanted it to be printed.
Rudbeck may have given up his lecturing, he may have devoted much of his
energy to the completion of his great *Thesaurus*, but he still seems to have kept a
sharp eye on the activities of the medical school.

About this time Linnaeus applied for the vacant post of gardener at the
Botanic Garden; but Rudbeck turned his application down, evidently thinking
that he was too good to be wasted on a menial job. Moreover, Rudbeck had
other plans for this clever young man; he had to find someone to hold, in his

35

The mines at Dannemora, water-
colour by C. G. Gillberg.

place, the important botanical demonstrations which were given each spring in the Botanic Garden. Preutz should have been the obvious choice; but his ignorance and inefficiency were now common knowledge. So Rudbeck did something which was quite unorthodox: after carefully examining Linnaeus and Preutz, in spite of the protests of Roberg he offered Linnaeus the job. On 4 May 1730 Linnaeus held his first demonstration.

One can imagine the sensation caused by the appointment of this eager second-year student to take over duties normally performed by tired old men. His demonstrations were crowded out; instead of the customary 70 or 80 students, Linnaeus sometimes found himself addressing an audience of 300 or 400. But Rudbeck's patronage did not stop here: after the course was over he invited his protégé to become tutor to his three youngest sons (a much married man, Rudbeck had had twenty-four children by his three wives), and in the middle of June Linnaeus moved into his house. Rudbeck also obtained for him a special grant from the Senate, and before long this was doubled. The days of penury were, for the time being, over.

Linnaeus showed his gratitude to Rudbeck by naming an American plant in his honour. 'So long as the earth shall survive,' he wrote to him on 29 July 1731, 'and as each spring shall see it covered with flowers, the *Rudbeckia* will preserve your glorious name.' To lend one's name to a plant was a sure way to live on in the memory of mankind: who, he asked, would remember Gentius, King of Illyria, were it not for the gentian?

He had carefully considered what plant would be suitable:

Triewald's machine, engraving by E. Geringius, 1734.

> I have chosen a *noble* plant in order to recall your merits and the services you have rendered, a *tall* one to give an idea of your stature; and I wanted it to be one which branched and which flowered and fruited freely, to show that you cultivated not only the sciences but also the humanities. Its rayed flowers will bear witness that you shone among savants like the sun among the stars; its perennial roots will remind us that each year sees you live again through new works. Pride of our gardens, the Rudbeckia will be cultivated throughout Europe and in distant lands where your revered name must long have been known. Accept this plant, not for what it is but for what it will become when it bears your name. . . .

Celsius appears to have approved of the step that Linnaeus had taken in going to live with Rudbeck, for his friendship with Linnaeus remained unclouded.

At Whitsun Linnaeus took, as a paying pupil, another student to Dannemora, about thirty miles to the north of Uppsala, returning in due course with a number of new plants which delighted Celsius. In the famous Dannemora iron-mines they saw in operation 'the fire machine which Mårten Triewald had designed; it is driven by water and steam pressure, and there has never been another in Sweden. Not far away I saw the Österby foundry, where there were iron hammers. What a labour! Here the men wear nothing but shifts, with socks and slippers on their feet.' There were also in the Dannemora mines shrew-mice 'as tractable and tame as dogs, which came and fed out of people's hands. They are considered sacrosanct and nobody harms them.' 'I was three hundred feet below the surface,' Linnaeus wrote to Stobaeus, 'and searched for stones, collecting as many as I could conveniently bring home in my trunk.'

Then in June he went with Celsius to Börje, near Uppsala, in pursuit of an

37

'Pedicularis Sceptrum Carolinum',
from *Flora Danica*.

uncommon and exciting plant – Sceptrum Carolinum (Charles's sceptre). This golden-yellow flower with a lion's mouth and bloody under-lip had been named in 1701 by its discoverer, the younger Rudbeck, in honour of Karl XII, who had just won the Battle of Narva. Unfortunately it was not in flower, but in the autumn, on a second expedition, they found it in seed; and on yet another occasion Linnaeus took Rudbeck's youngest son, Johan Olof, to see it in order that he might write a dissertation on the subject. This dissertation was in fact composed by Linnaeus to earn a little money – a secret confession that he subsequently sadly noted on the back of the title-page but which he did not at the time betray: 'I have written this thesis in one day for thirty copper dalers; another has received the credit for it.' Linnaeus was later to list Sceptrum Carolinum as a species of *Pedicularis*, or lousewort – a name less flattering to the warrior-king.

Throughout the autumn and winter Linnaeus worked with his usual energy on the material he had accumulated during the summer. He had begun to doubt the adequacy of Tournefort's system of classification; he now therefore decided to arrange his plants according to a plan of his own, dividing them into classes by a consideration of the number of stamens and pistils and their relative disposition. Thus was born the 'sexual system of Linnaeus' which, in its subsequently modified form, was and has remained the most practical artificial method of classification.[1]

It was for Linnaeus a time of enormous mental activity: innumerable schemes were germinating in his mind. Already he was beginning to write what before very long would be given to the world in his *Bibliotheca Botanica*, *Classes Plantarum*, *Critica Botanica* and *Genera Plantarum*. He was also working on Swedish birds and insects. He made many long overdue improvements to the Botanic Garden and drew up his *Adonis Uplandicus* in which he listed, for the benefit of his students, the plants growing there. When some months later this thesis, now revised and arranged according to his own system, was presented by Rudbeck to the Royal Society of Science, 'the Society [wrote Linnaeus, who was present] thought at first that I was mad; but when I explained my intention they stopped laughing and promised me their support'.

'In November [Linnaeus told Stobaeus] I gave lectures on botany and had many of the nobility among my audience. I generally received a ducat [twenty-four copper dalers] a head.' Some of the students, however, paid for their tuition in kind, and elsewhere Linnaeus lists gifts that ranged from a copy of Bauhin's *Pinax* to a pair of stockings and a tooth-pick.

In March 1731 the long absent Nils Rosén returned to Uppsala after taking a medical degree in Holland. He was a brilliant young doctor, only a year older than Linnaeus and in line to succeed the seventy-year-old Rudbeck. He at once brought the anatomy school to life and also attempted to take over from Linnaeus the botanical demonstrations at the Botanic Garden, but this Rudbeck forbad. Thus Linnaeus became, he himself wrote, 'the object of jealousy, with such far-reaching repercussions that they cannot be specified here', but which will be discussed later.

At the end of the summer Linnaeus went in Rudbeck's post-yacht and by inland waterways to Stockholm, where he lodged with Apothecary Warmholtz whose son was his pupil. By 24 July he was back at Uppsala, studying medicine privately with Dr Rosén and pursuing his various literary activities. Then there were the three Rudbeck boys to coach, and no doubt many other pupils also; he was endlessly busy. Sadly, however, in December something went wrong with his relations with the Rudbecks. Linnaeus is not explicit; he writes: 'The unfaithful wife of Librarian Norrelius now visited the Rudbecks, with the result that Linnaeus became the object of such hatred to his hostess that he had to leave.' Possibly this hussy played Potiphar's wife to him, and Fru Rud-beck was jealous.

In any case Linnaeus, who had not seen his parents for more than three years, was about to return home for Christmas. His relations with his mother, after his refusal to become a priest, had at first been strained. She had made up her mind that he would never rise higher in the medical profession than an army surgeon, and (wrote Samuel) 'her love for him had almost grown cold'; but all had changed when she learned that her son, though only a second-year student, had been chosen to 'lecture for a professor', and now she eagerly awaited his return.

In the event, however, his homecoming was a sad one. News had already reached him that his mother was seriously ill, but he also found on his arrival that his youngest sister, the eight-year-old Emerentia, was critically ill with smallpox. Remembering, he said, David, 'who when old took two young girls into his bed so that by their healthy transpiration they might revive him', he had a sheep killed and flayed and laid the child in the skin, thus 'drawing her from death'; his mother, however, seems to have recovered without resort to such disagreeable treatment. Later, in his *Lachesis Naturalis*, Linnaeus was to advocate taking David's advice literally: 'If one has a cold and is put to bed between two young people,' he wrote, 'one quickly recovers.'

4.

The Lapland journey:
Lycksele Lappmark

In Lappland sind schmutzige Leute,
Plattköpfig, breitmäulig und klein;
Sie kauern ums Feuer, and backen
Sich Fische, und quäken und schrein.[1]

Heine

A visit by Linnaeus to his parents was overdue, and his mother's illness will have made him doubly anxious to return home. Perhaps, however, there was a yet further reason for his going to Stenbrohult: he may have wanted to consult them about an important and adventurous project which he had in mind. His troubles in the Rudbeck household, though they had not cost him the friendship of Rudbeck, had undoubtedly unsettled him, and possibly he had already aroused the jealousy of Rosén; it was therefore hardly surprising that Linnaeus felt that he would like to get away from Uppsala for a while. Now Rudbeck must often have told him of his journey to Lapland, the fruits of which had mostly perished in the fire of 1702. He will have described this vast and desolate wilderness, with its nomad inhabitants who spoke a strange language and indulged in ritual magic, with its rich bird life and unfamiliar flora, as a scientifically virgin land awaiting an investigator and a chronicler. And Linnaeus's imagination had been stirred; he resolved that if he could get a grant from the Royal Society of Science he would follow in Rudbeck's foot-steps and see for himself this remote and mysterious land.

It might perhaps be imagined that to travel from end to end of one's country was not, even two centuries ago, a very ambitious or daring undertaking – nothing more dangerous than, say, Dr Johnson's journey forty years later to the Hebrides. But Lapland, though missionaries and bailiffs had of course found their way there, had at that time been little explored, and conditions were even more primitive than those obtaining in Scotland.

True there had been one or two other pioneers. Anders Olofsson Holm and Jonas Giädda had been there and had produced in 1671 a description and a serviceable map of whose existence Linnaeus does not seem to have been aware; he appears, however, to have consulted Johannes Scheffer's *Lapponia* (1673), some of whose attractive woodcuts are reproduced in this book. The French comic poet Jean-François Regnard was in Lapland with two companions in 1681. Linnaeus nowhere mentions his name and may have known little or nothing of his journey; he certainly could not have read his *Voyage*,[2] which had been published, posthumously, in France only a few months earlier. Nor does he seem to have known of Aubry de la Motraye, whose travels through Torne

[1] 'In Lapland the people are dirty, flat-headed, wide-mouthed and small; they huddle round the fire, frying themselves fish, croaking and shrieking.'

[2] An English translation will be found in Pinkerton's *Voyages*, vol. I.

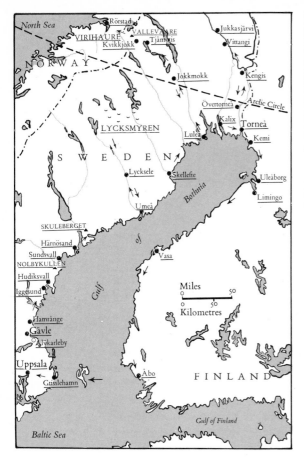

Lappmark had been published in English in 1723 and in French four years later. But in contemplating the exploration of Lapland Linnaeus, who had little of the explorer in him, was none the less considering embarking upon a real adventure.

As was only to be expected, it was Christina Linnaea who was the most apprehensive, the most upset over his news; and no doubt her anxiety was aggravated by her illness. She quoted an old tag:

> In thy country born and bred,
> By God's bounty duly fed,
> Be not lightly from it led!

But Nils took a more sensible view. 'You have only one life to provide for,' he told his son. 'If you are confident that this journey will advance your career, then ask God for guidance and help. He is everywhere, even among the wildest fells. Trust in Him. My prayers will go with you.'

Probably Linnaeus had already as good as made up his mind to go if he could get a grant – he was, after all, nearly twenty-five now and earning his living – for before leaving Uppsala he had approached the Royal Society of Science for help;

41

Swedish medal struck in 1957 for the 250th anniversary of Linnaeus's birth. The insect on the reverse is *Chrysoclista linéella*.

he suggested the sum of 600 copper dalers for what he estimated as a four months' journey of 1,600 miles. In a lengthy document he gave his reasons for wishing to explore Lapland and for believing that he was well fitted to do so. Its natural history he said, was 'as unknown as that of the most barbaric tract in the whole world'; yet it was enormously rich in wild life, especially birds. There were probably vast mineral resources, and there was certainly an interesting and little known flora. Then there were the Lapps themselves – a very valuable field for ethnographical study.

And what, he asks, are the necessary qualifications for anyone who undertakes such a journey? The man should be a Swede, so that no foreigner might reap the credit for what Sweden had financed. He should be young and active, very fit, very tough, and a bachelor. He should be a doctor, and a natural historian with both theoretical and practical knowledge of all three natural kingdoms – qualifications 'more difficult to find than a bird of paradise, because few botanists are at home in two kingdoms and there is hardly one who has knowledge of all three'. And finally, he should be able to draw. Then Linnaeus stood back and looked at himself. Admittedly he was no artist, and his mineralogy was still weak; but did he not in almost every other respect satisfy the conditions he had laid down? Would the Society be prepared to give him those 600 copper dalers towards the cost of such a journey? But many weeks passed and there was no reply.

Perhaps Rudbeck or Celsius, who were of course both members of the Royal Society of Science, now gave him a hint that, though the sum he had asked for was little enough, he would be wise to show himself ready to accept even less. He wrote again, this time suggesting 450 or even 400 copper dalers, and on 15 April the lesser sum was promised him. The Society should not, however, be accused of meanness, for even this pittance almost exhausted the small fund allotted for such purposes. It is necessary constantly to bear in mind how impoverished Sweden was at this time.

A month was spent in preparing for the journey and in waiting for better weather. Linnaeus was briefly in Stockholm, and there was a dissertation that he was anxious to finish. Then at last the great day came, and with a light heart he set out on what was to prove the most important and influential scientific exploration ever undertaken in Sweden.

We may start Linnaeus on his travels in his own words from the opening pages of his *Iter Lapponicum* (*Lapland Journey*). A little unpunctuated prose-poem precedes the text of what is really a diary never intended for publication and which, indeed, still remained unpublished at the time of his death:[1]

> *Småland* gave me birth
> *Sweden* have I travelled through
> *Seen* 450 ells deep into the bowels of the earth
> *Climbed* six miles up into the skies
> *Summer* and *Winter* seen in one day and on the same day lived in
> *Clouds* have I passed through
> The *World's End* have I visited
> Seen the *Sun's* overnight refuge
> In one year travelled more than 6,000 miles by land

[1] It was in fact first published in an English translation, oddly misentitled *Lachesis Lapponica*, in 1811. The original Swedish text appeared in 1889 and a new English translation is in preparation.

Then comes the first page of the text, which is headed:

O ENS Entium miserere mei!
(O Being of Beings, have pity on me!)

Having been appointed by the Royal Society of Science to travel through Lapland for the purpose of investigation of the three kingdoms of Nature there, I prepared my wardrobe and other necessaries for the journey as follows.

My clothes consisted of a little unpleated coat of West Gothland cloth with facings and a collar of worsted shag, neat leather breeches,[1] a pig-tailed wig, a cap of green fustian, a pair of top boots, and a small leather bag, nearly two feet long and not quite so wide, with hooks on one side so that it can be shut and hung up. In this bag I carried a shirt, two pairs of half-sleeves, two nightcaps, an ink-horn, a pen-case, a magnifying-glass and a small spy-glass, a gauze veil to protect me from midges, this journal and a stock of sheets of paper, stitched together, to press plants between (both in folio), a comb, and my manuscripts on ornithology, my *Flora Uplandica* and *Characteres Generici*.

A short sword hung at my side, and I had a small fowling-piece between my thigh and the saddle; I also had a graduated 8-sided rod for taking measurements. In my pocket was a wallet containing my passport from the Governor of Uppsala and a letter of recommendation from the Society.

Thus equipped I left Uppsala on Friday 12 May [Old Style] 1732, at 11 o'clock. I was twenty-five years old, all but about half a day.

Linnaeus was young and eager. His whole life lay before him and, more immediately, the prospect of a thrilling and adventurous journey. It was spring, which after a long northern winter makes an impact that no southerner can hope to understand. As he rode out alone through the northern gates of the city the radiant beauty of the morning stirred the poet that could never long remain silent in one who saw in the miracle of Nature the hand of the Creator of the universe. Oblivious of the hardships and possible dangers ahead he opened his notebook that evening and wrote:

Now the whole land laughs and sings, now sweet Flora comes to lie with Phoebus.... The winter rye was already five or six inches high and the barley was showing its blades. The birches began to break into green; only the aspen and alder still withheld their leaves. . . . Everywhere beside the road I saw mares grazing with their little foals. . . . There were geese too, with tiny yellow goslings. The lark, trembling in the air, sang to us[2] all the way. . . .

The day was fine and warm, with a light and cooling western breeze; then clouds came up from the West. [At Högsta] the forest became more dense, and the sweet lark, which till now had been in attendance, sang no more; but another bird, the song-thrush, welcomed us to the forest and with his amorous warblings to his beloved from the tops of the firs delighted us also: yes, so high and so ingeniously does he sing that often his song surpasses that of the nightingale, the master-singer.

Linnaeus was for ever dismounting to gather and record the name of a flower or to examine a pebble; nothing in Nature was too small or too mean to arouse his interest. He was 'like a wide-eyed child among new toys'. And so it was to continue, day after day of patient observation all carefully noted in his Journal.

Handle of a walking-stick carved with *Linnaea borealis*, said to have been made by Linnaeus when in Lapland.

[1] He mentions elsewhere that he had bought these second-hand at an auction.

[2] To himself and his horse.

43

That night he lay at Mehede. For one who was little accustomed to riding he had made a good start: he had covered a distance of about forty-three miles.

It took Linnaeus eleven days to reach Umeå, the capital of Västerbotten (West Bothnia) – a small town lying a few miles from the sea at the point where the Gulf of Bothnia shrinks to its narrowest. This stage of his journey, which he estimates at about 400 miles, was over well beaten tracks and may therefore be dealt with briefly.

Near Elfkarleby he heard the first cuckoo and saw the famous waterfall and the salmon-fishery. It was a Saturday when he reached Gävle, the capital of Gästrikland, where the Provincial Governor gave him a letter of recommenda-tion to officials in the northern provinces. As was his invariable custom on a Sunday, the following day he did not leave until he had been to church. Beyond Gävle he came upon considerable quantities of a plant which he here calls *Campanula serpyllifolia* – a name given by Caspar Bauhin in 1596 – but which he later caused to be renamed *Linnaea borealis* in his honour. (In a famous passage in his *Critica Botanica* Linnaeus wrote with mock modesty: '*Linnaea* was named by the celebrated Gronovius and is a plant of Lapland,[1] lowly, insignificant, dis-regarded, flowering but for a brief space – from Linnaeus who resembles it.'

Heavy rain, fog, thunder and lightning were now successively his lot. At Iggesund he visited an iron-foundry, and on the sixth day came upon his first Lapps, seven men who were driving a herd of reindeer and their calves; they proved to be coastal Lapps who spoke good Swedish. At Norby he took a guide and climbed the local mountain, sliding most of the way down the steeper southern face but interrupting his descent to snatch a young horned owl, one of three, from its nest. The nest also contained a single wind-egg which broke as he picked it up, 'emitting such a disgusting stench that I shall not attempt to describe it for fear of making my readers sick'.

The greater part of his way now lay near the seashore, which at one point was strewn with the wreck of a ship. The sight reminded him of a student, Elias Tilliander (1640–93), who had been so 'harassed by Neptune' during his voyage across the Gulf of Bothnia from Stockholm to Åbo that he returned home overland – a journey of perhaps 2,000 miles instead of 200 – and changed his name to Tillandz ('by land'). Tillandz became a distinguished botanist, and Linnaeus named in his honour the *Tillandsia* – a plant which cannot tolerate a damp climate.

The 18 May was Ascension Day and Linnaeus spent it quietly at Fjähl, 'partly on account of the festival, partly to rest my weary and shaken body'. It was hardly surprising that he felt shaken, for no doubt he could afford to hire only very inferior horses from post-house to post-house. At Härnösand he found himself already so weighed down by the minerals he had collected that he had them packed up for dispatch to Uppsala. Next day, 20 May, he climbed with two very reluctant natives to a cave which was said to be inaccessible, and while doing so was nearly killed by a falling rock. Snow still lay several inches deep in many places, and he was grateful for the hare-skin coverlet that he found that night on his bed.

Nordmaling, which he reached on 23 May, was Artedi's birthplace, and probably he called upon the mother of his friend to bring her the latest news of

[1] It is also a rare native of parts of Scotland and northern England, and a variety with stronger coloured flowers is found in North America.

44

796. Fruit and Flowers. JAN van HUYSUM. B.1682. D.1749. Dutch School.

her son. Next day, after being ferried across the River Umeå by a 'Charon' whom he describes as a 'canus, calvus, torosus [hoary, bald, brawny] old greybeard' – he often slipped like this from Swedish into Latin – he arrived at Umeå.

Andromeda polifolia, and below, *Linnaea borealis*, photographed by R. C. Elliott.

Linnaeus remained several days at Umeå, which he found had not yet recovered from the damage it had received in the late wars. Here he called upon Baron Grundel, the Provincial Governor – 'a most good-natured man who received me very kindly and showed me his collection of curiosities'. Among these were several caged crossbills and an otter, the latter so tame that when taken down to the lake it would neither dive into the hole cut in the ice for fish, nor eat live fish. The Baron was a keen gardener and proudly displayed to his guest his flowers, herbs and vegetables. But gardening in Västerbotten was hard and often un-rewarding work; potatoes, Linnaeus learned, grew 'no bigger than poppy-heads', and roses, apples, pears and plums were virtually impossible to cultivate.

Linnaeus was particularly interested in the local brand of half-boots, called *kängor*, which were comfortable, cheap, and completely waterproof. They had no heels: Nature, Linnaeus observed, had not given high heels to man and Nature always knew best, for the wearers of these buskins could run as nimbly as if they went barefoot.

So far Linnaeus had kept to the regular and tolerably frequented route, never too far from the coast, which continued beyond Umeå right round the Gulf of Bothnia into what today is Finland; now he was to turn inland, travelling due west, and for a fortnight explore the wild, difficult, and largely unknown country inhabited by the Lycksele Lapps. His real adventures were about to begin.

It was a depressing start, for it was still raining heavily and the only nag he could hire was a more than usually wretched animal. Moreover, as far as Umeå he had been able to command a horse at any post-house, but now he was obliged to beg and grovel to get one at all. With every mile the road grew worse, and his mount constantly stumbled. 'In this desolate wilderness I began to feel very lonely and longed for a companion. . . . The few natives I came upon spoke with a foreign accent.' Towards evening he reached Jämtböle, where there was nothing to eat but a capercailzie that had been killed and dressed a year before; however, it tasted better than it looked. The rain was now so torrential that he decided to go no further that day. He slept well beneath a reindeer-skin, his head resting on pillows stuffed with reindeer hair.

Next day was wet as ever and the going even more difficult. No doubt what Dr Shaw was to write in his *Linnaeus in Lapland* was true:

> New scenes his raptur'd sight surveys
> Amid Lapponia's peaceful soil;
> And while with ardent zeal he strays
> Fair science crowns his pleasing toil.

But the stanza that followed better described Linnaeus's present situation:

Umeå, 1701.

Through many a forest dark and drear,
O'er many a desert's trackless side,
With fearless foot he ranges round
With Heaven and Nature for his guide. . . .

'Never have I known a worse road,' he wrote, 'for all the elements combined against me. It was a mass of boulders, with great twisted tree-roots and between them pot-holes full of water.' Slender birches, bowed down by the rain, lashed his face. Great pines, 'overthrown by the wrath of Juno', barred the way, and there were swollen streams to be crossed over primitive, dilapidated bridges or just a fallen tree. To make matters worse, his horse had no saddle or bridle, and for reins simply a piece of rope tied to its lower jaw. Yet nothing could at any time deter him from studying, collecting, or recording whatever aroused his insatiable curiosity: the plants – especially mosses and lichens; the broad, horizontal collars of birch-bark, which people wore, pinned round the neck, as protection against the rain; the way of straining milk through plaited tufts of hair from the tails of cows: all were grist to his mill.

At Tegsnäs he pitied the inhabitants who were nearly fifty miles – two whole days' journey – from their parish church at Umeå, but who were heavily fined by their bullying priests and made to do penance for three consecutive Sundays if they absented themselves from any of the major festivals. The church at Granön was much nearer, but being in another parish attendance there presumably did not count. Elsewhere Linnaeus mentions that getting to church in parts of Lycksele Lappmark in spring often involved 'wading up to the armpits through icy water and arriving half dead from cold and exhaustion'. Sir James Smith,[1] in his edition of the *Lapland Journey*, here comments: 'This is no new instance of contrariety between the tyranny of man and the gospel of Christ, whose "yoke is easy and his burthen light".' Linnaeus was also told that when a Lapp refused to surrender his magic drum or his idols to the missionaries, his coat would be removed and he would be held down while the main artery in his arm was opened; he was then left to bleed until he had promised to come to heel – a procedure, says Linnaeus, that was 'often successful'. Smith, clearly a humanist, here makes another acid comment.

[1] Son of a rich Norwich manufacturer and a keen naturalist. In 1784 he acquired the Linnaean collections for England.

50

On the third day, which was Whitsunday, Linnaeus reached Granön in time for church at 9 a.m. Hardly a soul was present, the pike having impiously chosen that very moment to rise – an important event, then as now, in the Lapp calendar. The service lasted until eleven o'clock, by which time it was too late to leave for Lycksele, more than thirty miles away. In any case, this part of the journey had mostly to be made by water, and there was a strong headwind. The delay gave him the opportunity to examine and describe a small beaver that had been shot by one of the peasants.

Very early next morning he set out in perfect weather by boat up the River Umeå:

> It was an immense joy to observe at sunrise the tranquil stream, disturbed neither by the Naiads with their floods and torrents nor by the soughing of Aeolus, and to see how the woods on either side of it were reflected to provide for the traveller a subterranean kingdom beneath the surface. On both banks lay wide heaths, steeply sloped and covered with undergrowth. . . . Such of the giant firs as still defied Neptune smiled in the waters, deceptive in their reflection; but he and his brother Aeolus had taken their revenge on many of them, Neptune devouring their roots and Aeolus casting down their summits.

There was plenty of opportunity to study the water-birds, and from time to time the peasant who was rowing him stopped to take pike from nets that he had previously set near the bank. After some twenty miles the water became more difficult, till finally they reached three rapids which obliged them to land. What then took place Linnaeus not only describes but also illustrates with a whimsical drawing:

> The peasant handed me my things, put his bag of food on his back and, turning round to the boat, laid both oars over it crosswise so that each came under the opposite arm [and then put it over his head]. And thus he leaped with them over hill and dale, so fast that the devil himself could hardly have kept up with him.

At eight o'clock the following night they reached Lycksele, where Linnaeus was very hospitably entertained by the Pastor and his wife. These kindly people at first tried to persuade him to stay with them until the next *böndag* (prayer day); Lapps, they said, were apt to fire on strangers at sight, and it would be best for him to wait until those who then came to church could return home and give warning of his approach. Next morning, however, they changed their minds and recommended him to leave before the floods, always a danger when the mountain snows began to melt, grew worse.

During his brief stay at Lycksele Linnaeus found time to purchase a snuff-box of reindeer horn and to make several drawings of the caparison of a reindeer. He also visited the church – a miserable kind of a barn which leaked so badly that the congregation might just as well have been in the open, and whose seats were so low that one had to sit all hunched up. Finally, he examined a woman who believed she had three frogs in her stomach as a result of having drunk water containing frog-spawn. She maintained that she could hear them croak, and said that only *brännvin* (spirits) eased her discomfort. Another woman had some years earlier had the same complaint; she happened to take three *nuces vomicas* and

A Lapp and his magical drum, engraving by George Cooke from Pinkerton's *Voyages*, 1819. The religion of the Lapps, before the coming of Christianity, was a form of Shamanism.

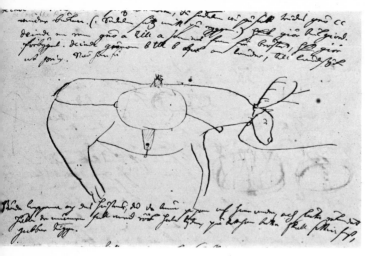

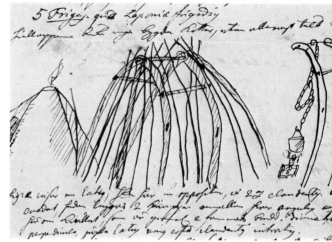

Linnaeus's drawing of a reindeer, from *Lapland Journey*.

Right: Linnaeus's drawing of how a Lapp tent is made.

recovered, but this one did not dare to. 'I recommended tar; but this too she said she had used, and it merely made her vomit.'

It would appear that there were weekday services at Lycksele, for Linnaeus left on a Wednesday 'after divine service was over'. In a letter he tells us that for the journey he took with him only three loaves of bread and some reindeer tongues, intending to buy *en route* what more he needed. He again went by boat, his destination now Sorsele (which in fact he was never to reach).

There is at this point, as also elsewhere in his narrative, much information about the customs of the Lapps, about the plants he was collecting and the birds and other animals he saw. He mentions that in parts of Lapland there were Finnish colonists – his boatman was one – who had been given leave to settle there and who had established excellent relations with the local inhabitants. He draws a *kåta* or Lapp dwelling. The Lapps, he observes, 'lie stark naked, with only reindeer-skin coverlets. There is no embarrassment when a man or woman stands up naked to dress.' The commonest illness was *ullem*, a kind of colic caused by drinking polluted water, 'for which they take soot, tobacco, salt and other remedies. The pain is often so violent that they crawl on the ground.' Asthma, epilepsy, pleurisy and rheumatism also occurred. 'For headaches they place a small piece of fungus on the spot where the pain is greatest, then set fire to it and let it burn till the part is excoriated.'

Linnaeus elsewhere in his Journal mentions another fungus (probably *Boletus suaveolens*) which was prized by young Lapps when they went courting. In his *Flora Lapponica* he writes more fully and in his most romantic vein on the subject:

> When a Lapland youth finds this fungus he preserves it carefully in a little pouch hanging from his waist, so that its grateful scent may make him more acceptable to the girl he is courting. O whimsical Venus! In other parts of the world you must be wooed with coffee and chocolate, preserves and sweets, wines and dainties, jewels and pearls, gold and silver, silks and cosmetics, balls and assemblies, concerts and plays; here you are satisfied with a little withered fungus!

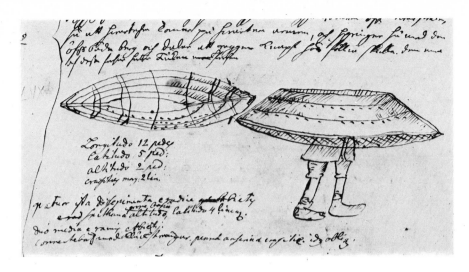

Linnaeus and his companion continued up the river all day and all the following night – 'if night it could be called, for it was as light as day, the sun disappearing below the horizon for only about an hour and a half'. It was exhausting work, he says, and cold at midnight. 'My companion had sometimes to wade, dragging the boat after him, for more than three miles at a stretch.'

In the morning they saw some tents and hoped that they might find a Lapp who would act as guide for the next stage of the journey; but they were empty. Towards evening, however, they came to an island on which some men had encamped for the pike-spawning season. 'They were peasants from Granön, a place about fifty miles away. They had built themselves a hut just like a bath-house except that there was no stove and the smoke issued through the door. They lie upon benches.' These fishermen were, however, too busy to help them, and the travellers went on their way. After many more weary miles they decided to leave the boat and turn inland. The going now was dreadful: all night in wind and rain they scrambled over fallen trees, waded knee-deep through bogs and waist-deep through icy streams. 'Had it been punishment for a capital offence it would still have been a cruel one. How I wished that I had never undertaken my journey!' At six in the morning they rested and managed to light a fire to dry their clothes and, hopefully, give them a short respite from the midges. Then, at a place that proved to be Lycksmyran ('Lucky Marsh' – it had more properly been called Olycksmyran, 'Unlucky Marsh', thought Linnaeus) they came upon a tent, and a man who agreed to go in search of a guide:

It was about 2 o'clock in the afternoon before he returned, completely exhausted. He was accompanied by a human being, but whether man or woman I could not at first decide. No poet can ever have portrayed a Fury to compare with her; she might have come from the Stygian regions. She was very tiny, her face blackened by smoke. Her eyes were brown and sparkling, her eyebrows black; and her jet-black hair hung loose about her head, on which she wore a flat red cap. Her dress was grey; and from her chest, which was like the skin of a frog, were suspended a pair of long limp brown dugs. She wore a number of brass bangles; round her waist was a belt, and on her feet Lapp boots.

The first sight of this Fury alarmed me, but she showed her compassion when she

53

addressed me: 'O you poor man! what cruel fate has brought you here? Wretched man! how did you come, and whither would you go? Do you not see the misery of our dwellings, the labour that it is for us to get to church?'

I asked her where I could go from here, either onwards or back again, so long as it was not by the way I had come. But she replied, 'No, Sir, there is no other way; you must return as you came. Ahead the river is in spate. We can do nothing for you. My husband, who ought to receive you, is ill. Our nearest neighbour is more than six miles away; if you could get to him perhaps he could help you, but I doubt whether it is possible.'

I asked how far it was to Sorsele. 'That I do not know,' she answered. 'But in these conditions it would take you at least a week to get there, my husband says.'

I, who was already ill and exhausted from such great exertions and long journeying, from carrying my own baggage (for the Lapp carried the boat), from sleepless nights, from having no cooked food and from drinking too much water (since there was nothing else to drink and nothing to eat but unsalted and often maggoty fish) – I would have died had it not been for a scrap of dried and salted reindeer's flesh which the pastor's wife had given me, though without bread it was very bad for the stomach and was evacuated undigested.

I longed for once to meet people, to eat cooked food, and not to try like a salmon to swim upstream to my total ruin. I asked if she had any food for me. 'No – not unless you will have fish.' I looked at the raw fish, whose mouths were full of worms, and the sight took away my appetite without fortifying me. I asked if I could get reindeer tongues, which the Lapps dry and sell and which for their fat are much prized by the best people; but she said it was not possible. 'Then reindeer cheese?' 'Yes – but it is nearly six miles away.' 'If you have any, could I buy one or two?' She replied, 'I would not want you to die of hunger in my country.'

A Lapp tent, from G. Acerbi's *Travels through Sweden*, 1802.

Opposite: Lapps cooking fish, from G. Acerbi's *Travels through Sweden*, 1802.

Somehow or other Linnaeus managed to buy one small cheese, but presumably from the peasant of Lycksmyran since he makes no mention of a twelve-mile walk; then, abandoning all idea of reaching Sorsele, he started back towards Lycksele.

As he had feared, the dangers were even greater than on the outward journey. The boat rushed headlong down the racing stream until finally it crashed against a boulder and was smashed to pieces. Fortunately the water was at this point shallow and he and his companion reached the bank without difficulty; but the Lapp lost not only his boat but also his axe and his pike, and Linnaeus a stuffed heron and sea-eagle. After they had stripped and dried their clothes in the sun they walked along the shore for six miles or more, through bushes and bogs, until they were lucky enough to come upon a settler who had pitched his tent up there to fish for pike. He produced some food and put them on their way.

Two days later, exhausted and hungry, Linnaeus reached Lycksele where the Pastor and his wife revived him, and by the afternoon of 8 June he was safely back at Umeå.

At Umeå he allowed himself four days to recuperate from his fortnight up-country; then he continued northwards along the coastal road, his destination Luleå.

It sometimes happened that a particular plant caught Linnaeus's fancy and stirred him to lyrical flights. (In Lapland small flowers would 'wave to him in friendship', wrote his student Sven Anders Hedin.) In the marshes not far from Umeå he came upon large quantities of a small, pink-flowered shrub 'at the

Andromeda polifolia, from Sowerby's *English Botany*.

Below: Linnaeus's drawing of Andromeda.

height of its beauty' – a plant previously known as *Chamaedaphne* but which he decided to place in a separate genus and name *Andromeda*.[1]

I noticed that she was blood-red before flowering, but that as soon as she blooms her petals become flesh-coloured. I doubt whether any artist could rival these charms in a portrait of a young girl, or adorn her cheeks with such beauties as are here and to which no cosmetics have lent their aid. As I looked at her I was reminded of Andromeda as described by the poets, and the more I thought about her the more affinity she seemed to have with the plant; indeed, had Ovid set out to describe the plant mystically *[mystice]* he could not have caught a better likeness. . . .

Her beauty is preserved only so long as she remains a virgin (as often happens with women also) – i.e. until she is fertilized, which will not now be long as she is a bride. She is anchored far out in the water, set always on a little tuft in the marsh and fast tied as if on a rock in the midst of the sea. The water comes up to her knees, above her roots; and she is always surrounded by poisonous dragons and beasts – i.e. evil toads and frogs – which drench her with water when they mate in the spring. She stands and bows her head in grief. Then her little clusters of flowers with their rosy cheeks droop and grow ever paler and paler. . . .

But Linnaeus is not content with words alone, and with his clumsy pen he illustrates his far-fetched allegory, using a newt to symbolize the dragon. Felix Bryk, in an article on Linnaeus as an artist, writes that this drawing always reminded him 'of the English Pre-Raphaelites – e.g. Rossetti or Moore. . . . What could they not have made of this idea if it had been their own!' More, at all events, than did Linnaeus. Bryk goes so far as to call Linnaeus 'an excellent draughtsman' – which is nonsense. He was less at sea when drawing a fly, whose structure he understood, than when attempting figures or a landscape; but I cannot even agree with Stearn that he was 'a good draughtsman when dealing with small objects', or indeed that the fact that he pasted the walls of his study with botanical prints really proves that 'he took a keen interest in pictures'. Matisse

[1] *Andromeda polifolia*, marsh andromeda or bog rosemary, also found in Wales, northern England, southern Scotland and central Ireland.

once said that his ambition was to draw like his little girl of five; Linnaeus achieved this effortlessly. It is, incidentally, impossible to accept as Linnaeus's work the four quite competent studies of flowers which Miss Gourlie reproduces in her biography (Plate IX).

One day, at a later stage in his journey, Linnaeus showed a Lapp some of his drawings. The man 'was alarmed at the sight, took off his cap, bowed, and remained with head down and his hand on his breast as if in veneration, muttering to himself and trembling as if he were just going to faint. . . .' This was not, however, an aesthetic reaction: clearly he thought that the drawings were magical, like those on the drums of his own country, and Linnaeus a wizard.

Linnaeus's drawing of a cranefly, *Pedicia rivosa*, syn. *Tipula rivosa*, made at Umeå; it shows the veining of the wings characteristic of this species.

A little further on, Linnaeus noticed, hanging beside the road,

> the under-jaw of a horse, having six fore-teeth, much worn and blunted, two canine teeth, and at a certain distance from the latter twelve grinders, six on each side. If only I knew how many teeth and of what kind every animal had, how many teats and where they were placed, I should perhaps be able to work out a perfectly natural system for the arrangement of all quadrupeds.

Here, comments Smith, 'the Linnaean system of *mammalia* seems first to have occurred to the mind of its author'.

Near Skellefteå, soon after midnight, Linnaeus saw an owl (*Strix ulula*) flying ahead of him and, in spite of the bad light, succeeded in shooting it without dismounting from his trotting horse. The bird was too damaged to stuff, so he sketched and described it. Shortly before reaching Old Piteå, a small port on the Pite Estuary about 150 miles from Umeå, he was

Linnaeus's drawing of an owl, *Strix ulula*.

> assailed by such swarms of midges as surpass all imagination. The air seemed to be solid with them. . . . They filled my mouth, nose and eyes, for they made no attempt to get out of my way. Luckily they did not try to bite or sting me, though they almost suffocated me. When I clutched at the cloud before me, my hands were filled with thousands of these insects, all far too small to describe, which were instantly crushed to death.

Outside the gates of Old Piteå he came upon 'a gibbet with a couple of wheels upon which lay the bodies of two decapitated Finns who had been executed for highway robbery and murder. Beside them was the quartered body of a Lapp who had murdered one of his relations.' Linnaeus makes no comment: in those days such happenings were taken for granted.

Linnaeus spent five days in and around Piteå, constantly on the watch for anything unusual. While walking in the fields at Piteå he suddenly saw a great herd of charging cattle:

> Even the leanest cows, which one would have thought were hardly able to walk, raced like deer in a field, their tails curling, running and leaping till finally they came to a pond, where they halted, thinking to have found a place of refuge from the enemy. I hastened to try to see what drove them with a force greater than the whip or even death itself, and found that it was something that I had already encountered,

namely *Oestrus bovi*. These gadflies do not attack the body, but the feet – between the larger and smaller hooves: the insect seldom if ever flies more than two or three spans from the ground and mostly at half that height. The cattle run until they find water in which to stand, so that the gadflies cannot harm them.

Linnaeus left Old Piteå on the morning of 21 June and the same evening reached New Luleå – 'a very small town, situated on a peninsula surrounded by a kind of bay' – which had been founded in the seventeenth century. Finding little to interest him there, he continued his journey the next day – by sea, since he could not hire a horse – to Old Luleå, about three or four miles distant. In the Gothic church there he was shown a fine altarpiece with statues of martyrs, the tops of whose heads had been scooped out to hold water which, by means of pipes leading to the eyes, could produce at will the effect of weeping. There were also two statues of saints whose arms could be raised, as if in veneration, by a concealed mechanism. In Old Luleå Linnaeus was the guest of Pastor Unnaeus, 'a venerable and pious old man who entertained me extremely well'. He also received hospitality from Lars Vallman, who gave him a Lapp woman's cap; this is probably the one which Linnaeus is shown as wearing in the well-known portrait of him in Lapland dress.

'A Lapland fantasy', by Linnaeus.

58

5.

The Lapland journey:
Lule and Torne Lappmark

he up-country expedition which Linnaeus now made took him five weeks. The greater part of the outward journey was in a north-westerly or west-north-westerly direction up the Lule River; then, crossing the watershed into Norway, he reached the coast at Sørfold, on the southern arm of the Foldenfjord, and returned approximately by the way he had come. The distance from Luleå to Sørfold is, as the crow flies, rather over 200 miles – about that from London to Darlington.

There were sailing-boats on the lower reaches of the Lule, and Linnaeus embarked in one of these. Here he soon made friends with another passenger, a mining engineer from Kalix named Seger Svanberg who was on his way to inspect a newly discovered lode of silver ore near Tjåmotis. Svanberg offered to show him the mine and, if at a later date he could manage to get to Kalix, to give him a short course in assaying.

On the second day they crossed from Västerbotten into Lule Lappmark to reach Storbacken. From there they travelled on foot to Pajerim, where they passed the night 'in a smoky hut, ventilated only by holes in the roof'. On the fourth day, 'after much labour', they reached Jokkmokk, today a popular tourist centre, lying exactly on the Arctic Circle.

The church at Jokkmokk was the principal one of the district, but if Linnaeus is to be believed, its pastor and the local schoolmaster (who was also in holy orders) were no ornaments to their professions:

The priests – Herr Malming the schoolmaster and Högling the pastor – entertained me with their stubborn clerical follies. I was amazed that such great arrogance and ambition, such great want of understanding and such vulgarity, such obstinacy and meanness in discussion, should be found in a priest, who is commonly supposed to be an educated man; moreover, that anyone who had been a student for more than twelve years should not be better read. I understood only too well why these barbarians were kept far from civilization.

The pastor began to discuss the clouds in Lapland, how they sweep over the mountains carrying away with them stones, trees and animals. I ascribed this to what it may well have been – the violent winds, and said that clouds never lift anything. He smiled at me, saying I had never seen such clouds (who had never been in the mountains). Yes, I answered; when there is mist I walk in the clouds, and when the mist falls it immediately rains on me. At such sophistry he smiled sardonically. Still less acceptable was my talk on water bubbles which can rise into the air etc., and he told me that clouds were solid. When I denied this he supported himself with a scriptural text, smiled at my simplicity, and said that he himself would teach me how after rain a slime remains on the mountains where the clouds had descended on it. When I said that that was called *nostoc* and was vegetable, I was judged, like St Paul, to be mad, too much science having made me crazy. . . . He advised me to trust people who understood such things and not, the moment I got home, write a thesis full of such nonsense.

The other (the pedagogue) reproached me for paying too much attention to worldly vanities at the expense of spiritual matters, and said that many souls were lost through hankering after learning. Both wondered at the Royal Society choosing such a student, instead of relying on finding a knowledgeable and responsible man on the spot who could explain all these things.

It was unusual for Linnaeus to write with such venom, nor were his opinions of these two men to be mellowed by the passing of time; when, after his return to Uppsala, he compiled a list of the people who had entertained him in Lapland and elsewhere, he seized the opportunity to pour yet further scorn on their ignorance and arrogance.

In a paper published in 1740 in the *Proceedings* of the Swedish Royal Academy of Science Linnaeus discussed the lemmings, one of the animals that the Lapps believed to be carried by the clouds, and offered his explanation of the origin of this myth. In the mountains of northern Scandinavia strong winds some-times bring dense fog and darkness

in which it is easy to stumble into a crevasse formed by the water, and be buried in it; this is the origin of their belief that the clouds carry away Lapp and reindeer and hurl them down the mountainside. But cloud is no more able to lift anyone than is mist – not even these lemmings, which breed like other animals in the fells and in certain years swarm from them in enormous numbers. In olden days, when these animals suddenly invaded the whole countryside in those provinces which adjoin Lapland, the people were dismayed; for this was something unfamiliar, and they imagined it to be a punishment sent from God because they had failed to observe their prayer days. . . .

The extraordinary story of the periodic invasions of these lemmings – the locusts, as it were, of the North – and of their long, slow march 'towards death and distant seas', can be read in any popular work on zoology.

Beyond Jokkmokk the travellers came to Purkijaur, in whose vicinity was a pearl-fishery which Linnaeus was able to visit and describe on his return journey. The fisherman made use of a primitive raft on which he lay, drawing the mussels from the river-bed with a long pair of wooden tongs – a procedure which Linnaeus illustrates with a naive sketch. The pearl, he knew, was caused by a disease; but an all-too-rare one, for several thousand mussels had to be opened for every worthwhile pearl found. Reflecting on this later, he came to a conclusion that was to bear important fruit: 'Anyone who could induce this illness in mussels could make them produce pearls; and if one could, what could be more profitable?'

60

Next day, Saturday, 1 July, a few miles short of Tjåmotis, Linnaeus had his first view, through a gap in the hills, of the high, snow-covered mountains of the Lapland fells. 'In the evening I arrived at Tjåmotis, where I saw the midnight sun above a high mountain called Harrevarto, opposite the sacristan's house. I held this to be not the least of Nature's miracles. . . . O Lord, how wonderful are Thy works!'

After a leisurely Sunday at the parsonage he set off early the following day with Svanberg and an army quartermaster to visit the new silver-mine. Two days later, provided with a week's provisions and a Lapp to act as guide and interpreter, he continued his journey, presumably up the lakes by boat, to Hyttan ('the Hut', now called Kvikkjokk). Of the Pastor of Kvikkjokk, doubtless his host there, and of his family Linnaeus was to write many years later in his *Nemesis Divina*, that curious compendium of examples of divine retribution: 'The pastor's wife [Christina Groth] in Kvikkjokk whores with regimental quartermaster Kock. The pastor in despair takes to the bottle; his daughter becomes a strumpet and is tumbled by a Lapp.'

Linnaeus was at this time much concerned with the life and habits of the reindeer which, here and elsewhere in his Journal, he describes fully. The reindeer is to the Lapp what the coconut is to the Sinhalese – the supplier of nearly all his daily needs. In addition it provides him with transport; it is 'his estate, his cow, his companion, and his friend', and he has no less than twenty-four different names for it. The gelded animal was the most valued, as being bigger and fatter than the ungelded, and Giuseppe Acerbi, in his *Travels through Sweden.* . . . (1802), adds the information that the Lapps, 'when speaking of any one whom they think worthy of the very highest degree of praise, say *uærtzeketz*, or, *he or she is absolutely a castrated rein-deer*'.

Linnaeus discovered what caused the curious castanet-like noise which reindeer make when trotting over snow: their hooves were hollow and clacked as the animals moved. He also solved the problem of the perforations which spoil the appearance and reduce the value of all reindeer skins. They were generally believed by scientists to be the result of smallpox, but the Lapps understood the real cause – that they were made by the larvae of another species of gadfly, *Oestrus tarandi*, which torments the reindeer by depositing her eggs in their skins. Many years later, in a dissertation (*Cervus rheno*, 1754), Linnaeus put in order his accumulated knowledge of the reindeer and discussed this gadfly, whose pricks he whimsically compared to those of Cupid's darts:

61

The pregnant gadfly pursues the reindeer all day long, up hill and down dale, perpetually trying to lay her eggs on their backs (and so that she may survive in these icy mountains, the Creator has completely covered her with hairs). The reindeer, even if there is a herd of a thousand of them, kick, snort and never stop frisking about as long as a single weak, defenceless little fly is buzzing over them; not until after she has gone do they desist for a second, so that if an egg has chanced to fall upon one of their backs it may be dislodged.

All day long in summer they roam the eternal snows of the fells, and if there is no one tending them they always run at top speed into the wind so that no fly can follow them. . . . They hardly trust themselves to graze, being always on the alert, with watchful eyes and pricked-up ears, lest a fly should be anywhere in the neighbourhood. But the fly continues her pursuit until she drops on the snow from sheer exhaustion. As soon as she is rested, however . . . her desire is once more aroused to seek out the object of her longing.

Oh, with what a variety of arrows Cupid inflicts his wounds!

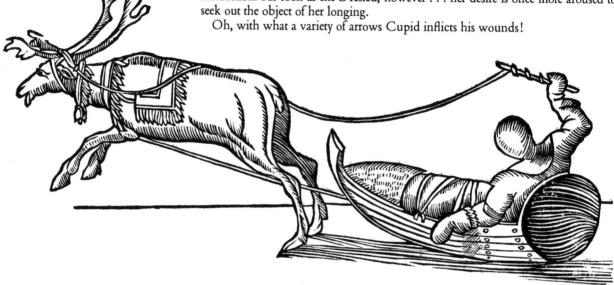

Reindeer and sleigh, from Scheffer's *Lapponia*, 1673.

Leaving Kvikkjokk, Linnaeus set out to climb Vallevare, a near-by mountain whose height he estimates at about 8,000 feet:

When I reached its slopes, it seemed as if I were entering a new world; and as I climbed higher I did not know whether I was in Asia or in Africa, for the soil, the situation and all the plants were strange to me. I had now reached the fells. All around me were snow-covered mountains; I was walking on snow as if in midwinter. All the rare plants which I had seen before and rejoiced in, were here as if in miniature; indeed there were so many that I feared I was taking away more than I would be able to deal with.

At this point Linnaeus's Narrative[1] gives a fuller, though possibly an exaggerated, description of what is also recorded in the Journal:

Here there were no more trees – nothing but mountains, each one bigger than the last and all covered with frozen snow. There was no road, no track, no sign of human habitation. Summer's green seemed to be banished, driven down into the deepest valleys. There were hardly any birds other than Alpine ptarmigans running about

[1] See page 68.

62

in the valleys with their young. . . . I climbed to the highest point to see the midnight sun. . . . Then I sat down to sort and describe the plants I had collected [he lists thirty of them], oblivious of the passing of time, so that my guide had to remind me that we still had thirty-five or forty miles to go to the next Lapp tent and that if we hoped to get any reindeer meat we would have to hurry. So we continued, up hill and down dale, to right and to left, across the snowbound mountains, the going becoming each moment more difficult; there were loose stones everywhere. . . .

Among the Alpine plants collected on Vallevare (though actually on the return journey) was another species of *Andromeda* – a plant today known as *Cassiope tetragona*. In his *Flora Lapponica* Linnaeus describes how he came to find it:

> At midnight – if such I may call it when the sun never sets – I was walking rapidly, facing the icy wind and sweating profusely . . . but always on the alert, when I saw as it were the shadow of this plant, but did not stop to examine it because I took it to be an *Empetrum*. A moment later, however, I suddenly thought that it might be something new, and retraced my steps; I would again have taken it for an *Empetrum* had not its greater height made me examine it more carefully.
>
> I don't know what it is that at night in our mountains disturbs our vision and makes objects far less distinct than by day, for the sun is just as bright. But from being near the horizon its rays are so level that a hat affords no protection to the eyes. Moreover, the shadows are so extended, and by gusts of wind made so confused, that things not really a bit alike can hardly be told apart. . . .
>
> The *Andromeda* was over, and setting seed; but after a long search I managed to find a single plant still flowering; the flower was white, shaped like a lily of the valley but with five sharper divisions.

Every plant-collector will at one time or another have had a similar experience. The Journal adds a further and agreeable detail about Linnaeus and the Alpine ptarmigans:

> Small Alpine ptarmigans, woodcock-coloured, with white wings, were there with their young. I picked up a chick, and the mother rushed at me and kept flying round me so that I could easily have caught her. A hundred times I could easily have killed her had I not considered a mother's feelings and reflected that to do so would be to leave her tiny young one defenceless. So I gave her back her son.

At last, after many hours, Linnaeus and his companion reached a Lapp tent. This consisted of a simple wooden framework covered with cloth, the floor being overlaid with reindeer skins, hairy side uppermost:

> The people – there were sixteen of them – lay naked. They washed themselves by rubbing themselves *down*, not up, and did not dry themselves. They cleaned their bowls with their fingers, spitting water out of their mouth on the spoon, and scooped out their boiled reindeer milk which was thick like milk-and-egg soup and very strong.
>
> In the morning about two thousand reindeer came in and were milked by both men and women, who knelt on one knee. . . . I was given whey to eat. . . . It tasted good and strong, but my appetite was spoiled by the way the spoon was cleaned; for the husband took water into his mouth and spat on the spoon, then cleaned and

Linnaeus's drawing of top, *Saxifraga stellaris*; centre, *Rhododendron lapponicum*; bottom, *Pedicularis flammea*.

63

Linnaeus's drawings of *Dryas octo-petala* and *Erigeron uniflorus*.

Andromeda tetragona, now *Cassiope tetragona*, from the *Botanical Maga-zine*, 1832.

dried it with his fingers. The wife cleaned with her fingers the bowl that held the milk, licking them after every stroke.

To this description may be added that of another tent of a couple of mountain Lapps which Linnaeus subsequently visited:

I sat with my legs crossed, to the right of the entrance. Opposite me was an old woman with one leg straight, the other bent. She wore a silver belt, and her dress came no lower than her knees; her grey hair was hanging down; her face was wrinkled and her eyes bleary; her features were typically Lapp, and her fingers big and horny. [Here follows a detailed description of her *pudendum*.] Beside her sat her husband, a young man of about thirty-eight who had married this old hag ten years since for the sake of her reindeer.

Next day there was a heavy hailstorm. Linnaeus, not adequately protected against such cold, borrowed the gloves and reindeer-skin jacket of the guide, who was presumably left to shiver. It grew late and still there was no sign of a tent; in fact there can be little doubt that the Lapp, now far from his home, was completely lost. But eventually they came upon fresh reindeer droppings, which after three more miles led them to a dwelling. Miss Gourlie, who spent a winter with the Lapps and knows the country well, says that Linnaeus must have come down to the south-eastern angle of Virihaure and the mouth of the River Staloks.

They rested in the tent for a whole day, Linnaeus busy writing up his notes on reindeer, drawing an infant in its cradle, and observing local customs. For example: 'When my guide came in, he put his nose close to that of the person he wanted to greet, as if he intended to kiss him. . . . I asked whether they actually kissed each other, and he said, no, that they only put their noses together and that it was only relations who greeted one another thus.' In fact the Lapps lay cheek to cheek, not nose to nose.

For two more days they continued their way across the mountains that divide Sweden from Norway, mountains that Linnaeus called 'the Alps' and which he alleged to be in places 'more than a Swedish mile high' – that is to say, a good deal higher than Everest. Once he fell into a crevasse and had to be pulled out, wet and bruised, by two men with ropes; he seems at this stage to have had a second companion, both men being glad to make the journey at his expense so that they could buy *brännvin* in Norway. Finally, they came to the watershed – and there, far below them, green and beckoning and looking deceptively near, lay the foothills and coastal plain of Norway:

We descended – and so long was the slope and so steep that I feel as if I were descending still. But down below there were no more rock plants.

When at last we reached the bottom, what a relief it was to my tired body! I came from cold, freezing rocks down into a warm and shimmering valley (I sat down and ate wild strawberries); instead of snow and ice I saw green plants in charming meadows (I had never seen such tall grass anywhere before); instead of wild weather there was a wonderful smell of flowering clover and other plants. *O formosissima aestas!* Oh how beautiful is summer!

That evening they reached the coast at Sørfold, where one of the Lapps, who presumably was making his first acquaintance with the ocean, scooped up some of the sea-water in his hands and was perplexed to find it undrinkable. They were put up by a shipmaster; and what pleasure it was, Linnaeus thought, to sit once again on a real chair, drink cow's milk, and eat delicious *Sebastes marinus* (rose-fish or Norway haddock) 'which tasted almost like salmon'. He was quite worn out; yet the two Lapps – one was fifty and the other nearly seventy – who had carried his baggage all the way, seemed fresh as paint and immediately began romping together and running around. Rosén had asked him to try to find out why Lapps were so swift-footed, and he now turned his mind to the problem. He believed that probably there was not just one reason for this but many, though the heel-less boots might well be the most important. A meat diet might be another, as also the fact that they ate in moderation whereas 'Finnish peasants cram themselves with turnips, those of Scania with as much flummery as they can hold, while the Dalecarlians gorge themselves till their bellies are tight as drums. . . . Lapps are always small and slim; I never saw one with a big belly. Milk also helps to make them active.'

And why, too, were Lapps so healthy? Here again there were a number of reasons. Pure air and pure water, he thought; well dressed food eaten cold: 'they do not spring upon it with boots and spurs' – that is to say, rush at it as soon as it comes off the fire; tranquillity of mind – they are not jealous and they never squabble; moderation in eating – and in drinking also, for *brännvin* was not easy to come by; a Spartan upbringing; and their meat diet, 'for carnivorous animals are long-lived'.

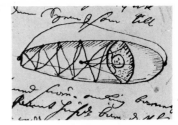

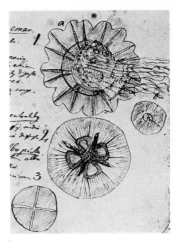

Above: Linnaeus's drawing of a baby Lapp.

Linnaeus's drawing of medusas.

On his first day at Sørfold the sea was very rough, and if truth be told Linnaeus was probably more than thankful that a long expedition he had intended to make to the Lofoten Islands to study the Malstrøm – a dangerously strong current, later made famous by Jules Verne, which wrecked many fishing-boats – was pronounced impossible. So he passed the time pottering on the beach, observing and drawing crabs and jellyfish and whatever caught his fancy. He returned to find that his two Lapps had not only filled their dried reindeer bladders with *brännvin*, they had also consumed it in such quantities that they were dead drunk.

A Lapp tent, from Scheffer's *Lapponia*, 1673.

65

Above: Lapp fishermen, from Acerbi's *Travels through Sweden*, 1802.

Linnaeus's drawing of a fish.

Next morning the water was calmer and he was taken down the Sørfolden by boat, to be landed towards evening at Rörstad, near its junction with the Norfolden, where he was the guest of Pastor Johan Rask and his 'quite remark- ably beautiful eighteen-year-old daughter, Sara'. Rask was a much travelled man, having been in the West Indies as well as Africa; he had published an account of his journeys in which he described various fish and plants he had seen. The visit was a success: Linnaeus was overwhelmed by Sara's beauty. Rask, after giving his guest a rather frigid reception, soon warmed to him, while Sara confessed that 'she had never expected to meet an honest Swede' but that here was the exception that proved the rule. Linnaeus was royally entertained, given by Sara various recipes for making bread (including one for what we now call Ryvita), and by her father, at his departure, a fine and valuable venus's shell.

Two days later, on 15 July, Linnaeus set out from Sørfold on his homeward journey. Though reluctant to leave Sara he was eager to be off, for he found the Norwegian coast very relaxing; as soon as he was back again in the mountains his languor vanished. He was convinced that mountain air provided a far better health cure than did the fashionable spas, which were often low-lying and which encouraged over-indulgence in food and drink. He was much ahead of his time in thus advocating high Alpine resorts.

There is no need for us to follow Linnaeus step by painful step on his return journey, as

> . . . down Luleå's haunted stream
>   His vent'rous bark pursues its way,
> While round the waving meteors gleam,
>   And cataracts urge their dashing spray.

It was 'the mixture as before', and was made by approximately the same route. At the end of July he reached Luleå, where he was again the guest of Pastor Unnaeus; then, working his way further up the Gulf of Bothnia, he crossed the linguistic frontier to enter Finnish-speaking territory and on 3 August arrived at Torneå, at the head of the Gulf.

Torneå, now the Finnish Tornio, is situated on an island near the mouth of the River Torne which today marks the boundary between Sweden and Finland; the Swedish town of Haparanda, on the mainland, was not founded until 1829. Linnaeus spent six weeks in and around Torneå. He visited a few places in the immediate neighbourhood, such as Kemi and Kalix, and on 19 August set out on a fortnight's expedition by boat up the River Torne, getting as far as Vittangi before the cold and the dearth of interesting new material drove him back to the coast. At one moment he considered exploring East Bothnia; but in East Bothnia they only spoke Finnish, and he thought that once he was off the beaten track he would not be able to make himself understood. He was a bad modern linguist, but he can hardly be blamed for finding Finnish impossible. Yet might he not, as in Lapland, have used an interpreter?

While at Torneå he was shown much hospitality by a number of its citizens, including Dean Abraham Fougt who added to other kindnesses the loan of a

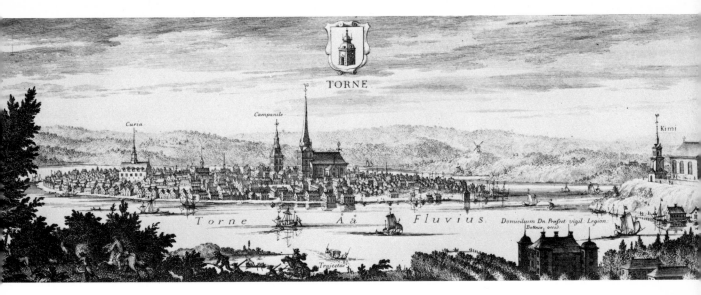

TORNE

Curia Campanile Kimi

Torne Aä Fluvius. Domicilium Dn. Præfect. vigil. Legion.
Botniæ, oriens

Trajectus

Torneå, 1701.

hundred copper dalers to help him home, and who much impressed his guest by his ability to preach in both Swedish and Finnish. Linnaeus made himself popular in the neighbourhood by solving the mystery of a distemper which each year killed large quantities of cattle; it was caused, he found, by their eating the highly poisonous water-hemlock which grew in profusion in the water-meadows there. One day he climbed the church tower, from whose summit, in June 1694, King Karl XI had observed the midnight sun – an event which had been commemorated by a medal showing on one side a bust of the King and on the other the sun half above the horizon.

At Kalix, about forty miles to the west of Torneå, he was the guest of a circuit judge named Hoijar, and also of Svanberg who gave him his promised instruc-tion in assaying and whose kindness he repaid by acting as godfather to his infant son. At Kemi, to the east (and now in Finland), he lodged with the hospitable pastor, whose curate was the father of the famous Cajanus, known as 'the long Finn', a giant who exhibited himself in various parts of Europe and who had been rejected for Friedrich Wilhelm's Prussian Guard for being a head taller than any other man in the regiment. At Kemi Linnaeus also saw the salmon-fishery, and here and elsewhere enjoyed, night after night, splendid displays of the aurora borealis.

In the middle of September Linnaeus finally turned his steps homeward, setting out along the eastern (now Finnish) shores of the Gulf of Bothnia through East Bothnia towards Abo, from where he could complete the journey by a short sea voyage; he confessed that he had no desire whatever to sail down the whole length of the Gulf.

He now found himself among Finns, with their difficult language and un-hygienic habits; though doubtless a certain amount of Swedish would be understood at the post-houses along the coastal road, for safety's sake he armed himself with a few useful phrases. He did not care for Finns. Almost all of them were bleary eyed from living in smoky, unventilated huts: 'If *I* had the

67

management of these Finns,' he wrote, 'I would tie them up against a wall and flog them till they promised to build chimneys.' And further: 'The peasants of Upper East Bothnia, being children of darkness indoors, are unkempt. They wear enormous trousers, reaching to their feet and made of white fur stitched from top to bottom. Quarrelsome. Indoors was a disgusting stench of a sour white fish like Baltic herring. Dirty indoors. They speak nothing but Finnish.'

On 30 September Linnaeus reached Åbo (in Finnish, Turku – Finland's oldest city and ancient capital) where he was obliged to borrow some more money. A week later he crossed by way of the island of Åland to Grisslehamn, and on 10 October about one o'clock in the afternoon, came safely to Uppsala. He closes his Journal with the praise of his Maker who had brought him unharmed through so many dangers. The greatest adventure of his life was over.

We come now to something which, though it shows Linnaeus in an unattractive light, must not be shirked.

As we have already said, Linnaeus kept a day-to-day account of his travels in a Journal, written at the time, which he never intended for publication and which was not in fact published until more than thirty years after his death. But on his return to Uppsala he drew up and submitted to the sponsors of his journey a brief 'Narrative' in which, in order to magnify the hardships and the extent of his sojourn in Lule Lappmark, he distorts various facts and even wholly invents at least one long expedition which he cannot conceivably have made. His early biographers are for the most part discreetly reticent on the subject; but Miss Gourlie draws attention to it, though she considers as 'all rather humorous and pathetic' what most people would call a deliberate and clumsy attempt to deceive for the purpose of gain.

First, there is mention of a long excursion by sea, made when Linnaeus was at Sørfold. This was no doubt the trip that he intended to make to Malstrøm but which the weather conveniently prevented; all that Linnaeus did at Sørfold, so far as we can tell, was to potter about for an hour or two in a rowing-boat and then allow himself to be rowed in it a dozen or so miles to Rørstad, at the mouth of the Sørfolden. But worse was his story of a long and dangerous expedition from the Norwegian coast to 'Caituma', in the Torneå fells. (Incidentally, the misleading map reproduced in the first volume of Mrs Caddy's biography shows Linnaeus as almost reaching the North Cape.) Had he really made this great detour to Kaituma he would, according to the dates and distances given in the Narrative, have covered about 840 miles in a fortnight – an impossible average of sixty miles a day; as Miss Gourlie, now almost indignant, rightly says, 'it is naughty to fib'.

Here is Linnaeus's account of this purely fictitious journey to Kaituma:

In the morning [of 16 July] we began to climb the mountain and continued thus all day, sweating unbelievably because it was so steep and so unpleasantly high; but when we reached the snow we were able to cool ourselves. We then made towards the Torneå fells, which were said to be more than 260 miles away. . . . Oh, how many weary steps we took up that steep mountainside, how we sweated, how exhausted we were before we reached Caituma! Sometimes we were enveloped in clouds which half blinded us; sometimes we had to make a detour to avoid a stream, sometimes to strip and wade through icy water. Had we not had this cold snow-water to revive us in the heat we could never have survived. We reached the top of Caitumbyn, where the inhabitants were completely wild and ran from their tents when they saw us although we were still a long way off. I did not want to go any further, particularly as we had finished our bread a fortnight before.

A fortnight! The whole journey to Luleå took our Munchausen only a fort-night and it is inconceivable that neither the lovely Sara nor the shipmaster at Sørfold would have provided him with a few loaves to take with him. He con-cludes: 'I remained four days at Kvikkjokk to recruit my strength, then descended the river again to Luleå.' That at least was approximately true.

The two weeks' journey from Torneå up the River Torne to Vittangi and back – a journey which, incidentally, brought Linnaeus to within twenty-seven miles of Jukkasjärvi – must have involved him in at least a mild adventure or two; yet in his Journal he dismisses it all in a few lines. After the fantasies of Lule Lappmark the reader may well be excused for wondering whether Linnaeus is not again straying from the realm of fact into that of fiction. But those best qualified to judge seem to be satisfied that he really did make this quite considerable expedition; had he invented it he would, perhaps, have made it more exciting.

It is understandable, if regrettable, that Linnaeus wanted to impress the officers of the Society by exaggerating his distances and his miseries: he felt that they had treated him stingily and hoped to extract more money from them; what is curious, however, is that he should have submitted to them an account contain-ing such clumsy inconsistencies. And how truthful, one is forced to ask, was he when he wrote his Journal? Since it was written on the spot, kept daily, and never intended for publication, it is safe to conclude that in it he told the truth with no more exaggeration than must be expected from any traveller exploring a relatively unknown country.

Incidentally, Baedeker, in writing of Jukkasjärvi, states that 'among savants who have penetrated to this point are Regnard, who came in 1681, Linnaeus in 1732 and Maupertuis and [Anders] Celsius in 1736'. Of these four men, only Regnard actually reached Jukkasjärvi, and his visit with two French com-panions is properly authenticated. He wrote from this remote spot:

We spent the rest of this day and all Tuesday morning cutting on stone a permanent record to inform posterity that three Frenchmen had travelled till they could go no further; that they had achieved this in spite of difficulties which had frightened many others; and that they had come to erect a monument at the world's end, being prevented from going further not by lack of courage but by shortage of supplies.

Another question poses itself: how daring, in fact, were these explorations of Lapland? Regnard reaching 'the world's end' at Jukkasjärvi and Torneträsk (he left inscriptions in the churches of both these places) only to find Christian churches and resident priests – was not this something of an anticlimax: another Tartarin arriving at the Hotel Rigi-Kulm? And as for Linnaeus, he never even reached Jukkasjärvi! Were not the real heroes of exploration the missionaries

69

who had brought Christianity to these wilds and had built churches there?

Linnaeus's journey, judged by the risks taken and the hardships endured, was, after due allowance has been made for exaggeration, probably not much more adventurous or hazardous than many made today by enterprising under-graduates to relieve the boredom of a long summer vacation. Compared with Wilfred Thesiger's travels in Arabia it was about as dashing as a walking-tour in the Lake District. What makes it so important is the richness of the information gleaned and accurately recorded; to do this justice would require a whole book.

The botanical fruits of his journey did in fact receive one: the *Flora Lapponica*, which was published in its final form in Amsterdam in 1737 and which re-mains important because Linnaeus, when naming Arctic-Alpine species in his *Species Plantarum*, continually cited it. Other material was also used later in dissertations or in various of his longer works. But for many of his observations made in Lapland the student must do what was not possible for Linnaeus's contemporaries: turn to the delightful pages of *Iter Lapponicum*.

There he will find how to cure chilblains with toasted reindeer cheese and boils with a poultice of birch bark, how to cement broken pots by boiling them in milk, how to exterminate house-crickets, and how to castrate reindeer. He will learn how to make thread from the tendons of reindeer hooves, and how to play *tablut* – a kind of mixture of chess and draughts with Swedes and Muscovites as pieces. Marriage ceremonies are described, and courtship in a cold climate: 'To begin with, the lover addresses his beloved in a jocular manner, to find out how the land lies. . . .' There is information about food and cooking, about fishing, embroidery, tanning leather, and the entertainment of guests; about trapping ptarmigans and shooting wolves; about the crossbows with which a Lapp can hit a small twig at thirty paces; about sicknesses, hobgoblins, love-potions, skis, sledges, lemmings, and the seasonal changes in the size of reindeer droppings. Of Lapp music Linnaeus wrote: 'They know only the *lur* [a kind of trumpet] and pipes made from the bark of the rowan. In church only the educated sing.' And perhaps one should put 'sing' in inverted commas, for else-where Linnaeus wrote, 'No *Laplander* can sing, but instead of singing utters a noise resembling the barking of dogs.'

Writing of the dress of the Lapps, he favourably contrasts their sensible, loosely fitting clothes with the tight garments of the Swedes:

> The Lapps protect their necks by means of thick collars, without which they would never survive in such intense cold. For these sensitive parts of the body, which have so many nerves, muscles, windpipes, veins and marvellous arteries, are inevitably, as the smallest and least warm, the most susceptible to injury. And so, unfortunately, our girls and youths tie scarves round their necks until they are as red as if they were strangulated. We Swedes are swaddled in our clothes. Neckcloth, jacket, waistcoat, breeches, stockings, overcoats, etc., are all tight-fitting; and the tighter they are, the more fashionable. . . .

Linnaeus in the course of his travels had formed a great admiration for the Lapps, and in some respects an envy of their way of life. Hard though their existence was, it had, he thought, something of the tranquillity of the Silver Age of Ovid or the pastoral life of Virgil. 'Their soil is unwounded by the plough, their lives by the clash of arms. They have not found their way into the bowels of

Linnaeus's drawing of a Lapp woman's headdress.

Linnaeus's drawing of ski and ski-stick.

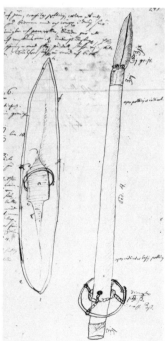

the earth; they do not wage wars to establish territorial boundaries. They wander from place to place, live in tents, lead the patriarchal life of the shepherds of old.'

It sounds idyllic. But as Linnaeus proudly strutted about Uppsala in the Lapland dress he had brought back with him (much of it the gift of his various hosts), as he told and retold to his friends those stories of his adventures which lost nothing in the retelling, he could not disguise from himself the fact that he was glad, very glad indeed, to be back once again in civilization.

A footnote must be added to this account of the Lapland adventure. In 1935, during repairs to the house in the old Botanic Garden at Uppsala in which

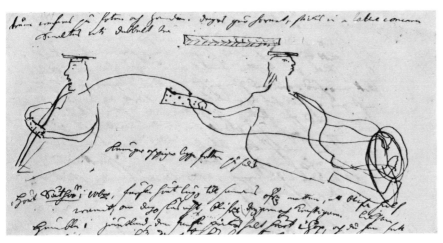

Making thread from reindeer tendons, drawing by Linnaeus, woodcut from Scheffer's *Lapponia*, 1673.

Left: 'Recollections of Lapland', drawing by Linnaeus.

Linnaeus lived for more than thirty years, a little notebook was found buried in a pile of rubbish under the floor-boards. It proved to be the actual pocket notebook that Linnaeus had carried with him throughout that memorable journey, containing a list of persons visited, distances travelled, and so on, together with the brief selection of useful Finnish phrases already mentioned. There is also a kind of writing-tablet on which jottings could be made in pencil and then erased; very possibly Linnaeus used this tablet to make, as he travelled, notes from which to write up each evening the account which was published after his death.

Linnaeus's notebook for the Lap-land journey.

6.

Work and play

Back at Uppsala, Linnaeus found himself faced with both a worry and a disappointment.

The worry was the old familiar one: money. His journey had proved much longer than the 1,600 miles for which he had budgeted, and for which in any case he had received from the Society only two-thirds of the 600 copper dalers he had asked. The actual distance covered was probably upwards of 3,000 miles – a figure which, in order to touch the hearts (and, more particularly, loose the purse-strings) of the officers of the Society, he inflated to over 4,000 miles. He even managed to add up incorrectly the figures that he submitted. In November 1732 he appealed for an additional 122 silver dalers; the Society replied that they would do something – but did nothing. The following February he tried again, now reducing his claim to 78 silver dalers; finally he was given, from a reserve fund, 40 silver dalers to cover an outstanding debt. Linnaeus was highly indignant: 'After all I have suffered,' he wrote, 'I must pay those 38 silver dalers myself! . . . Would anyone in the whole world, I ask, undertake such a journey at such a price? I wouldn't make it again, not if I were offered two thousand plåtar.' (One plåt equalled two silver dalers.) To make matters worse, his Royal Scholarship in the medical faculty was about to expire and was not renewable. The Consistory was, however, gracious enough to promise him an annual grant of sixty plåtar, payable half-yearly, from the Wrede Fund.

Such were his worries; his disappointment was a literary one. Linnaeus had undoubtedly hoped that his report to the Society, which contained more than 200 observations on the natural history of Lapland and much else besides, would be published in the Academy's periodical, *Acta Literaria Sveciæ*. In fact only a small fragment of this material was printed at the time: the first part of the *Florula Lapponica* (*Brief Lapland Flora*), the promised publication of the second part of this *opusculum* being delayed for another six years. The *Florula* is important for being the first printed work in which Linnaeus employed his 'sexual system' of classification.

He did, however, submit to the Academy a paper dealing with three matters which had aroused his interest during his travels: 'The causes of cattle death in Torneå', 'The use of Aconite as a food in Medelpad', and 'A makeshift bed in the wilderness'. This was read to the members in February 1733 but was

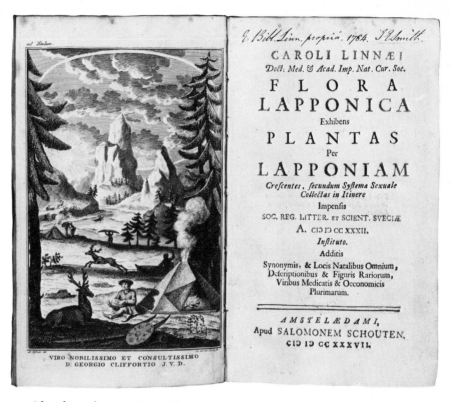

CAROLI LINNÆI
Doct. Med. & Acad. Imp. Nat. Cur. Soc.
FLORA
LAPPONICA
Exhibens
PLANTAS
Per
LAPPONIAM
Crescentes, secundum Systema Sexuale
Collectas in Itinere
Impensis
SOC. REG. LITTER. ET SCIENT. SVECIÆ
A. CIↃIↃ CC XXXII.
Instituto.
Additis
Synonymis, & Locis Natalibus Omnium,
Descriptionibus & Figuris Rariorum,
Viribus Medicatis & Oeconomicis
Plurimarum.

AMSTELÆDAMI,
Apud SALOMONEM SCHOUTEN.
CIↃIↃ CC XXXVII.

VIRO NOBILISSIMO ET CONSULTISSIMO
D: GEORGIO CLIFFORTIO J. V. D.

Frontispiece and title-page of *Flora Lapponica*.

considered overlong and therefore not printed. 'Thus,' he laments, 'is economy practised in Sweden.'

But if Linnaeus was indignant and disappointed, he was by no means discouraged. All through the autumn and early winter he toiled away at his *Flora Lapponica*, the major work for which the *Florula* was as it were a sketch, and at putting in order his Lapland and other treasures. The room in which he lived and worked soon became a 'cabinet of curios', which grew richer with each month that passed, and which a year or two later was thus described by one of his friends:

You would have admired, enjoyed – yes, quite fallen in love with his museum, to which all his students had access.

On one wall was his Lapp dress and other curiosities; on another side were big objects of the vegetable kingdom and a collection of mussels, and on the remaining two his medical books, his scientific instruments, and his minerals. In a corner of the room, which was a high one, were the branches of a tree in which lived about thirty different kinds of tame birds, and in the window recesses stood great pots, filled with earth, for growing rare plants. It was a joy, too, to look at his collection of pressed plants, all gummed on sheets of paper; there were more than three thousand Swedish plants, both wild and cultivated, as well as many rarities from Lapland. Further, there were a thousand species of Swedish insects and about the same number of Swedish stones, tastefully displayed in spacious boxes and arranged according to the entirely new system founded on his own observations.

74

Christmas 1732 was now approaching and Linnaeus decided to spend it with his family; no doubt he was looking forward to telling them all about his adventures in Lapland. He reached the Rectory at Stenbrohult on Christmas Eve, just as his father was saying grace before dinner. Before he returned to Uppsala he told his brother of his presentiment that he would never see his mother again; she was only forty-five, but perhaps she had never entirely recovered from her illness of the previous year. His fears proved to be justified: 'On 6 June 1733, at 6 o'clock in the evening, my dearly loved and most pious mother died, in my absence, to my unutterable sorrow, anguish and loss.'

At Uppsala the spring term of 1733 opened inauspiciously for the medical students: there were the usual absentees in high places, with the resultant dearth of lectures. Linnaeus seized the opportunity to give a private course in assaying, a subject new to the University and one in which he himself was little more than a tyro; the course was well patronized and he received two plåtar from each

Some of Linnaeus's instruments, preserved in his house at Uppsala.

student who attended. Like Ruskin, who said that when he wanted to find out about a subject he wrote a book on it, Linnaeus even compiled a short textbook on assaying, which was well received by the authorities. The rest of his time was devoted to his *Flora Lapponica* and to the compiling of a number of papers on botanical and other subjects. In a letter written during the following autumn he listed no less than thirteen manuscripts in various stages of completion, and it is obvious that what was to prove his life's work had already taken clear shape in his mind.

The success of his lectures and textbook aroused the jealousy of Rosén, whose own lectures on anatomy Linnaeus had not attended. Fries, the author of the standard biography of Linnaeus, deals at enormous length with the unfortunate quarrel that ensued, and establishes that the story, once current, that it ended in a duel was quite untrue. It was of course only to be expected that these two clever young men should watch each other's progress with some concern, and Linnaeus was, on his own admission, *praeceps in iram* – 'quick to anger'. Yet were there really any serious grounds for jealousy? It was not a case of two men chasing one job; there were *two* jobs at Uppsala which must of necessity soon become vacant, for Roberg was now seventy and Rudbeck seventy-three. But the fact remains that Linnaeus was no longer happy at Uppsala, and that his relationship with Rosén was the cause of this unhappiness. He even began to dream of a peaceful life in the country, away from the 'rat-race':

Had I been brought up to it [he wrote], I would like to have been a rich farmer; or better still – if it weren't so cold up there – a rich mountain Lapp. I now wished that I owned a small freehold property on a conveniently situated island where without too much trouble I could get enough to eat and converse with a few simple friends . . . where I could watch from a distance the futile wrestling and wrangling of others attempting to make a living.

In the spring Linnaeus had been obliged to pawn a piece of silver; but as a result of the success of his lectures, and of his foregoing a summer holiday, by the autumn he found himself in better financial shape. When a fellow student, Claes Sohlberg, invited him to spend Christmas with his family in Falun, he felt justified in accepting: he needed a break.

But in the event it proved in part a working holiday; for Falun was an important mining centre and Sohlberg's father an inspector of mines, so that Linnaeus very naturally seized the opportunity to go down the big copper-mine and a silver-mine, and to visit a smelting-works. He has left a graphic account of his descent into 'Pluto's restless, infernal kingdom', the Falu Gruva – the oldest and most celebrated copper-mine in Europe:

We went the whole way down by wooden ladders, mostly of twenty rungs each, hanging vertically and free of the wall. Often they were joined in pairs and only supported at their ends, so that they swayed about. Down below the drifts were so low that we had to stoop or crawl, and so narrow that many a time we had to turn our bodies sideways in order to move forward; again and again I knocked my head on projecting bits of the roof – a roof that was covered with crystallized vitriol of a curious blackish colour. All the men carried torches in their mouths. At the bottom

there blew a cold wind strong enough to turn a windmill. The horses which drew the winch were driven by a man who stood close to the axle, and there were stalls, hay and a smithy. The ore was carried in wheelbarrows or small four-wheeled waggons.

In these gloomy places to which no daylight ever penetrates, these doomed creatures – there were about twelve hundred of them – lived and had their being; yet they seemed to be content, because they fought to get jobs there. They are surrounded on every hand by rock and gravel, by dripping corrosive vitriol, by smoke, steam, heat and dust. There is a constant risk of sudden death from the collapse of a roof, so that they can never feel safe for a single second. The great depth, the dark and the danger, made my hair stand on end with fright, and I wished for one thing only – to be back again on the surface. These wretched men live by the sweat of their brows, working naked to the waist and with a woollen rag tied over their mouths to prevent them so far as is possible from inhaling fumes and dust. The sweat poured from them like water from a bag. It was only too easy to fall into a hole, to miss one's footing on the rung of a ladder; or a rock might come crashing down and kill some miserable man instantly. Every aspect of hell was here for me to see. . . .

Over Christmas, however, Linnaeus really did bring himself to relax; indeed this advocate of the simple and sober life seems to have let himself go with quite unprecedented abandon. To a friend he now wrote: 'Dalecarlia's sirens have beguiled me into forgetfulness of friends, cares, nagging thoughts, troubles, home, studies, and time itself. I am soothed by their songs. They sing that trouble comes all too soon without our meeting it half way. They have taught me to drink a half, even a whole measure – yes, joking apart, I have been thoroughly enjoying myself.'

What does Linnaeus mean by 'joking apart'? That his participation in this riotous living, which seems so out of character, was not really all that he pretended? Later, however, he was to write of these 'Falun mining gentlemen' that they 'vied with one another in drinking, all day and every day', and that they eventually died of drink unless a sharp and timely illness brought them to their senses. 'The foundry owners,' he continued, 'put a firkin on the table, and the cups race over the table as briskly as the piss-pot under it, until the firkin is empty. I saw Forsling incapable of lying down as the beer gushed out of his full

Mines at Falun, from *Suecica Antiqua et Hodierna*, 1701.

Bishop Browallius, by J. G. Geitel, 1754.

stomach, and Eric Sohlberg squeeze his belly so that the beer spurted on to the opposite wall. . . .' The picture is not a pleasant one, and it is hard to visualize Linnaeus so nastily employed.

'Keeping term'[1] at Swedish universities seems to have been a very casual affair at this time, for it was March before Linnaeus, closing the journal of his travels with a little hymn of praise to God, returned to Uppsala:

> Almighty God, Creator and Preserver of all things, who
> On Lapland fells suffered me to ascend so high,
> In Falun mines to descend so low,
> On Lapland fells showed me *diem sine nocte*, day without night,
> In Falun mines *noctem sine die*, night without day,
> On Lapland fells suffered me to be where cold is never-ending,
> In Falun mines where heat is never-ending,
> On Lapland fells suffered me to see in one place all the four seasons,
> In Falun mines not one of the four seasons,
> In Lapland led me unharmed through so many mortal dangers,
> In Falun through so many perils to health,
>   Praised be all Thou hast created
>   From the beginning to the end.

Vague too must have been the distinction between graduate and under-graduate; for though Linnaeus was still a student, more of his time seems to have been spent in giving than in attending lectures. He was now lecturing not only on mineralogy and botany but also, to private pupils, on a subject in which he had lately become much interested: diet. His lecture notes on the subject, begun at this time and constantly added to in later years, together with a bundle of loose sheets and various extracts from notebooks kept by students, have been published by A. O. Lindfors under the title *Linnés Dietetik* (Uppsala, 1907). Linnaeus was frequently to lecture on diet in Uppsala between 1742 and 1772, and the subject will be discussed in a later chapter.

While at Falun, Linnaeus had made friends with Johan Browallius, later Bishop of Åbo but at that time Chaplain to the Provincial Governor of Dalecarlia, Baron Nils Reuterholm, and tutor to his sons. (It was in fact Browallius who wrote the description of Linnaeus's museum in Uppsala.) Through Browallius Linnaeus had come into contact with Reuterholm, who had been impressed by his account of his Lapland journey and who talked rather vaguely of the possibility of a similar survey being made of his own province. Linnaeus had not treated this as a serious proposition; but there now came from Reuterholm a definite offer to finance such a survey, together with a money-order to cover the cost of his journey to Falun to discuss the project. Linnaeus was delighted and hurried to Falun, where he was handsomely entertained by Reuterholm and given a generous grant. Seven of the ablest students in the medical faculty at Uppsala now asked if they might join the expedition at their own expense. 'Of course I accepted their briskness with the due thankfulness,' wrote Linnaeus (according to a translation made by Dr Hartmann, into what he quaintly believed to be English).

The eight members of the Societas Itineraria Reuterholmiana (the Reuterholm

[1] There were two terms a year: 28 January to 23 June, and 1 October to 20 December.

78

Travel Club), as they rather pompously styled themselves, were well equipped, the expedition efficiently organized; it was a very different affair from the one-man, shoe-string exploration of Lapland two years earlier. Linnaeus designated himself the Club's President, and to each of the seven other members special duties were assigned. Reinhold Näsman was appointed the geographer; he had also to read prayers each day and preach on Sundays – services unlikely to be demanded of a member of such an expedition today. Carl Clewberg, an all-round scientist, was to analyze soil, investigate mineral springs, calculate altitudes, record the weather, and act as secretary. Ingel Fahlstedt was the mineralogist, and also groom in charge of the horses; Claes Sohlberg was physicist, botanist and quartermaster, and Eric Emporelius the zoologist, with instructions to include in his duties the provision of fish and game for the larder. Pehr Hedenblad was to observe economic conditions and to act as Linnaeus's adjutant. Finally, Benjamin Sandel, who had been born in America, was steward and treasurer, responsible too for foddering the horses. All but Linnaeus and Clewberg were Dalecarlians with some knowledge of the country, Näsman having also made a special study of local dialects. The whole team was urged to make drawings whenever possible.

The journey was in a north-westerly direction, through some of the most beautiful parts of Sweden, the objective – or at all events the furthest point reached – being Røros, about forty miles across the Norwegian border in the mountains which separate Sweden from Norway; it took forty-five days in all, and the distance covered was some 520 miles. The little band of eager young men – Stoever describes them as 'a kind of caravan of naturalists' – set out from Falun on the morning of 3 July 1734, though it appears that from time to time the party split up in order to cover more ground. Sometimes they travelled on horse-back, sometimes by boat; sometimes a friendly pastor gave them beds, sometimes they slept in barns. Each evening the accumulated experiences of the day were duly recorded in a journal.

At first they journeyed over relatively well known and not particularly interest-ing country. After three or four days they reached Orsa on the lake of the same name, a village renowned for its grindstones and, noted Linnaeus, for the con-sequent prevalence of diseases of the lung. The men, he wrote, 'seldom live beyond the age of twenty, thirty or forty. . . . In church we did see a few grey-haired old men, but they proved to be tailors and shoemakers who had never worked in the mines.'

Lake Siljan, with its gently wooded slopes, was a district famed for its tough fighting-men who had formed the backbone of Gustavus Vasa's army in the sixteenth century, and at Mora, at the head of this lake, the travellers were the guests of Dean Johan Emporelius, father of one of the party, who had a fine library. They also joined in the village dancing, and again at Nås where the three local specialities were 'the "Heart dance"; the "Jäfvund dance", named after a village in Venjan – a most agreeable and delightful dance that would be acclaimed at Court if it had come from Spain and were performed by a French dancing master' – and the pretty 'Six men in a dance'. Diagrams in the Journal show the steps of these dances.

At Älvdalen, the last stronghold of runic letters in Sweden, they stayed with Pastor Näsman, father of the party's geographer and prayer-leader, who had

Browallia demissa, by S. Edwards, from the *Botanical Magazine*, 1808. Philip Miller gave seeds, gathered near Panama, to Linnaeus, who changed the name of the plant from Dalea to Browallia.

achieved local fame by introducing the potato into Dalecarlia. Beyond Åsen the country became wilder, the route less well defined and finally, as they neared the Norwegian border, virtually non-existent. Crossing the watershed they reached the little copper-mining town of Røros, and four or five days later began to retrace their steps, but varying the way in places. By 18 August they were back in Falun.

Stoever, with his sharp eye for the whimsical, adds that

> the tour through *Dalecarlia* also mentions . . . how the inhabitants masticate a certain kind of rosin, and dress it in a still more disgusting manner as an aliment; how they bury in the earth a species of rotten fish, which is called *Lunsfisk*, and dig them out again to prepare them for their food. The same transactions describe a kind of bed called *Jullar* [jällar], in which the girls amuse themselves with their lovers. . . .

Soon after his return to Falun Linnaeus wrote to his friend and patron Baron Gyllengrip, the Governor of Umeå, telling him of the 'extraordinary observations in natural history and economics' that he had made during his journey:

> I have ideas as to how the fells could be cultivated by growing root-crops. . . . Oh, if only one could travel like this through all the Swedish provinces, visiting one each summer, how much one could discover that would be of value to our country! How much one could learn from one province of how best to cultivate another. I keep on thinking that this would be of far greater value to Sweden than all the poetry, Greek and metaphysics [i.e. physics] taught in our Academies – and it would cost the public far less. I am staying on at Falun for as long as Baron Reuterholm continues to put me up, then I shall have to go back to that wretched Uppsala. How I shall fare in the future is in the hands of Almighty God, who has given me the support of such powerful patrons. I hear that Dr Rosén has been urging that no reader in medicine should be appointed; clearly this is principally aimed at me. . . . I pray you, my Lord Governor, to bear me in mind if any opening should occur. . . .

So Linnaeus remained for the time being at Falun, teaching assaying and mineralogy to Reuterholm's two younger sons and Dr Browallius, and in his leisure moments writing up his travel material or availing himself of the opportunity to read in the Baron's well stocked library. Part of his instruction in assaying, he tells us in his Autobiography, was in the form of public lectures given before large audiences in the Assaying Room of the Falun mines:

> After his return from Lapland, Linnaeus had given a good deal of attention to mineralogy, and his chief reason for visiting Bergslagerna had been that there was no better place for making the mineralogical studies necessary to him for the formation of his system of classification; this system he now explained to the miners, who were delighted. Here at Falun Linnaeus felt that he was in a different world – a world where everyone liked him and was eager to help him. He got together quite a large medical practice. But Browallius was convinced that if he wanted to succeed in life he ought to go abroad and take his degree; after that he could come back and settle down wherever he liked. But for this he needed money, and to his friends there seemed that there was only one thing for him to do: to marry it. In theory Linnaeus approved the idea, but in practice he did not find any of the proposed candidates acceptable.

Fig. 2.

Fig. 1.

TAB. CII.

Fig. 3.

But the promise of financial aid was soon to come from another quarter. Sohl-berg, in whose house Linnaeus had spent the previous Christmas, now sug-gested that Linnaeus should take his son Claes to Holland and, for a salary of 300 copper dalers a year, continue coaching him. The Dutch were at this time among the best educated peoples in Europe: they had scholars and patrons of natural history, fine gardens stocked with plants brought back from their overseas empire, and, incidentally, excellent printers of whose services Linnaeus might be able to avail himself. So he gladly accepted Sohlberg's offer. Soon afterwards he returned to Uppsala to make preparations for the journey and to sit for the theological examination which every student intending to study abroad had to take before he could obtain a passport. This proved to be the only examination that Linnaeus ever underwent in a Swedish university.

Next he spent a fortnight in Stockholm on various errands including the purchase of clothes; by mid-December 1734 he was back at Uppsala, and two days before Christmas, after fighting his way through a blizzard, he arrived half-frozen at Sohlberg's hospitable house in Falun. Once again Linnaeus relaxed. There were parties every day until Twelfth Night, and it was at one of these that he met a girl with whom he found he had 'the desire to live and to die' (and who would, incidentally, bring a fairly substantial dowry with her).

This was Sara Elisabeth (Sara Lisa) Moraea, the eighteen-year-old daughter of Falun's Town Physician, Dr Johan Moraeus. Linnaeus immediately began to pay court to 'the Fair Flower of Falun' (as she is inevitably dubbed by Mrs Caddy). On 2 January he waited on her, dressed to kill in his famous Lapland costume, and the following day he took advantage of the absence of her parents to call again. Other visits followed, besides meetings at the houses of mutual friends. On 16 January he spent the whole day with her, proposed, and was accepted.

Dr Moraeus, after his own experiences as a medical man, was not at first pleased with the idea of his daughter marrying a doctor; nor was the mother, who had probably hoped that the girl would make what the world would consider a better match. In the end, however, they capitulated, on the under-standing that the marriage should not take place for three years and that Linnaeus should abide by his plan to go abroad. So rings were exchanged and the customary Vow of Fidelity was written by Linnaeus, after which a month was spent in visits to friends and future relations and in the preoccupations of young lovers.

Linnaeus also took stock of his financial position. He found that he had 260 silver dalers – a good deal less than he had thought. One or two friends made him presents of money, and from Fru Sohlberg came the welcome gift of some fine linen underwear. But Sohlberg, after many kindnesses in the past, now miserably and unexpectedly let him down:

No further mention was made of the yearly salary of 300 copper dalers. All I got was 12 plåtar. I could not now draw back from my journey, nor could I say anything to the old man who had housed and fed me for six months. . . . The Sohlbergs already owed me an agreed sum of thirty plåtar for my assaying. However, I put everything into the hands of God, who so far had wonderfully advanced me into the world; and I continued faithfully to serve my travelling companion, knowing that God always rewards us according to our deserts.

'Cupid inspiring plants with love', stipple engraving after Reinagle from the *Temple of Flora*. 'And thou, divine LINNAEUS! traced my reign O'er Trees, and Plants, and Flora's beauteous Train. . . .'

85

Dr Johan Moraeus.

Before leaving Linnaeus wrote a poem – 'A Lover's Farewell' – to his fiancée in which, in seven very trite stanzas, he spoke of the anguish of leaving her for so long; then he set out from Falun with Claes Sohlberg. The journey south was leisurely, with halts on the way to inspect mines and to visit friends. At Växjö they spent a few days with Dr Rothman, and on 19 March reached Stenbrohult. It was a sad home-coming for Linnaeus: 'My mother was missing, and I felt her loss. In the house everything was in confusion.' He found his father depressed, lonely in spite of the company of his younger son and his three daughters, in dread of the future, and unhappy that he was not in a position to contribute anything towards the expenses of Carl's journey.

On 15 April Linnaeus took leave of his family. He was embarking on his second great adventure and, as on the day he left Uppsala for Lapland, spring was waiting to speed him on his way. 'The weather was glorious,' he wrote. 'The rye was sprouting, the birches beginning to put on their leaves. The birds made the woods a paradise with their singing. . . .' In his luggage was a bundle of manuscripts and, needless to say, his famous Lapp dress – drum and all.

PART II

In search of fame
1735–1738

Collinsonia canadensis from *Hortus Cliffortianus*, 1738, drawn by Ehret, engraved by Wandelaar.

I.

Germany

'Time is never so dearly bought as when people go abroad for the sake of languages only.'

Linnaeus, Autobiography

The events of the next few weeks are described by Linnaeus in his *Iter ad Exteros* (*Journey Abroad*), first published in 1919 – a fragment of a travel diary in which five sheets (corresponding to the last ten of the eighteen days he spent in Hamburg) have been left blank, and which ends abruptly on 24 May (Old Style) 1735.

The two young men reached Helsingborg on Saturday 18 April, and the following day, after attending morning service, crossed 'the little mile' of water to Helsingör (Elsinore) in Denmark, where they found an inn which offered them bed and breakfast at one silver daler a head. In Helsingör they ran into a fellow-countryman from Stockholm, a man named Slyter, who befriended them and showed them the sights of the town – the Royal Garden, which they found dull, and the church which was 'also not to our liking'. But the town itself, with its well built timbered houses, they admired. 'It is as big as Kristian-stad,' wrote Linnaeus, 'and not fortified. The inhabitants are rather different in character from the Norwegians.' After listing, as he always did when travelling, the flowers that he saw, he continued: 'There are pumps everywhere, cavaliers and soldiers dressed in scarlet but *fides pauca* [of little honesty]. The town built like Malmö.'

Having waited in vain for five days for a ship bound for Holland, Linnaeus and Sohlberg decided to accept the chance of a passage to Travemünde (near Lübeck) in the *Tobias*:

But there was a head wind, and we had to lie in the Sound where sixty craft of various nations were also awaiting a favourable wind. Those who sail the seas usually drink three handfuls of sea water as soon as they go aboard, to prevent sea-sickness. . . . It makes a great difference whether one lies lengthways or athwart. My companion, who lay athwart, was tossed about and became sick and dizzy, whereas I, who lay lengthways, ate tough salted meat, cheese, etc., and was not sick. . . .

The 23rd. No change in the weather. We remained all day on board. Ships are always sour and stink of bilge-water; it would be a very good idea to have dried sweet rush strewn on the bunks for the sake of its aromatic smell. For food we had French bread made of rye and roasted chestnuts; it was as white as bread made of wheat, and very palatable. Gruel noon and evening every day. Nothing to drink but French wine that at first tasted good, but in the end we grew very tired of it and longed for water. It neither digested the food nor quenched the thirst. . . .

Opposite: 'Linnaeus fell on his knees and wept for joy when he saw for the first time the long heath of some English upland made yellow with the tawny aromatic blossoms of the common furze. . . .' (Oscar Wilde, *De Profundis*).

There were two green parrots on board. . . . Everywhere along the shore a poisonous stench of rotting seaweed.

The 24th. At dawn there arose a good wind from the north-west, and it was delightful to see how all of a sudden every ship in the Sound was rigged, and anchors raised. The weather was wet and the sky overcast. We passed on our left the island of Hven, ten miles long, Landskrona and Malmö; on our right came Sjælland and Copenhagen, where the masts of ships rose like a forest. . . .

On 26 April they reached Travemünde where they took the coach to Lübeck, a distance of about thirteen miles. After the four days spent at sea the country 'with its flat fields and charming arable land, its groves of beech and oak, was a paradise. It was glorious summer weather. . . . Gorse with its lovely yellow flowers was growing among the heather. . . .' There is a widespread legend that Linnaeus, when he came to visit England in August of the following year, saw gorse for the first time and fell on his knees to give thanks to God. The story caught the fancy of the Victorians; Oscar Wilde repeats it at the end of his *De Profundis*, and more than one female poetaster saw its potentialities – for example Emily Carrington, who wrote in *Aunt Judy's Magazine*:

> *Linnaeus and the Gorse*
> Over the heath the golden gorse is glowing,
>   And making glad the breeze;
> And lo! a traveller by the wayside going
>   Falls low upon his knees,
> And thanks God for such a glorious vision,
>   And such a rich perfume,
> As met him in what seemed a dream Elysian,
>   Far from his northern home.
>
> So felt the great Linnaeus, when before him
>   The yellow gorse spread out. . . .

Linnaeus found Lübeck a clean town, 'as big as Uppsala or even bigger, in pleasant surroundings; the suburbs fortified'. The streets were lit all night, and at every street corner were shutters which could be closed in the event of fire. He particularly noticed the lime trees, which had been planted close to the houses and trained so as to form arbours. The following day being a Sunday they went to church, where they were bored by the excessive singing of hymns – 'about fourteen of them. . . . On Sundays all the men wear black, and most of them had black cloaks although it was not raining.'

Next morning at six a.m. they left in the daily post diligence for Hamburg, a distance of about fifty miles. The way was pleasant and flowery, and it is almost unnecessary to add that a nightingale was singing in every tree. Soon too they heard the first cuckoo of the season. Dusk was falling and they were nearing their destination when an unpleasant incident occurred:

Shortly before we reached Hamburg our coachman drove the coach too near a field. A peasant immediately appeared on the scene and wanted to seize one of the horses and beat the driver until he gave him some money. After they had stood arguing for

a long time I told him to take the coachman to the courts and not to hold up the post.
He immediately went purple in the face and came at me with an axe. Had it not
been for my companions I would have taken him on.

How accurate, one may wonder, is this account of the brave young man so
eager to fight, single-handed, a raging farmer armed with an axe, desisting only
when restrained by his fellow travellers or in order to spare them an ugly
spectacle? And was it in Latin that he addressed him?

'The first appearance of the free imperial city of Hamburg is very disgusting and
ugly,' wrote a young German, Baron Caspar Riesbeck, when he visited the
town in the second half of the eighteenth century. 'Most of the streets are narrow,
close and black, and the populace in them is fierce, wild and, generally speaking,
not very clean.' But in the houses of the rich merchants he found 'taste, cleanliness,
magnificence and at times even profusion'. He praised, too, the beauty of the
Alster Lake, 'in a summer evening . . . almost completely covered with gondolas,
which have not such a melancholy aspect as those in Venice', and the good food
and fine wines that were served in the houses of the rich. Each dish had its
appointed wine: 'Burgundy is the standing vehiculum of green pease. Oysters
must of all necessity swim in Champaigne', etc.

Linnaeus, however, liked the general appearance of Hamburg. Many of the
houses were large and beautiful, and the Exchange, which was partly covered in,
'like a fine market-place. At midday it was full of people – mostly Jews, of
whom there are a great number here.' He found the inhabitants handsome,
amiable and polite, and noted that they 'followed the French fashion' in dress.
But he was even more struck than was Riesbeck by the filth and stench in the
streets. 'The beautiful town of Hamburg stinks like a privy,' he wrote, 'for
excrement flows into the gutters like water. It is a miracle that its inhabitants are
not all ill.'

In Germany at this time several periodicals were published which dealt with
scientific and learned subjects. One of these, the *Hamburgische Berichte von Neuen
Gelehrten Sachen* (*Hamburg Reporter of New Scholarly Matters*), had three years
earlier contained an article in which mention had been made of an *opusculum*
by Linnaeus and of his future literary projects; and in a local bookshop he now
came upon copies of the Nuremberg *Commercium Litterarium* in which also his

91

praises were sung. One or two of Linnaeus's biographers charitably assert that the information for these articles was supplied by Anders Celsius and other friends and admirers of the young Swede; but there is no lack of evidence that Linnaeus was never shy of blowing his own trumpet – and blowing it *fortissimo*.

The Editor of the *Hamburgische Berichte* was Professor Kohl, 'a most cultured man who showed me every possible kindness' and who continued to keep Linnaeus's name before its readers. Fries mentions and quotes from a long article which presumably appeared while Linnaeus was still in Hamburg. 'It opens,' he says, 'with an account of part of the work which Linnaeus had brought with him in manuscript to get published abroad, together with his collection of about a thousand insects from Lapland and Dalarna "all beautifully gummed on to paper"[!], and his complete Lapp dress with the magic drum whose use [for divination] he was always ready to explain and which never failed to arouse the greatest interest and admiration.' Then he quotes from the article:

> All that this well informed man thinks and writes is methodically treated, and he never rests until he has brought the science or the current problem into line with the appropriate system of classification; for he has an altogether remarkable power of judgment combined with an innate power of observation. His eagerness, endurance and industry are exceptional. . . .
>
> He is also a tireless reader, and as he reads he industriously makes notes and drawings; thus he has acquired great experience and so thorough an insight into many fields that, although he is only twenty-eight, he stands ahead of most of his seniors. His intellectual superiority is graced by an equally delightful disposition which reveals itself in his courteous modesty when in the company of scholars, his love of truth, his genuine piety, and in particular in his great affection for his fellow men – an affection that is free from envy, jealousy and slander.

With such publicity, it was hardly surprising that Linnaeus soon found himself sought out and hospitably entertained by all the scientists and scholars in the town. Kohl was the first to call on him, and it was no doubt he who proudly introduced his tame lion to his circle of intellectual friends. Among these was a Dr Jaenisch, to whom Linnaeus later refers as 'the only real friend' he made in Hamburg; probably there would have been more about him had the blank pages of the Diary been duly filled in. There was a lawyer named Johann Heinrich von Spreckelsen (commemorated in the genus *Sprekelia*), who had a fine garden and many exotic plants in his orangery; Linnaeus mentions forty-five kinds of aloes and fifty of mesembryanthemums. He also had 'a big collection of fossils; I've never seen a larger', and a splendid library from which his guest was allowed to borrow a copy of Patrick Blair's *Botanick Essays* (1720). In return, Linnaeus produced and displayed his collection of insects.

Another day 'we saw Dr Fabricius's incredibly large library, consisting of a series of rooms whose walls were as if papered with books. . . . He lent me Ray's *Historia [Plantarum]* and Bradley's works. A man of about sixty, slim.' In the house of the Swedish envoy he was shown a camera obscura. Then there was the High School library, much smaller than Uppsala's and stocked with out-of-date books on medicine and physics. The former Reformed church had been converted into Hamburg's largest wine-cellar; Linnaeus visited it, put his head inside one of the vats and was 'nearly stupefied by the sulphur dust. We each drank one and a half *ösel* of wine, which was quite enough.' He must have been less lucky than Riesbeck, for after dining with a man named Schoning he complained that 'everything you get to drink in Hamburg is wretched stuff'.

Linnaeus had mentioned the number of Jews to be seen in Hamburg. At this time Jews were not allowed to enter Sweden, and he therefore studied them with particular interest. 'Every Jew', he wrote, 'wore a beard, which was trimmed so that it left only a narrow strip up to the ear and a tuft under the lower lip. On the chin it was like a Lapp's beard. Their hair was pitch black, their beards blackish or red, their eyes brown. The Rabbis (their priests) all wear coats and ruffs like our country pastors.' And one Saturday he went to Altona – then a separate town in Danish territory but now a part of Hamburg – to see the synagogue there:

> The synagogue consisted of two houses, one for the men and the other for the women. All the Jews had Hebrew books from which they read. Beside the altar, on which stood a large seven-branched candelabrum, was a lighted lamp and a candle. The priest sang quite nicely, trilling. He put his fingers to his ears, and stamped with each of his feet in turn, just as though he badly wanted to pass water; and all the Jews who were reading did the same. When the priest sang something, the others joined in and continued it in antiphon. . . . On his head the priest had a black cap, like a Lapp's only larger. I tried to tip the boy who had shown us round, but he refused money because it was the Sabbath.

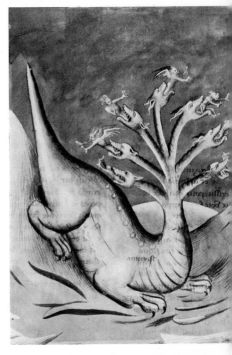

Seven-headed dragon, from a medieval manuscript.

But Hamburg had something even more curious to offer Linnaeus than its Jews: its famous stuffed seven-headed Hydra. Formerly the property of Count Königsmark, who had looted it in 1648, after the Battle of Prague, from the altar of a local church, the monster had eventually passed into the hands of the Burgomaster of Hamburg and his brother. Albert Seba, a famous Amsterdam apothecary whom Linnaeus was soon to meet, had been sent a drawing of the 'Hydra, or seven-headed Serpent' which he published in 1734 in the first volume of his *Thesaurus (Treasury)* of natural history. 'Many people said it was the only one of its kind in the world,' wrote Linnaeus, 'and thanked God that it had not multiplied.'

Even today there is curious credulity where fabulous animals are concerned: Britons need look no further than the Loch Ness monster. Seba, who admittedly had not actually seen the Hydra, never for a moment doubted its genuineness, and listed and described various other monsters reputedly seen in Venice, Brussels and elsewhere. But Linnaeus, who was taken by Kohl to inspect it, at once detected the fake. On examination he found that the jaws and clawed feet were those of weasels, and that the body had been covered with snake-skins neatly joined and glued. That the creature had seven heads was in itself enough, in his opinion, to establish the fraud: 'Good God,' he cried, 'who never put more than one clear thought [*tanke*] in any of Thy created bodies!' He presumed that the Hydra had been manufactured by monks as a representation of an Apocalyptic beast, and makes no mention of Greek mythology.

The Burgomaster had for some time past been trying to sell his Hydra, and had at first asked an enormous sum for it. It was said that the King of Denmark had made an unsuccessful bid of 30,000 thalers; but latterly the price had been steadily dropping, and when Linnaeus tactlessly made public his discovery it fell to nothing at all. Fearing the vengeance of the Burgomaster he thought it best to leave Hamburg forthwith. On 16 May the travellers said good-bye to their friends and went to Altona where they were to spend the night before embarking in the little two-masted ship which was to carry them to Amsterdam for the very modest sum of one ducat a head.

The district between Hamburg and Altona served as a brothel for the citizens of Hamburg, and Linnaeus, on his way to the synagogue at Altona, had observed with distaste 'the whore-houses in which violas, oboes, flutes, trumpets and the waltz were always to be heard'. Riesbeck reported that in his day the 'extremely pretty' daughters of the local farmers 'allure the young men of the city to their cots; and many quarter themselves here under the pretence of a milk diet'. One is left with the impression that Riesbeck may well have availed himself of the facilities provided; but Linnaeus and Sohlberg, who that evening made a brief tour of inspection of the neighbourhood, returned speedily 'without having had the least conference with the womenfolk'. Their dislike of Altona was increased by the 'ill treatment' they received at the hands of their inn-keeper, who presumably overcharged them.

They went on board next morning at dawn in order to be ready to sail with the ebb-tide down the Elbe to the open sea. The Baltic being virtually tideless, Linnaeus was much impressed by the ebb and flow of this great river – 'as big as the biggest river in Lapland'. The voyage took them sixteen days and for the most part the weather was dreadful. On 19 May, which was Whit-Monday, a contrary wind forced them to anchor off Wewelsfleth. Here the Swedes were able to make amends for missing church the previous day by attending a service in the village church, 'which was decorated with branches till it looked like a wood, making it impossible to see either the pulpit or the altar. The farmers were dressed like rich burghers in velvet breeches with silver buttons and buckles, and embroidered waistcoats. The women had a thousand fantasies on their caps; one could fall into ecstasies over such a quantity of droll inventions.'

But there were long days on board with little enough to do, and to pass the time Linnaeus jotted down one or two things which he had not had time to record in Hamburg. For example, he noted that German frogs 'croaked very loudly – three or four times louder than Swedish frogs; and each had its own voice. Some sang so beautifully that it cheered the heart and banished all disagreeable thoughts, others so mournfully that one almost died of melancholy.' When they finally reached the open sea the ship kept so far as was possible in the shallow waters between the chain of Frisian Islands and the mainland. Whenever she was obliged to anchor, Linnaeus and Sohlberg were soon on shore looking for specimens on the beach, 'wading up to their knees to examine the sea-bed' or buying fish from the local fishermen; all that they found or acquired was immediately recorded and described by Linnaeus. The bad weather pursued them right into the Zuider Zee, and no one was more thankful than Linnaeus when, early on the morning of 2 June (or 13 June by the New Style which was in use in Holland) they reached Amsterdam and for the first time set foot on Dutch soil.

2.

Holland

It is a misfortune for us that Linnaeus's travel diary came to an end before he reached Amsterdam, for we have no record of the impact made upon him by that handsome city which, like Stockholm, derives so much of its beauty from the presence of water. We know, however, from some jottings he made in a little pocket calendar, that he and his companion spent three or four days there, that during that time they visited the Botanic Garden (still extant, and commonly known as the Hortus) and made the acquaintance of two men who were both to play a part in Linnaeus's life: Johannes Burman and Albert Seba.

Burman, a brilliant young botanist born a year before Linnaeus, had at the early age of twenty-one been appointed Professor of Botany and Director of the Hortus; he was now at work on a Flora of Ceylon, *Thesaurus Zeylanicus*, using primarily a herbarium which had been formed in the 1670s by Paul Hermann. Linnaeus must have been thrilled by his first sight of tropical plants, but it is said that all did not go well at this initial encounter; the two young men were, however, destined soon to meet again in more favourable circumstances.

Seba was an internationally famous apothecary, a German by birth and now in his seventieth year. After several voyages to both the East and the West Indies, from which he had returned with a big collection of curiosities of every kind, he had established himself in Amsterdam where he soon prospered and grew rich. Through useful connections that he had formed during his travels, and by boarding newly arrived ships from distant parts and judiciously distributing medicines to the crews, he had been able to acquire further treasures at very low prices, till finally his collection became the most remarkable of its day. In 1717 he sold it in its entirety for 15,000 gulden to Peter the Great, who carried it off to St Petersburg. But Seba was an irrepressible collector; he immediately started all over again, and soon the new cabinet surpassed the earlier one.

Such 'cabinets of curios', brought together by apothecaries for the concoction of their strange nostrums, or to satisfy the curiosity of men interested in natural history, or, in due course, merely because it became fashionable, had long been known in various parts of Europe; even Shakespeare's impecunious apothecary in *Romeo and Juliet* (v. i) had possessed

> . . . a tortoise hung,
> An alligator stuff'd, and other skins

Amsterdam in the eighteenth century, by Hendrik Kenn.

Of ill-shaped fishes . . .
Green earthen pots, bladders and musty seeds,
Remnants of packthread and old cakes of roses. . . .

The cabinets of Gessner in Zürich, Belon in France, Cesalpino and Aldrovandi
in Italy, and the two Tradescants in England had all been much admired and
much visited; and in 1736 Linnaeus was to see Sir Hans Sloane's famous
collection in London.

Linnaeus paid two visits to Seba's cabinet. The old man was still at work
on his *Thesaurus* – his great and superbly illustrated survey of natural history in
four bulky folio volumes, two of which had already been published; but he
saw that he had little time left, and he was looking for someone to help him
finish it. He did not immediately invite Linnaeus, of whose ability he as yet
knew little or nothing, to take the task in hand. Doubtless, however, he marked
him down as a possible collaborator; but when, soon after, he came to make the
offer, Linnaeus was too busy with his own books and felt obliged to refuse.

From Amsterdam the two Swedes sailed the thirty-five miles to Harderwijk,
in Gelderland on the southern shores of the Zuider Zee, where they arrived on
17 June. The little fishing town was the seat of a university which did a thriving
trade in cut-priced 'instant' degrees for which only the briefest residence was
required, and Linnaeus, like many of his countrymen, proposed to take
advantage of the facilities it provided for clever but impoverished students.
There was a jingling couplet which once went the round:

Johannes Burman.

Left: Albert Seba aged sixty-six, by J. M. Quinkhard, engraved by J. Houbraken; frontispiece of his *Thesaurus*.

Harderwijk is en stad van negotie,
Men verkoopt er bokking, blauwbessen en bullen van promotie –

that is to say, 'Harderwijk is a commercial town where they sell bloaters, bilberries and degrees.' Indeed rumour had it that as soon as a foreigner arrived there the beadle called to inquire if he intended taking a degree.

The whole procedure of graduation could be completed within a week, after which the newly qualified doctor usually went on to Leyden to get his education. The day after his arrival Linnaeus had his name entered in the *Album Studiosorum* of the University and handed in a thesis, written before leaving Sweden, on 'A new hypothesis as to the cause of intermittent fevers' – his theory being that they resulted from living on a clay soil. An oral examination followed, after which he wrote an exposition of two of Hippocrates' *Aphorisms*, diagnosed and prescribed treatment for a case of jaundice, and was duly declared a medical candidate. Next day his 'promoter', Professor Jan de Gorter, returned the thesis marked 'imprimatur'; it was immediately passed to the University printer who, well accustomed to these rushed jobs, promised it in time for the debate on 23 June.

The three days of waiting were spent by Linnaeus and Sohlberg in attending private lectures by de Gorter and in sightseeing with him and his son David. Then came the debate, after the successful conclusion of which de Gorter presented Linnaeus with the customary gold ring, silk hat and diploma, and inscribed his name in the *Album Doctorum*. Thus, at the age of twenty-eight, the clever young student became a doctor of medicine, 'recognized as having . . . the right to advance to the upper (or doctor's) chair, publicly to justify medical treatises, to teach the craft of a physician, to visit the sick, to prescribe for them, to hold disputations etc., etc.'

Miss Gourlie, who visited Harderwijk in 1930, found the town itself seemingly little changed since Linnaeus's day:

> Its alleys of lime trees with their branches interlacing overhead, the walls protecting the inhabitants from the sea, the narrow twisting paved streets, the gaily painted houses, the shining brass door-handles and knockers, the stiff white lace curtains, all the brilliant, dazzling if perhaps superficial cleanliness, are the same as in the days when he strolled around. . . . Old women clad in numerous bunchy petticoats, with gold helmets and wooden sabots, tottered about the charming old almshouses close to the church, all of them so ancient and wrinkled of skin that they too seemed to have been there since Linnaean times.

But in one important respect the life of the place had altered, for in 1818 Napoleon had closed the University. The brief visit Linnaeus paid to it has not, however, been forgotten: in a niche of the wall of the so-called Little Tower of Linnaeus – a tower once used for the incarceration of rebellious students – there was placed, in 1869, a bust of the great Swedish botanist.

From Harderwijk Linnaeus returned to Amsterdam, but four days later he moved to Leyden. Sohlberg was still with him; gradually, however, he fades out of a story in which he rarely receives a mention, and it is not even known at what moment he went back to Sweden. One must hope that he now helped Linnaeus financially, as he certainly did on a later occasion, in return for tuition, for Linnaeus's funds were running dangerously low and he had begun to wonder how much longer he could afford to remain in Holland.

But at that time nobody with scientific interests could have contemplated leaving the Netherlands without paying his respects to Dr Herman Boerhaave in Leyden. Boerhaave was the most famous physician and teacher of medicine of his day, a chemist also and an ardent botanist; so universal, indeed, was his

Leyden in the eighteenth century.

reputation that a letter from China addressed 'à Monsieur Boerhaave, Europa' reached its destination. Even a Pope (Benedict XIII) had sought his advice by letter, and Boerhaave, after studying the reports of the Vatican doctors, had successfully prescribed riding. Peter the Great of Russia, while working as an artisan in Holland, had called on him in person, choosing what to us seems the curious hour of five a.m. for his visit; but Voltaire, who came to Leyden in 1737 on the recommendation of Frederick (not yet the Great) of Prussia, arrived while Boerhaave was at table and was refused admission, the Doctor announcing that he was not prepared to rise for someone who did not rise for God.

Boerhaave was now in his late sixties. He had retired from the chairs of medicine, chemistry and botany which he had held with such distinction at Leyden University, and had handed over the charge of the Botanic Garden to a younger man, Adriaan van Royen; but he still had his practice, and still gave lectures and clinical demonstrations which Linnaeus was to attend. In a passage which might have come straight from Aubrey's *Brief Lives*, Linnaeus described Boerhaave as 'corpulent, tall, curly-haired, hook-nosed, going bald. Had not visited his nearest neighbours or his relations for twenty years. Saw patients daily from 9 to 11 a.m., lectured in public at 11, from 1 to 2 in private, at 3 publicly. . . . Slept without a nightcap, never had a fire in his bedroom, drank no wine, tea or coffee, and never smoked.' He said, 'If I dress before a fire when I get up, I am soon tired; but if I dress in the cold I am brisk.'

Linnaeus's first attempt to meet Boerhaave failed; no one had warned him that the maidservant in his house expected a handsome tip – what Jackson calls 'jingling methods of persuasion' – for the service of procuring access to her master. Nor, it would seem, did he have any letter of introduction. But he was successful in getting to know another distinguished local doctor and botanist, Johan Gronovius the Younger, to whom he showed the manuscript of his *Systema Naturae* – a work in which he put forward, in outline, his plan for the classification of the three kingdoms of Nature. Gronovius was deeply impressed: 'I don't believe,' he informed an English friend, 'that since the time of Konrad Gesner there was a man so learn'd in all parts of natural history as he; and that not superficial, but to the bottom. . . .' He readily agreed to give Linnaeus a letter to Boerhaave. Thus armed, and no doubt also provided with the appropriate *douceur* for the maid, Linnaeus called again on Hippocrates Redivivus – as Boerhaave had been nicknamed.

Herman Boerhaave, by Aert de Gelder, *c.* 1723.

Even now, however, there were difficulties. On 10 June, soon after Linnaeus left Hamburg, the following notice had appeared in the *Hamburgische Berichte*:

> Herr Carolus Linnaeus, the famous Swedish doctor and botanist whose renown has more than once been mentioned in earlier numbers of this periodical, recently passed through here on his way to Holland, where he intends to stay for several years in order to frequent the famous men there, and in particular Herr Boerhaave with whom he has already carried on a scholarly correspondence, and thus still further perfect his already outstanding knowledge of medicine, physics and botany.

Boerhaave had seen the notice and was indignant; he had never corresponded with Linnaeus whom, rightly or wrongly, he held to be responsible for this fiction. Himself the most modest of men, who all his life scorned the honours

Botanic Garden, Leyden, 1710, from H. Boerhaave's *Index Plantarum*.

that were showered upon him, he considered the young Swede bumptious and pushing. 'It is strange that Boerhaave cannot stand Linnaeus,' said Sohlberg to a friend after the two great men had finally met. Was it really so very strange after all?

So when Linnaeus delivered his letter of introduction Boerhaave kept him waiting for a whole week before receiving him. But if Boerhaave disliked conceit, he was the first to recognize merit; he saw Linnaeus's great gifts and before long was doing all in his power to help him. Indeed, Boerhaave quickly overcame his initial mistrust, and eventually the two men became good friends; the lines that he wrote at their first meeting in Linnaeus's *Liber Amicorum* – the 'autograph book' that it was at that time fashionable to carry when travelling abroad – were few and dry, and he declined an invitation to provide a preface for the *Flora Lapponica*; but two years later he willingly accepted, and graciously acknowledged, the dedication of the *Genera Plantarum*, thus assuring it of an auspicious start.

The visit to the Doctor's town house, which took place on 5 July, was followed by visits to his large country estate of Oud-Poelgeest. Boerhaave was particularly fond of trees; indeed there is a pleasant story – now, alas! considered apocryphal by the best authorities – that he always took off his hat when he passed an elder tree, in recognition of its therapeutic properties. At Poelgeest he had space to plant trees on a scale which had been impossible in the little University Botanic Garden in the town. Linnaeus considered Boerhaave's arboretum 'a paradise, Holland's miracle whose equal no mortal can imagine'.

The biographies of botanists are strewn with stories of botanical 'one-upmanship'. In the arboretum grew a tree which its owner declared to be a great rarity not as yet described by any naturalist. Linnaeus immediately recognized it as a species of *Sorbus*, and added that Vaillant had described it in his *Botanicon Parisiense*. Boerhaave challenged this; he possessed the book and had studied it carefully. The book was sent for, and Linnaeus proved right.

Linnaeus learned much from Boerhaave that was to be valuable to him in later life. One such lesson is mentioned in a letter which the former wrote in 1748 to the brilliant and versatile Swiss scholar, Albrecht von Haller:

> If you will but listen to me as a friend, I would advise you to write no letters to Hamberger and such people. He is not on a par with you; and the more he is your inferior, the more consequence you give a man who would otherwise remain in obscurity, known only to those in his immediate circle. Our great example, Boerhaave, never answered anybody. I recollect his saying to me one day, 'You should never reply to any controversial writers. Promise me that you will not.' I promised him accordingly, and have benefited very much thereby.

It was, incidentally, a lesson that Rousseau regretted that he had never learned from Linnaeus: 'If only I had imitated the Uppsala professor,' he wrote, 'I would have won a few days of happiness and years of peace of mind.'

On the morning of 8 July, three days after Boerhaave had finally consented to receive Linnaeus, the latter had suddenly seen, in a tavern in Leyden, a familiar figure; it was none other than his old friend of Uppsala days, Peter Artedi, who had just arrived from London. England, thanks to the pioneer work of John

Ray and Francis Willughby fifty years before and their great joint work on fishes, *Historia Piscium* (1686), was still the Mecca of the ichthyologist, and Artedi had been studying there until his money ran out.

The two men had lost touch, and the meeting was purely accidental; but

> nothing more delightful could have happened to either of us [wrote Linnaeus later], and our tears showed what joy we felt. I told my story, and he his: what kind of life he had led in London; the many splendid observations which he had made among the ichthyologists; how he had enjoyed the favour of various scholars, especially that of the illustrious Sloane, the kindness and generosity of whose reception he lovingly described; the many museums he had visited; the affection and high opinion therefore entertained by him of England and the English. He now wanted to take a doctorate in medicine; but he had been made penniless by the expenses of his journey and was worried about how to get clothes, food, and all the books he needed for his work. He was therefore thinking of returning home.

How short he was of clothes and money to buy them with is revealed by the inventory made of his belongings after his tragic death ten weeks later, for it includes 'three day-shirts marked with an S belonging to Sohlberg' and other things which Linnaeus's companion had generously lent or given him.

By a stroke of luck Linnaeus happened to be in a position to be of at least some help to his friend. The third volume of Seba's *Thesaurus*, with which Linnaeus had been unable to lend a hand, dealt with fishes; he therefore took Artedi to Amsterdam to meet Seba, who immediately agreed to employ him. Artedi was also able to be of help to Linnaeus, especially by explaining to him his system of classifying fishes. This was something very timely, for Linnaeus was just putting the finishing touches to his *Systema Naturae*.

Linnaeus had brought with him from Sweden a number of botanical and other manuscripts in various stages of completion, hoping that he might find in Holland the opportunity to have some of them published. Gronovius had been so greatly impressed by the originality of his *Systema Naturae* that he felt it should be published at once. So too did a young Scots doctor, Isaac Lawson, who was studying in Leyden, and the two men generously offered to have it printed at their own expense. This slim volume – it ran to a mere fourteen crowded folio pages – is today a great rarity. Twenty-nine copies (two of which are in the Library of the Linnean Society) are known to exist, and one which was sold by public auction in London in 1959 fetched £2,900. There subsequently appeared no fewer than sixteen enlarged editions or reprints; twelve were issued under Linnaeus's personal supervision, the last, which was published in 1766–8, being in three octavo volumes and containing no less than 2,300 pages. In gratitude to Lawson, Linnaeus named the *Lawsonia*, the henna of the East, in his honour; to his other benefactor he awarded the *Gronovia*, described in his *Critica Botanica* as 'a climbing plant which grasps all other plants, being called after a man who had few rivals as a "collector" of plants'.

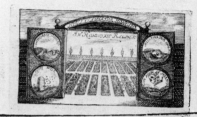

CAROLI LINNÆI
Naturæ Curioforum *Diofcoridis Secundi*

SYSTEMA NATURÆ

IN QUO
NATURÆ REGNA TRIA,
SECUNDUM.
CLASSES, ORDINES, GENERA, SPECIES,
SYSTEMATICE PROPONUNTUR.

Editio Secunda, Auctior.

STOCKHOLMIÆ
Apud GOTTFR. KIESEWETTER.
1740.

Title-page of *Systema Naturae*, second edition, 1740.

3.

George Clifford

ncouraged though he was by the publication of his *Systema Naturae*, Linnaeus could not forget that his funds were running low; but when he talked of returning to Sweden both Boerhaave and Gronovius attempted to dissuade him. Linnaeus wrote of Gronovius that of all the men he met in Holland 'he was the one with the greatest thirst for knowledge'; and how highly the latter admired the talents of the young Swede can be gauged (even when allowance has been made for the flattery customary on such occasions) from the lines that he wrote in Linnaeus's *Liber Amicorum* when it seemed that he was determined to leave:

> Even though the earth should disintegrate and stagger in its course, even then the fearless man, though the falling ruins might strike him down, will remain undaunted. Adversity is conquered by *learning to live with it*! Leave your home for foreign lands, and a new life will then begin for you. But never bow before adversity! Your name will travel from the farthest banks of the Danube to the frozen North.
>
> With this parting gift I bid farewell to the most famous and learned man, Doctor CAROLUS LINNAEUS – pre-eminent on account of the several very dangerous journeys which he has undertaken for the benefit of the community – journeys during which he so felicitously investigated the three kingdoms of Nature. May he prove himself a match for the troubles which so often overtake those who live abroad, and may he return safely to his family and friends.

Boerhaave, in his eagerness to persuade Linnaeus to make his career in Holland, offered to arrange for him a voyage to the Cape and thence to America at public expense to collect plants for Dutch gardens, with the bait of a professorship at Leyden on his return. But Linnaeus excused himself on the grounds that the heat would be intolerable to one brought up in a cold climate. In fact the Swede disliked extreme cold almost as much as he disliked extreme heat, and Lapland had taught him that he did not care for 'roughing it' anywhere.

Since Linnaeus's journey to Sweden was to be made by way of Amsterdam, Boerhaave urged him to take the opportunity when there to call once again on Burman; provided now with a letter from Boerhaave he would be assured of a favourable reception. A typical anecdote is related of this second meeting of the two young botanists. Burman produced a specimen of a rare plant for Linnaeus to identify. Linnaeus moistened it in his mouth and proclaimed it a *Laurus*.

'No, it is not a *Laurus*,' said Burman.
'Yes; a *Laurus* – and a *Cinnamomum*.'
'A *Cinnamomum*, admittedly – but. . . .'

Then Linnaeus explained why, in his opinion, the two genera ought to be united. Both plants belong to the Laurel family (Lauraceae); but later botanists have found cause again to separate them, and Burman's plant, the valuable cinnamon, is now *Cinnamomum zeylanicum*.

Burman, impressed by his guest's knowledge, now proposed that Linnaeus should stay with him and help with the preparation of his *Thesaurus Zeylanicus*, tempting him with the offer of a bed, board at his own table, and a good room to work in. At this juncture Sohlberg produced some welcome money for him from home; Linnaeus therefore agreed to remain with Burman over the winter. Burman also assisted Linnaeus with two books on which he was working at the time – his *Fundamenta Botanica* and *Bibliotheca Botanica*. The latter, in which the authors of botanical works were placed in sixteen classes, he now in gratitude dedicated to his host.

Soon after Linnaeus had established himself in Burman's house he met there a man who was to become his greatest patron and benefactor in Holland: George Clifford.

Clifford was an enormously rich, fifty-year-old Anglo-Dutch financier and a Director of the Dutch East India Company (but not, as is often stated, at any time Burgomaster of Amsterdam). He was also an enthusiastic horticulturist and zoologist, and his garden and private zoo at the Hartekamp, his country estate about five miles from Haarlem on the way to Leyden, were famous throughout Holland; their upkeep was said to cost their owner no less than 12,000 gulden a year. On 13 August 1735 Linnaeus went with Burman to the Hartekamp.

Linnaeus had no doubt been told of the splendours that awaited him; but what he found surpassed anything that he had been able to imagine, and later he was to enumerate them in the dedication to Clifford at the beginning of his *Hortus Cliffortianus*. First there were the gardens themselves – 'masterpieces of Nature aided by Art' – with their 'shady walks, topiary, statues, fishponds, artificial mounds and mazes'. Then came the zoo, 'full of tigers, apes, wild dogs, Indian deer and goats, peccaries and African swine'; with innumerable varieties of birds (which he lists) 'that made the garden echo and re-echo with their cries'. But still more exciting to him were the 'houses of Adonis', or hot-houses:

> I was amazed when I entered your houses of Adonis, so full were they of such a variety of plants that they bewitched a Northerner, who could not imagine into what foreign land you had led him. In the first house you had the plants of southern Europe – the flora of Spain, southern France, Italy, Sicily and the Isles of Greece. In the second, treasures from Asia such as cloves, poincianas, mangosteens, coco-palms. . . . In the third the plants of Africa, plants whose structure was unique and their nature indeed monstrous, such as mesembryanthemums and aloes of many different kinds, carrion flowers, euphorbias, crassula and protea species. . . . In the fourth our beloved Americans, all the progeny of the New World: innumerable cacti;

'*Laurus zeylanica*' (*Cinnamomum zeylanicum*), from the *Botanical Magazine*, 1818.

Title-page of *Hortus Cliffortianus*, 1738.

orchids, passion flowers, magnolias and tulip-trees; the calabash tree, acacias, tamarinds and peppers. . . . Among these rioted the earth's strangest wonders: bananas, exquisite hermannias, silver-leaved proteas and valuable camphor-trees.

When, finally, I entered your truly regal house and splendidly equipped museum, whose collections spoke no less of their owner's renown, I as a foreigner felt quite carried away, for I had never seen their equal. I desired above all things that you might let the world have knowledge of so great a herbarium, and did not hesitate to offer to lend a helping hand.

Clifford was much impressed by Linnaeus's ability to classify Indian plants that were new to him, simply by opening a flower and examining its parts. As for Linnaeus, he was seized with a sudden longing to be invited to take charge of this wonderful garden and its hot-houses and to have the run of Clifford's fine library and herbarium. Though it has often been stated (and even by Linnaeus himself at a later date) that Boerhaave, who was Clifford's doctor, finally brought about the realization of Linnaeus's dream, it is now known that this was not so; in fact Linnaeus made an intermediary of Gronovius, who put the suggestion to Clifford 'as of his own accord'. The proposal was that Linnaeus should go to live with Clifford, who was something of a hypo-chondriac, in the double capacity of house physician and superintendent of his garden.

Clifford was as enthusiastic as Linnaeus, who wrote: 'Captivated as I was by these delights, stuck fast on these Siren-rocks, you bade me lower my sails; and you prevailed without any difficulty.' But there was still an obstacle to overcome: Linnaeus had pledged himself to stay with Burman over the winter; how could he justify this desertion after only a few weeks? It must have been during a second visit to the Hartekamp that the proposition was put to Burman, and it was at once apparent that he was far from pleased. However, while they were looking round Clifford's library Burman noticed a splendid book that he had not seen before: the second volume of Sir Hans Sloane's *Natural History of Jamaica*. It was obvious to Clifford that he coveted it. 'I happen to have two copies,' he told Burman. 'I will give you one if you will let me have Linnaeus.'

So on 24 September Linnaeus, bartered as it were for a book, was installed at the Hartekamp. It was agreed that he should be paid a thousand florins a year, with free board and lodging; his principal duties would be to supervise the hot-houses and classify and put in order the specimens in the herbarium, to prepare an account of the latter and of the plants which Clifford grew, and to keep a watchful eye on the health of his patron. Linnaeus pledged himself to stay through the winter; as things turned out he was to remain at the Hartekamp for more than two years. He lived there 'like a prince', with a free hand to buy what books were needed for the library and what plants he coveted for the garden and hot-houses; he had leisure for his own work and access to all the reference books that were necessary for it. At last he was – to use a botanical metaphor – 'in clover'.

During the opening weeks of September, while Artedi was working for Seba and Linnaeus was with Burman, the two Swedes, though they were both living in Amsterdam, had hardly seen anything of one another. Artedi was something of a recluse and he kept strange hours: 'He lived a lonely life, went to the tavern from 3 to 9, was at work from 9 to 3 in the night, and slept from 3 till noon.' But shortly before Linnaeus left Amsterdam for the Hartekamp he took the completed manuscript of his *Fundamenta Botanica* (in which the science of botany is reduced to 365 aphorisms) to show to his friend, who for his part had by this time almost completed his work for Seba.

The session proved a long one. Artedi insisted upon reading to Linnaeus all he had so far written of his book on ichthyology, after which there inevitably followed an endless discussion of various points upon which they held differing opinions, and an examination of all Artedi's manuscript notes. Linnaeus was weary and wanted to get away: 'He kept me long, too long, unendurably long (which was unlike our usual practice),' he wrote, 'but had I known that it was to be our last talk together I would have wished it even longer.'

A few days later, on the night of 27 September, Artedi was invited to dine with Seba. It was a convivial evening and the party did not break up until the small hours. Artedi, not too familiar with the streets of Amsterdam, missed his way in the dark, stumbled into an unfenced canal and was drowned. 'Thus in the flower of his age and strength,' wrote Linnaeus, 'died one who was the ornament and glory of his nation! Thus too early did Fate pluck this unique genius! Thus did the most distinguished of ichthyologists perish in the waters, having devoted his life to the discovery of their inhabitants! . . .'

Linnaeus was at the Hartekamp at the time of the accident, and it was Sohlberg who two days later brought him the tragic news. Artedi's body had been recovered and taken to the City Hospital; Linnaeus therefore went there at once:

> When I saw the stiff and lifeless body, the livid, pale and foam-flecked lips; when I thought of the loss of so old and excellent a friend and remembered the sleepless nights, the laborious days, the journeys, the midnight hours of exhausting study which had preceded his attainment of that learning in which he had no rival to fear – then I burst into tears. And when I foresaw that all this scholarship, which should have earned immortality for him and glory for his country, would perish with his death, then the love which I still felt for my friend commanded that the pledge we had once made – that the survivor would give to the world the observations of the other – must be honoured.

But in carrying out his promise Linnaeus soon came up against a difficulty. Though Artedi's family in Sweden had immediately agreed to his taking possession of their son's papers,[1] the young man's landlord in Amsterdam refused to hand them over until the money still owing to him for board and lodging had been paid; if it was not, then there would be a public auction of his effects. Seba had contributed fifty florins towards the cost of the funeral, but he refused to do more – some said because he himself hoped to acquire the papers at the sale. However, in the nick of time Clifford came to the rescue.

As soon as he could find a spare moment Linnaeus began to prepare his friend's book for publication. He mentions this in a letter to Haller, written some time in 1737:

> I am now employed in printing the posthumous works of my late friend Peter Artedi, in which, if I mistake not, you will see more perfection than can be expected in botany for a hundred years to come. He has established natural classes [orders],

[1] So Linnaeus wrote, two years later. But it is inconceivable that a letter to Sweden could have been received and answered in so short a time.

Georg Dionys Ehret, by George
James, A.R.A., 1767.

natural genera, complete characters, a universal index of synonyms, incomparable
descriptions, and unexceptionable specific definitions.

This was no exaggeration. In the first chapter of the book, which is untouched
by Linnaeus, is to be found in a fully developed form the Linnaean method that
the two young men must have evolved in collaboration in Uppsala days. Indeed,
Artedi had the finer intellect of the two, and had he lived he would probably
have had an equal share in the renown which in the event fell to Linnaeus alone.
Ichthyologia (*The Natural History of Fishes*), prefaced by a short account of the life
of Artedi from which the biographical passages quoted above have been taken,
was published the following year in Leyden, and later Linnaeus named a plant
of his friend's favourite family, the Umbelliferae, *Artedia* in his memory.

Soon after Linnaeus had gone to the Hartekamp there arrived on foot from Leyden, with a letter of introduction to Clifford from the Margrave of Baden, a young German botanical draughtsman named Georg Dionys Ehret, who was destined to become the greatest flower painter of his age. The news that Linnaeus was with Clifford had made him doubly eager to visit the Hartekamp, and in his autobiography he describes how he showed Clifford some drawings which he had recently made in England:

> I showed him my work in the presence of Mr Linnaeus, than whom no one was more eager in the characters of plants. There were some quite new plants among them. Mr Clifford then asked me if I wished to sell them, and what my price was, took almost everything that I had with me, and paid me what I asked, namely 3 Dutch gulden a piece. He kept me more than a month at Haarlem; and in that time I completed all the figures which came out in the *Hortus Cliffortianus* – *Collinsonia*, *Turnera*, etc., which I had brought from England. I profited nothing from [Linnaeus] in the dissection of the plants; for all the plants in the *Hortus Cliffortianus* are of my own undertaking, and nothing was done by him in the way of placing all the parts before me as they are figured: for I had done all this, as the noble Dr Trew knew, many years before I had ever heard of Mr Linnaeus. . . .
>
> During the time I was with Mr Clifford I was treated courteously. I did not then know that Linnaeus intended to publish a *Hortus Cliffortianus*. Linnaeus and I were the best of friends: he showed me his new method of examining the stamens, which I easily understood, and privately resolved to bring out a Tabella of it. As my work with Mr Clifford was now coming to an end I returned to Leyden and published the plate. . . . With this Tabella I once more earned some money; for I sold it at 2 Dutch gulden a piece and almost all the botanists in Holland bought it of me.

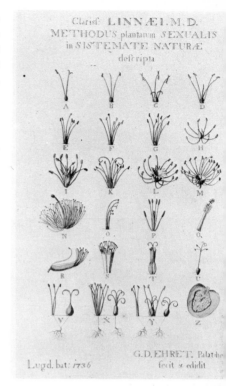

Ehret's original drawing illustrating Linnaeus's Sexual System, 1736.

Though Ehret had stated, in the title of his *tabella*, that he was indebted to Linnaeus for the system that he illustrated, Linnaeus included it without acknowledgment in his *Genera Plantarum*; as Ehret sadly noted, 'When he was a beginner [Linnaeus] appropriated everything for himself which he heard of, to make himself famous.'

After staying a few weeks at the Hartekamp Ehret returned to England and settled there permanently, soon making friends with all the leading men of science of the day. By the middle of the century he had become a popular figure in London society; the 'highest nobility in England' clamoured to receive instruction from him, and in his autobiography he proudly inscribed the names of the duchesses and countesses whom he numbered among his pupils. 'If I could have divided myself into twenty parts,' he added, 'I could still have had my hands full.' Yet he found time to paint a large number of superb flower pictures on vellum, two of which are reproduced in colour in this book. He died in 1770 at the age of sixty-two, working to the last.

In one of Clifford's hot-houses was a 'pisang', or banana (*Musa paradisiaca*). No one in Holland had ever succeeded in getting a banana to flower, still less to fruit; but within four months of his arrival at the Hartekamp Linnaeus, no doubt with the help of Clifford's able gardener Dietrich Nietzel, had coaxed the plant into flower. This miracle was worked by setting it in a rich soil, keeping it quite dry for some weeks, and then deluging it with water in imitation of tropical

Banana at the Hartekamp, drawn by Hoffman, engraved by A. vander Laan, from *Musa Cliffortiana*, 1736.

storms. Distinguished botanists flocked to the Hartekamp from all over Holland, and even old Boerhaave made the fourteen-mile journey to hear his young protégé hold a demonstration.

Linnaeus hastily produced a treatise, *Musa Cliffortiana*, illustrated with two large engravings – a slim folio important as being his first botanical monograph and interesting as, in the opinion of one English contemporary, an early example of what today would be called a 'coffee-table' book. Thomas Knowlton, Lord Burlington's gardener at Lanesborough in Yorkshire, writing to Dr Richardson, says:

> But now you mention his *Musa Cliffortiana*, pray what is there more than a compliment to the grate Mr Clifford, and to tell us it has flower'd in his garden, which is the first time in Europe, etc. . . . these books are made for pompe, to fill a library, and more for outward show than real use, etc., having very little within, as many I could name.

In the text Linnaeus discusses, among other things, whether the banana could be the 'forbidden tree' of the Garden of Eden. This possibility is mentioned by John Gerarde (who was sent a banana 'in pickle' from Aleppo) in his *Herball* (1597). The plant, he says,

> is called Musa by such as travell to Alepo. . . . The Jewes also suppose it to be that tree, of whose fruit Adam did taste; which others thinke to be a ridiculous fable. . . . It is called . . . in that part of Africa which we call Ginny [Congo], *Bananas*: in English Adam's Apple tree.

In adopting the generic name *Musa*, which is in fact derived from the Arabic, Linnaeus chose to associate it with Antonius Musa, Physician to the Emperor Augustus; thus was a 'barbaric' name, normally condemned by Linnaeus, rendered respectable! Incidentally, Dioscorides had given to a plant, and Linnaeus had adopted, the name *Euphorbia* in honour of Antonius Musa's brother Euphorbus, physician to King Juba; the two brothers were fortunate to be thus immortalized.

In 1737 Clifford's banana fruited still more splendidly, and Linnaeus greatly impressed the French botanist Antoine de Jussieu, who had never managed to flower his plant in Paris, by sending him a fruit. At a later date Linnaeus was to succeed with the banana in Uppsala also. Its fruit was sent to the royal family, who were probably the only people in Sweden to taste bananas before the Swedish Banana Company started to import them shortly before the First World War.

The deep-purple Lilac

4.

A month in England

As the traveller's tales of the younger Rudbeck had inspired Linnaeus with the desire to explore Lapland, so now it was doubtless Artedi's account of his experiences in London, of the fine cabinets and libraries he had examined there and the distinguished naturalists whom he had met and from whom he had received so much kindness, that made him eager to visit England. Clifford readily agreed to release him, stipulating only that he should not stay away too long, and gave him money for the journey and the commission to bring back as many plants as possible for the Hartekamp.

Linnaeus left Amsterdam on 21 July 1736, and after looking in on Boerhaave set sail from Rotterdam. Unlucky as always with his weather, he took nearly a week to reach London, where he found lodging with Tobias Björk, Pastor of the Swedish church in Prince's Square. This was close to the notorious Ratcliff Highway (now St George Street), a rough neighbourhood just to the north of the London docks, and no doubt Linnaeus, who spoke not a word of English,[1] was wise in carrying with him an addressed envelope (still piously preserved among his papers) in case he got lost or was waylaid.

His first call was paid on Sir Hans Sloane, the seventy-six-year-old physician and doyen of British naturalists, for whom he had a letter of introduction from Boerhaave. Sloane had become an institution, almost a legend. He had known Ray and Boyle; as a young man he had studied in France under Tournefort and Magnol. His *Natural History of Jamaica* was the result of fifteen months spent as a physician in the West Indies from 1687 to 1689. In 1712 he bought the Manor of Chelsea, though he did not occupy it until his retirement thirty years later, and in 1721 he presented to the Society of Apothecaries the freehold of the site, previously leased to them by Lord Cheyne, of what is best known as the old Chelsea Physic Garden. By way of return he asked only that each year the Royal Society should receive pressed specimens of 50 different species of plants until the number had reached 2,000; this herbarium is now in the Natural History Museum, London. In 1727, on the death of Sir Isaac Newton, Sloane achieved the height of his ambition by becoming President of the Royal Society. He died in 1753 at the age of ninety-three. His names and the name of his daughter, Lady Cadogan, are daily on the lips of Londoners, few of whom have any idea whom Hans Crescent, Sloane Square and Cadogan Gardens commemorate.

[1] It is a pity that Ifvar Kraak's *English Grammar for Swedes* (1748) had not yet appeared, for it contains some helpful specimens of English conversation for the traveller. For example: 'Where is the wash ball?', 'Let's fetch a walk', 'I have but a puny stomach', 'What will you drink? Any thing that's wet.'

MILLER.

De la société Royale de Londres
De l'académie des Botanistes de Florence
Et Directeur du Jardin de Botanique
Des Apothicaires de Chelsea

Sir Hans Sloane, by S. Slaughter
(1660–1753).

Right: Philip Miller.

Sloane had formed a fabulous collection which was said to have cost him £50,000 and which after his death became the nucleus of the British Museum. One of the Trustees nominated by Sloane was Horace Walpole, who wrote somewhat irreverently to Sir Horace Mann of his 'guardianship of embryos and cockleshells'. Sloane, he added, had valued his collection 'at four-score thousand [pounds]; and so would anybody who loves hippopotamuses, sharks with one ear, and spiders as big as geese! It is a rent charge to keep the foetuses in spirits! You may believe that those who think money the most valuable of all curiosities will not be purchasers. . . .'

Gronovius and Lawson had paved the way for Linnaeus's, visit to the great man by sending him, some months earlier, two copies of the *Systema Naturae*; one was for Sloane himself, the other for the Royal Society. But Sloane must have read with surprise, and possibly with irritation, what Boerhaave had written in his letter of introduction: 'Linnaeus, the bearer of this letter, is particularly worthy of seeing you, and of being seen by you. He who sees you together will look upon a pair of men whose equal is hardly to be found in all the world.' Thus prophetically, though perhaps tactlessly, Boerhaave placed on an equal footing the world-famous septuagenarian and an almost unknown Swede still in his twenties.

It is stated in Lemprière's *Universal Biography* (1805) that Sloane 'did not pay [Linnaeus] that respect and attention which his merits deserved, and this probably prevented the intended settlement of this immortal philosopher here';

but on his return to Holland Linnaeus wrote thanking Sloane for showing him his 'incomparable Museum', tactfully omitting to mention what he said to others, namely that he found it in a state of chaos. Sloane replied cordially. Although too set in his opinions to approve of the new system of classification, he not long afterwards arranged for Linnaeus's description (from the *Flora Lapponica*) of how gadflies attack reindeer, to be read before the Fellows of the Royal Society, where it was warmly applauded.

In charge of the Apothecaries' Garden at Chelsea was Philip Miller, author of the celebrated *Gardener's Dictionary* of which Linnaeus was to say, 'It is not a Dictionary for *gardeners* but for *botanists.*' In its earliest form it was a small two-volume octavo book, published in 1724; the first volume of the folio edition appeared seven years later, when Miller was forty, and such was its success that many further editions and translations followed. In the seventh edition (1759) Miller, a disciple of Ray and Tournefort, reluctantly changed over to the by then fashionable Linnaean system and in his eighth and last edition (1768) adopted the Linnaean binomial nomenclature for species.

Miller's father was a Scot – one of the many 'northern lads who have invaded the southern provinces' – and it was said that Miller would employ none but Scots; no one, however, accused him of the meanness often ascribed to his countrymen, for he was 'of a disposition too generous and too careless of money to become rich'. But success went to his head, until in his old age 'he considered no man to know anything but himself' (John Ellis to Linnaeus, 1770); and a year later, 'for his impertinence to the Apothecaries Company, his masters', he lost his job. In 1736, however, he was rightly looked upon as a horticulturist and botanist of the greatest promise, and Linnaeus was eager to meet him, to see his garden, and to extract, if possible, some interesting plants from it for Clifford.

His visit is described by one of his pupils, a German named Paul Giseke, who at a later date persuaded Linnaeus to talk about his early life and made careful and most valuable notes of these conversations:

> When I went to see Miller, which was the main object of my journey, he showed me the Chelsea [Physic] Garden and named the plants using the nomenclature then current – for example, *Symphytum consolida major, flore luteo* [Comfrey or great Con-sound with a yellow flower]. I remained silent, with the result that he said next day, 'This botanist of Clifford's doesn't know a single plant.' This came to my ears, and when he again began using these names I said, 'Don't use such names; we have shorter and surer ones,' and gave him examples. He grew angry and scowled at me. I wanted to get some plants from him for Clifford's garden, but when I returned I found he had gone to London. He came back in the evening and his ill humour had passed. He promised to give me everything I wanted. He kept his word, and I left for Oxford having made up a fine parcel for Clifford.

Besides living plants Linnaeus came away with herbarium specimens collected by William Houstoun in Central America. 'The English,' he wrote, 'are certainly the most generous people on earth.'

While in London Linnaeus also made the acquaintance of Peter Collinson – a Quaker, a mercer with trading connections in the New World, and an ardent botanist and entomologist in his leisure moments, who had been instrumental

Illustration from John Miller's *Illustratio Systematis sexualis Linnaei*, 1777.

Milleria annua, from *Historia Plantarum rariorum*, by John Martyn, 1728, named after Philip Miller.

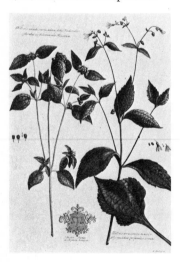

in introducing a large number of North American plants into England. Unfortunately his business commitments prevented him from seeing as much of Linnaeus as both would have liked, but they corresponded for many years. Collinson did all he could to make Linnaeus's *Systema Naturae* more widely known; the book, he told the American botanist John Bartram, 'is a curious [i.e. remarkable] performance for a young man, but his coining of a new set of names for plants tends but to embarrass and perplex the study of Botany.... Very few like it.'

Another acquaintance who became a regular correspondent was John Martyn, Professor of Botany at Cambridge and a medical practitioner in London; he had been responsible for the fine *Historia Plantarum Rariorum* (1728–36), the first botanical work to be illustrated in a kind of mezzotint printed in colour from a single plate. And probably Linnaeus again met Ehret, who mentions in his autobiography that 'Mr Linnaeus came to London; he stayed a month here, and I sent him plates to finish the *Hortus Cliffortianus*.'

The Oxford Botanic Garden, where Linnaeus intended to make propaganda for his system, was under the charge of Johann Jacob Dillenius, the Sherardian Professor of Botany.

Dillenius was a German by birth (a native of Darmstadt) and the great authority on mosses. He had been brought to Oxford in 1721 by William Sherard, a rich and widely travelled botanist who needed an assistant and who, shortly before his death in 1728, endowed a chair of botany on condition that Dillenius was its first occupant. Sherard's younger brother, James, had a fine garden at Eltham, which he had commissioned Dillenius to describe (*Hortus Elthamensis*, 1732). The first meeting of Linnaeus and Dillenius, like so many of his first meetings with those who later became his friends, was not a success. Linnaeus told Giseke:

> When I visited Dillenius I found James Sherard with him, to whom he said, 'This is the man who has thrown all botany into confusion'. I pretended not to understand. We walked together round the Garden where I saw for the first time *Antirrhinum minus*.[1] I asked Dillenius its name. 'What,' he said, 'don't you know what it is?' 'No. But if I may pick a flower I soon will.' 'Then do so,' he replied. I obeyed and at once recognized its genus.
>
> On the third day, seeing that Dillenius did not change his attitude towards me, and finding that my money was running low, I asked him to get one of his servants to book me a place next morning in the London coach. He did so, and I thought it my duty to say, 'I want to ask a favour of you. Will you please explain to me what you meant by that remark you made to Sherard when I first called on you?' For a long time he refused; but when I insisted he said, 'Follow me, and I will show you.' When we reached his library he produced my *Genera Plantarum*,[2] a part of which Gronovius had sent him at my request. I saw that he had written 'N.B.,' [*nota bene*] on almost every page. 'What does that mean?' I cried. 'Each N.B.', he said, 'means a false genus.'

Linnaeus maintained that it was not so, and one of the disputed flowers, a *Blitum*, was fetched from the Garden. Dillenius, like other botanists, had described it as having three stamens:

[1] The lesser snapdragon, now *Misopates orontium*.

[2] Not published until the following year. Gronovius had sent as much as was already set up in type.

114

I opened the flower and showed him that it had only one. 'No doubt it's an abnormal specimen,' he said. We opened several more, and they were all the same. We passed on to several other genera, and all tallied with my description of them. Dillenius was amazed and said, 'I shall not let you leave.' He kept me a month [in fact, only a week], and gave me all the live plants that I wanted for Clifford. . . .

After the reconciliation, he and Dillenius 'were not apart from one another for more than two hours, and when I finally left he was in tears. He presented me with his *Hortus Elthamensis*.' In view of the fact that Linnaeus spoke no English, it may perhaps be worth pointing out that 'botany' and 'confusion' being two words that any Classical scholar would recognize, he will have had no difficulty in getting the gist of Dillenius's offensive remark about him to James Sherard.

Linnaeus noted that he found the Oxford Garden well stocked with European plants, but that there was little in the hot-houses and orangeries; Clifford's orangeries, he proudly claimed, were undoubtedly the finest in the world. He saw William Sherard's herbarium with its unrivalled collection of European plants and a 'rather mouldy' one of exotics. The best trophies he carried back to Holland when he came to leave England were, he adds, live (North) American plants from Chelsea.

Johann Jakob Dillenius (1687–1747).

Linnaeus mentions another Oxford professor whose acquaintance he made and with whom he immediately found himself in sympathy. This was Dr Thomas Shaw, Fellow of Queen's College, Oxford, and for many years Chaplain to the English factory in Algiers, who was at that time working on his *Travels in Barbary and the Levant* (1738), a splendid book ('Fly, fly to secure it,' wrote a critic) containing valuable information about natural history. Shaw was 'a stout and fierce, but not ill-tempered, looking man', his features 'grotesque but marked most strongly with jocularity and good humour'. He had read *Systema Naturae* and had become an ardent Linnaean.

From Oxford Linnaeus returned to London. Probably he would gladly have protracted his stay in England; but Clifford had stipulated that he should not be too long absent, for he was eager for his protégé to start work on a full account of the plants in his garden and herbarium. Before the end of August Linnaeus was back at the Hartekamp and ready to begin what was to prove the most handsome of all his innumerable productions, his *Hortus Cliffortianus*.

5.

Hortus Cliffortianus

n his Autobiography Linnaeus refers to the book which Clifford had requested him to write, and explains why he very properly felt it his duty to accept, in spite of many other commitments, this laborious assignment:

> Since Clifford had not only been paying him a handsome salary but had also given him board and lodging and treated him like a son, Linnaeus undertook to prepare and write the extensive *Hortus Cliffortianus* and to correct the proofs. He finished in nine months what would have taken anyone else several years; and at the same time, whenever he felt in need of relaxation he would amuse himself by working on his *Critica Botanica*, which he arranged to have printed at Leyden. . . .

The *Hortus Cliffortianus* was the joint product of two men who were soon to be recognized as the greatest botanist and the greatest botanical draughtsman of their day, the latter supported by a competent engraver named Jan Wandelaar. Produced regardless of expense, it was as attractive aesthetically as it was important botanically, though collectors of 'fine flower books' will probably regret that the plates are uncoloured and the plants chosen for illustration not popular favourites. 'It marks,' writes Stearn, 'the beginning of a new era in botanical illustration since most of the plates give dissections of the flowers as well as portraying the habit of growth, and foreshadows the golden century of great flower-book production which extended from about 1760 to 1860'; but from an aesthetic standpoint this judgment is less than fair to the illustrators of several books of the previous century, and in particular to the three artists Nicolas Robert, Abraham Bosse, and Louis de Châtillon who were jointly responsible for the superb illustrations in Dodart's *Mémoires pour servir à l'Histoire des Plantes*.

The bulk of Linnaeus's fine folio is devoted to a description of all the plants growing at the Hartekamp or preserved in the herbarium there; it is for modern botany the most important of his books published before 1753, because of the frequency with which he adopted material in it, without alteration, in his *Species Plantarum*. But it contains much else besides, including a catalogue of the books in Clifford's library. For the majority of the plates Wandelaar used Ehret's drawings, but occasionally he was obliged to fall back upon his own. There is also a splendid Baroque frontispiece by Wandelaar (see page 128), the symbolism of which is thus described by Stearn, who based his interpretation on an article by C. Callmer and O. Gertz:

> In the centre of the picture a crowned goddess, Mother Earth or Cybele, sits upon a lion and lioness symbolic of her power; in one hand she holds a pair of keys indicating her right to the garden at any time; at her feet are a pot of *Cliffortia*, a plan of the Hartekamp garden and two cherubs [i.e. *putti*], one explaining Linnaeus's centigrade thermometer. . . . A negro brings her an *Aloe* from Africa, an Arabian woman a plant of *Coffea arabica* from Asia, a befeathered American Indian a plant of *Hernandia* from America. On a pedestal behind her stands a Janus-like bust wreathed with *Kaempferia* etc., the bearded head possibly portraying Clifford, against a background of topiary work. On the right overtopping all else is a banana in flower and fruit to indicate Linnaeus's success in its cultivation at the Hartekamp. A handsome young god, Apollo, steps forward below it, bringing light in his left hand and with his right hand casting aside the shroud of darkness around the goddess; he wears a wreath of laurel, and his face is the face of the young Linnaeus; underfoot he tramples the dragon of falsehood, slain with one of his arrows, an obvious reference to the counterfeit Hydra at Hamburg. . . . It thus graphically expresses Linnaeus's own opinion of his place in botany.

With regard to the thermometer in the picture – one that is now called the Celsius or, more often and less incorrectly, the centigrade thermometer – it is interesting to remember that Celsius made his zero the boiling-point of water and 100 degrees its freezing-point; Linnaeus did the opposite, and the thermometer which the *putto* is holding is clearly graduated according to Linnaeus. In a letter to a French correspondent he wrote: 'It was I who invented our thermometer in which the freezing-point of water is 0 degrees and the boiling point 100.' Celsius did not publish his plan until 1742, and thus Linnaeus clearly had precedence; how then did Celsius's name become associated with what was undoubtedly Linnaeus's thermometer? Can it be that the C which stands for Centigrade was mistakenly believed to stand for Celsius?

Some time during the summer of 1737 Linnaeus was offered through the good offices of Boerhaave the post of doctor to the Dutch Company in Surinam (Dutch Guiana), an assignment which would have afforded him a fine chance to study the flora of a tropical country; but once again the Swede feared the discomforts and perils of a torrid climate and the prospect of a yet longer separation from the bride who awaited him at home. Boerhaave then invited him to suggest a suitable substitute, and he proposed Johann Bartsch, a talented young German who was studying in Leyden. Linnaeus wrote:

> He was accepted and set out. But hardly had this unfortunate young man arrived when he found himself victimized by some Governor or other, who never allowed him a moment to himself. His dearest ambitions shattered, Bartsch succumbed at the end of six months, not to the dreadful climate but to the ill treatment he received. He deserved a better fate. The letters he wrote to me from Surinam were full of important observations, and his dissertation on Heat gives the measure of his worth.

Linnaeus was deeply distressed when he heard about Bartsch, feeling himself

'Linnaeus in his Lapland dress', mezzotint by Dunkarton after a painting by M. Hoffman, from the *Temple of Flora*.

to have been in part responsible for his fate. Later he named the genus *Bartsia* in honour of this 'most attractive young man, born to become one day the pride of his country. I knew him intimately when I was in Holland and was fortunate enough to inspire him with a love of natural history, for which he developed a wonderful talent.'

The year 1737 was one of almost unbelievable activity for Linnaeus. 'The books which bear the date 1737,' says Jackson, 'consist of nearly 500 pages in large folio and more than 1,350 pages in octavo', and other substantial works were on the stocks. Jackson purposely wrote '*bear the date 1737*' because the *Hortus Cliffortianus*, though so dated, did not in fact appear until the following year. Among the publications of 1737 was the first of many editions of the *Genera Plantarum*. In it, wrote Pulteney,

> our author found it necessary either to change or abolish more than half the number of the generic names which had been established by preceding authors, and the prodigious quantity of non-descript [i.e. not previously described] plants which had fallen into his hands, obliged him to frame *new* genera to the amount of more than double the number of those that were left as he found them. He tells us that he had examined the characters of 8,000 flowers before the publication of the first edition.

It was also some time during 1737 that Linnaeus sat – or rather stood – for the famous portrait in Lapland dress, best known from the mezzotints made after it for Thornton's *Temple of Flora*. The artist was Martin Hoffman, about whom all the standard art reference books are silent. Of this portrait, and the various copies (or replicas?) of it, Stoever wrote:

> In remembrance of LINNAEUS, his portrait, after life, and in a Laplander's dress, is still preserved there in Cliffort's house. From the original, drawn at CLIFFORT's, several copies were executed. In these portraits LINNAEUS had the most grotesque appearance. It represented him with boots of reindeer-skin, about his body a girdle, from which was suspended a Laplander's drum, a needle to make nets, a straw snuff-box, a cartridge-box and a knife; his neck was bare; his head was covered with a grey round hat; his hair was of a stiff brown colour; over his hands he wore Laplander's gloves; and in his right hand he held a plant, red from within and white from without [*Linnaea borealis*]. This portrait did not bear the least resemblance to LINNAEUS in his age and maturity of manhood, except the piercing hazel eye, and the wart on the right cheek.

Three versions of the oil-painting are known, two of them being now in Leyden and the third in Uppsala. Two different mezzotint engravings were used by Thornton in his *Temple of Flora*.

6.

Correspondents
and critics

In addition to working on his books Linnaeus had been carrying on an extensive correspondence with botanists all over Europe. Many letters written to him reveal admiration of the brilliance and the industry of this clever young man, but at the same time fear that his talents had been dangerously misdirected. Those addressed to him and to others by Dillenius are of particular interest.

Though Dillenius, after his initial mistrust of the cocksure young Swede, had soon realized that he was someone to be taken seriously, he was far from convinced that Linnaeus's new system would really prove satisfactory. Hardly had Linnaeus returned to Holland when Dillenius wrote to his old friend the veteran English botanist Dr Richard Richardson:

> A new botanist is arisen in the North, founder of a new method, based on the stamens and pistils, whose name is Linnaeus. He has printed *Fundamenta Botanica*, *Bibliotheca Botanica*, *Systema Naturae*, and is now printing in Holland his *Characteres*, and his *Flora Lapponica*. He is a Swede, and has travelled over Lapland. He has a thorough insight and knowledge of Botany, but I am afraid his method will not hold. . . .

The following spring Dillenius told Linnaeus himself what he felt about the sexual system and the rules of nomenclature as laid down in his *Critica Botanica*. On 16 May he wrote: 'You have achieved great things; but in order that you may achieve yet greater, I beg you to examine more and more species.' Linnaeus had in fact already carefully examined more than 8,000 species. The letter continues:

> I do not doubt that you yourself will one day overthrow your own system. You see, my dearest Linnaeus, how plainly I say what I think, for I count on your own frank nature to take it in good part. . . . I consider sexual differences altogether useless, superfluous, even misleading, for establishing the character of a plant. What is the point of it all? It is puerile; and it is quite enough that one botanist – Vaillant – should have had his head turned by them.

On 18 August he wrote again to air a very reasonable grievance, for Linnaeus had dedicated his *Critica Botanica* to him without permission:

> I am as disappointed with your *Critica Botanica* as I am pleased with your Lapland

Flora, and doubly so since you have, without my deserving such a compliment or knowing what you intended, dedicated the book to me. You must have known my dislike of all pomp and flattery. . . .

We all know that botanical nomenclature is an Augean stable which C. Hoffman, which even Gesner, was unable to cleanse. It is a task requiring much reading and wide and deep learning, and should not be undertaken precipitously or carelessly; you rush in and overturn everything. I don't object to Greek words, especially in compound names; but I think that the names of the Ancients ought not to be transferred rashly and indiscriminately to our new genera or to those of the New World. The time may perhaps come when the plants of Theophrastus and Dioscorides will be identified. . . .

I am not surprised at your refusing the medical post in Surinam, and I am glad that you did because the climate is very unhealthy. But if I were [you and] your age I would very much want to visit the Cape of Good Hope, or North America, before returning to your own barren land. . . .

The critical interest shown all over Europe in the sexual system and Linnaeus's new rules of nomenclature is testified by a very shrewd letter sent to Linnaeus on 15 November 1737 by Johann Amman, Professor of Botany at St Petersburg:

I see you are offended by what I wrote to Gronovius and Dillenius about your new method founded upon the stamens and pistils. Really I was only joking. I never supposed you would be seriously annoyed by what I said about the great concourse of husbands to one wife which so often happens, and which is so at variance with our local laws and customs. . . . I told Dillenius that your system was excellent for establishing and defining the genera of plants, though of little use where classes are concerned. I still think the same; for according to your method, plants which agree in the number of their stamens and pistils, though totally different in every other respect, are placed in the same class. . . .

You promise to account, in your *Critica Botanica*, for your numerous alterations of names. I presume that you have followed the rules you laid down in your *Fundamenta Botanica*. But many of these rules may not be universally approved, any more than your change of names. I beg you to consider what would happen if everyone were to lay down such laws and regulations whenever he felt so inclined, overturning names already known and approved by the best authors just for the sake of making new ones. Would it not lead to worse than the confusion of Babel? I write frankly and honestly, not just to wrangle or to contradict. . . .

Siegesbeck, a strange man, is printing a critical dissertation[1] in which your writings are harshly criticized. . . . The work is very short, but in my opinion its brevity is counterbalanced by its spite and arrogance. . . .

Admittedly Linnaeus, in his *Genera Plantarum*, had felt himself obliged to change or abolish more than half the names established by earlier authors. But with regard to Amman's criticism of his classes, it must be said in Linnaeus's defence that he never pretended that these were based on natural affinities.

The Siegesbeck whom Amman mentions was Johann Siegesbeck, a St Petersburg academician who vigorously denounced Linnaeus's 'lewd' system with its 'loathsome harlotry' which the Creator would never have tolerated in the vegetable kingdom. 'Who,' he asked, 'would have thought that bluebells, lilies and onions could be up to such immorality?' How could 'so licentious a method' be taught to the young without offence? Sir Thomas Browne had listed

[1] *Botanosophiae verioris brevis Sciagraphia (Short Outline of True Botanic Wisdom),* 1737.

120

the idea of sex in plants as a vulgar error; to Siegesbeck it was erroneous, and vulgar in another sense. Vaillant, incidentally, had been no less outspoken than Linnaeus.

Siegesbeck is remembered today, writes Stearn, 'only through the unpleasant, small-flowered weed which Linnaeus named *Sigesbeckia*', though it should in all fairness be mentioned that the plant had been so named before the two men had quarrelled. Stearn adds, 'In Flora's army-list . . . a revealing document drawn up about 1752 by General Linnaeus and headed by him, with Major-General Bernard Jussieu and Colonels Haller, Gronovius, Royen and Gesner as his chief officers, the lowest available rank is that of Sergeant-Major Siegesbeck, "Professor Petropolitanus"!'

Linnaeus hated opposition, and Siegesbeck remained a thorn in his flesh. 'I feel bound to say that you are not very patient under the attacks of your enemies,' Dillenius told Linnaeus. 'I am always ready to listen to criticism from anybody, in order to arrive at the truth; but I don't like wrangling for wrangling's sake.' For a time Linnaeus debated whether it were better to reply to Siegesbeck or to ignore him. In the end he decided to do the latter.

An extraordinary love-hate relationship seems to have existed between Linnaeus and his exact contemporary, that many sided genius Albrecht von Haller, the Swiss poet, philologist, anatomist, bibliographer, botanist, zoologist, physiologist and administrator, with whom he began in 1735 a correspondence which continued for many years.

Haller stood intellectually on a higher plane than Linnaeus, had much wider interests, made much more fundamental contributions to knowledge (particularly in anatomy and physiology), and knew Central European species of plants more soundly; but he was humourless and quick to take offence. His life held much tragedy. Botany, like everything else that he touched, he took in his stride, publishing in 1742 a volume on the Swiss flora and in 1768 an even more important work on the subject in three folio volumes. In 1736 he was appointed to the chair of medicine, anatomy, surgery and botany at Göttingen – a post he had held for seventeen years when he returned to Bern. He died in 1777.

It was said of Linnaeus and Haller that in botany 'they resembled Caesar and Pompey. One, our Linnaeus, suffered no equal, and the other, Haller, suffered no superior – or *vice versa*.' Over the years there were constant misunderstandings between the two men, both of whom seem at times to have suffered from a kind of persecution mania. Yet at other moments each of them – and Haller in particular – showed that he was capable of generosity and forgiveness. In 1738 Haller, who was thinking of leaving Göttingen to return to his beloved Switzerland, invited Linnaeus – 'of whom Flora has greater hopes than of any other botanist' – to succeed him. The letter was entrusted to a German priest who was returning to Stockholm but who took nine months to deliver it. Had it arrived more speedily Linnaeus might well have accepted, for he had been passing through a difficult time; but when it eventually reached him his circumstances had improved. He was, however, deeply touched, and replied in a letter full of gratitude.

All went well after this until the publication in 1745 of Linnaeus's *Flora Suecica*, when Haller took exception to some of his definitions of plants, seeing in

Sigesbeckia orientalis, drawn and engraved by Wandelaar, from *Hortus Cliffortianus*, 1738.

121

them a personal attack. 'Distinguished Linnaeus,' he wrote. 'You gratify your enemies, who are neither few nor impotent, when you thus attack your friends, as it cannot but abate something of their affection; whilst it raises, in their own estimation, those who wish you ill. . . .'

Linnaeus, in his reply, brushed these protests aside and told Haller of the tribute he intended to pay him in his *Flora Zeylanica*; but Haller nevertheless, when reviewing Linnaeus's *Fauna Suecica* (1746), savagely attacked his rival's zoological pretensions:

> The unbounded dominion which Linnaeus has assumed in the animal kingdom must upon the whole be abhorrent to many. He has considered himself as a second Adam, and given names to all the animals according to their distinctive features, without ever bothering about his predecessors. He can hardly forbear to make *man a monkey*, or *the monkey a man*.

What, one may ask, would Haller have said of Darwin?

So the bickering continued, to the credit of neither. In 1762 J. R. von Valltravers, who knew both men, attempted a reconciliation, bearing a friendly message from Linnaeus to Haller and adding his own regret that the two greatest naturalists in Europe should 'live at variance instead of uniting their endeavours in the pursuit of knowledge'. Haller responded, and his *Bibliotheca Botanica* (1771) contains a generous and magnanimous tribute to Linnaeus, whom he there describes as 'a man who brought about the greatest change in the whole of botany and who achieved his ends by making almost a fresh start to the subject'.

7.

Farewell to Holland

y the autumn of 1737 Linnaeus was so exhausted through over-work and so run down in health that he decided that the time had come for him to return home. 'And this,' he writes in his Autobiography,

in spite of the fact that he was living under ideal conditions; for he could go into Leyden whenever he wanted, to attend Boerhaave's lectures; he had the use of a coach-and-four in Amsterdam, where he could remain as long as he liked; the lovely gardens at the Hartekamp were always at his disposal; there were servants to wait upon him, and he could always entertain in style any who came to visit him.

When Clifford heard that Linnaeus intended to leave him, he suggested that he should stay in Leyden at his [Clifford's] expense for as long as he cared to, to hear Boerhaave; he begged him not to go before old Serrurier, the professor of Botany at Utrecht, died, as he could count on succeeding him. He said he would continue to pay him a salary. But in spite of all these offers, and the satisfaction he got from his reputation and from being treated as an oracle by every botanist who visited him, he took leave of Clifford. . . . He longed to be home again, and the Dutch climate does not suit Swedes.

It was Linnaeus's intention to return to Sweden by way of France and Germany. Clifford sadly saw him go, and with his customary generosity made him a parting present of a hundred ducats to mark his gratitude for the *Hortus*. From the Hartekamp Linnaeus went to Leyden to take leave of his many friends there, who one and all begged him to have second thoughts about abandoning Holland, where in less than three years he had made such a repu-tation for himself. It was van Royen who was the most insistent and who came forward with a positive proposal: he offered Linnaeus very advantageous terms if he would remain in Leyden over the winter to classify the plants in the Botanic Garden according to the sexual system.

The suggestion was tempting, but its acceptance presented difficulties. First, he knew that Clifford, to whom he owed so much and who had already himself offered to pay for him to remain in Leyden, must inevitably be hurt. Second, the plants in the Leyden Garden had been arranged by Boerhaave. As he told Giseke later, 'I owed too much to Boerhaave to agree to such a proposal, but van Royen was absolutely determined that the arrangement should be altered.

Three engravings from Thornton's *New Illustration of the Sexual System of Linnaeus*, 1799–1810. Above: Joseph Pitton de Tournefort and 'A zephyr disclosing to an aston-ished world the System of Tourne-fort'. Centre: Sébastien Vaillant. Right: Antoine de Jussieu.

"Very well," I said, "let us work out a method of classification which is neither Boerhaave's nor mine." Van Royen consented, and that was the origin of the van Royen method; but I don't want it to be known.' As for Clifford, he was too big a man to take serious offence. It may be worth mentioning that van Royen at this time bore Clifford a grudge because the latter had refused him the hand of his daughter; did van Royen perhaps feel that by taking Linnaeus from him he had had his revenge?

The winter passed agreeably enough for Linnaeus in Leyden. A particular pleasure to him were the meetings of a scientific club of which he had been made President and which held a *conversazione* every Saturday. On these occasions the host of the evening gave a demonstration in his particular field: Gronovius in botany, van Swieten in practical medicine, Lawson in history and antiquities, Lieberkühn (a portly Prussian) in microscopy, Kramer in chemistry, Bartsch (until his departure for Surinam) in physics, and Linnaeus himself in natural history. In a letter to Richardson, Gronovius, after praising Linnaeus's system and his prodigious industry, mentions the activities of the club:

Sometimes we examined minerals, sometimes flowers and plants, insects or fishes. We made such progress that by [Linnaeus's] Tables [his *Systema Naturae*] we can now refer any fish, plant or mineral to its genus, and thus to its species, though none of us had seen it before. I think these Tables so eminently useful that everyone ought to have them hanging up in his study, like maps. Boerhaave values this work highly and it is his daily recreation.

Linnaeus was busy enough in Leyden, but he was no longer overworking as he had been at the Hartekamp; consequently his health improved and he began to put on weight. His major occupation was the editing of Artedi's papers. Then there was his own *Classes Plantarum* – a survey of systems of classification from Caesalpinus (1583) onwards – on the stocks, and he made time to help Gronovius, not only with the Botanic Garden but also with his book on the Flora of Virginia. Van Royen paid him generously, and Lawson was per-petually trying to make him accept money: 'When I refused, he would press

124

sixty, eighty or a hundred gulden on me, saying that he had plenty for himself because he had had the foresight to save.'

But Linnaeus's good fortune was not to last. Shortly before Easter 1738 disturbing news reached him from Sweden that his 'best friend, B——'[1] had taken advantage of his absence to court Sara Lisa, and had made such headway with his suit that he had almost brought her to believe that her fiancé would never return. Linnaeus was about to pack his bags and hurry home when he was struck down by an illness.

> When hardly convalescent [he told Giseke] I rashly accepted an invitation from some Englishmen to eat oysters with them. I allowed myself to be persuaded; I ate one and then drank a large glass of wine. Next day I had a terrible attack of cholera. [typhoid?] Boerhaave prescribed laudanum, which I would never have dared to take had not my life been in danger. Over a period of twenty-four hours I took several drachms, and was cured; but I was so weak that I had to take daily a drop of oil of essence of cinnamon bark to sustain me.

Clifford, hearing of his illness, came to visit him. Forgiving his protégé's previous defection he carried him back with him to the Hartekamp to recuperate, giving him 'bed, board, and a ducat a day honorarium'. As a result of this good care, by May Linnaeus was well enough to travel.

Before leaving Holland he went to say farewell to old Boerhaave, who had been taken seriously ill and was believed to be dying. 'He labours under an asthma,' Linnaeus wrote to Haller. 'I fear a vomica [abscess].' He had refused to see anyone, and Linnaeus tells us that he 'was the only person allowed to enter, to kiss the hand of his great teacher with a sorrowful "Farewell!"'. . . . When Linnaeus returned to his house Boerhaave sent him a superb copy of his book on chemistry [*Elementa Chemiae*].' Boerhaave's condition was so grave that a rumour soon spread that he had died. On 22 July Gronovius wrote to a friend in England to contradict this; his letter shows his knowledge of the English language to have been imperfect: 'It is very strange that Dr Boerhaave is death in England, Switzerland and French; which is a great mistake. . . .' Boerhaave did in fact rally for a while; but the improvement was not maintained and on 23 September, four months after Linnaeus had left Holland, he died.

It might be imagined that Linnaeus, after his overlong absence from home and the disquieting news that had reached him from Falun, would now have returned post-haste to Sweden and his bride; in fact he set out for Paris, travelling by way of Antwerp, Brussels, Mons, Valenciennes, and Cambrai, and stayed there for a whole month, and it was only lack of money that made him abandon his intention of visiting Haller in Germany also. Either he had complete confidence in Sara Lisa's loyalty, or he felt that the benefit to his career of these French contacts outweighed the risk of losing her.

Paris proved in its way to be at least as stimulating as Holland had been. Tournefort and Vaillant were both dead; but the three Jussieu brothers, Antoine, Bernard and Joseph, were carrying on the distinguished tradition of botany in France, and it was these men whom Linnaeus particularly wanted to meet. Antoine, the eldest, was very hospitable; but besides being professor of

'Inauguration of the bust of Linnaeus at the Jardin des Plantes, Paris, in 1790.'

'Linnaeus returns from abroad', from *Through the Fields with Linnaeus* by Florence Caddy, 1887.

[1] Presumably Browallius. If so, his treachery must have been in part atoned for by his defence of Linnaeus against the attacks of Siegesbeck.

125

Oil-painting of Grinn (*Simia oedipus* L.), by G. Hesselius.
Below: 'Three people displaying a copy of Linnaeus's *Hortus Cliffortianus*', by Jacob de Wit (1695–1754).

Overleaf: frontispiece of *Hortus Cliffortianus*, described on page 117.

Turnera ulmifolia, painted by Ehret and engraved by Wandelaar, from *Hortus Cliffortianus*, 1738.

botany at the Jardin du Roy (Jardin des Plantes) he was an extremely busy doctor, and it was left to Bernard, a demonstrator at the Jardin, to take Linnaeus under his wing, to show him Paris, and to introduce him to his fellow scientists. Together they examined the herbaria of Tournefort, the Jussieus and Surian – 'all beautiful' – and Réaumur's cabinet; they also visited d'Isnard's fine library, which contained so many botanical books unknown to Linnaeus that it enabled him later to double the size of his *Bibliotheca botanica*. They saw Versailles and Saint-Germain; and the naturalist La Serre joined them for an expedition to Fontainebleau, where they stayed several days and found many wild orchids, some of which Linnaeus was later to discover in Sweden also, on the island of Öland. What made these excursions doubly delightful was that Bernard de Jussieu insisted upon paying for everything.

One day Linnaeus went on a botanical foray with Bernard and his students, one of whom played the time-honoured joke of concocting a spurious flower out of bits and pieces of various flowers and then inviting him to name it. Linnaeus, exposer of the bogus Hydra, was hardly likely to be deceived by such a flower; but tactfully he invited the student to ask Jussieu, since 'only Jussieu or God could do so'.

Among the botanists whom Linnaeus met in Paris were two of the Peintres du Roy – the seventy-three-year-old Claude Aubriet, and his young pupil Mademoiselle Madeleine Basseporte. It was the duty of these Court Flower Painters to record on vellum the rare plants grown in the Jardin du Roy, and by 1767, after little more than a century, the collection had swelled to fill more than seventy volumes. Aubriet, who had been closely associated with Tournefort and had accompanied him on his journey to the Levant in 1700, was one of the greatest of all botanical artists; his pupil, who had succeeded him in 1735, was much less talented, but she won for herself an influential position at Court, where she gave lessons to the children of Louis XV and advised Madame de Pompadour on interior decoration and other matters.

One June day Linnaeus was taken by Du Fay, President of the Académie des Sciences, to attend a session. At its close he was invited to become a Corresponding Member; further, if he were prepared to take French nationality and settle in France he would be made a full Member, with a salary and the prospects of a distinguished career. Linnaeus gratefully accepted the first honour, but the second he refused: the Dutch had begged him to stay, and now the French wanted him; but Sweden called him.

In his Autobiography Linnaeus tells us that as he had now seen 'all that was remarkable' in Paris, 'and since he did not intend to learn French manners or foreign languages' he prepared to return by sea to Sweden. He landed at Helsingborg, and on his way northwards broke his journey at Stenbrohult to visit his father. It was no return of the prodigal, but of a son who had made good; one can imagine with what pride Linnaeus showed him the books he had published, and how eagerly the old man must have listened to Carl's stories of his triumphs – triumphs which no false modesty will have obliged him to underestimate – in Holland and France. A fortnight later he set out for Falun and his patiently waiting bride.

PART III

The prince of botanists
1738–1778

Loeflingia hispanica, from *Petri Loe-
fling . . . Iter Hispanicum*, edited by
Linnaeus, 1758.

I.

Physician in Stockholm

ow Linnaeus was formally engaged; but there was to be no question of his marrying his Sara Lisa until he had a steady job. Though 'fonder of meddling with plants than with patients', he saw no immediate prospect of earning his living as a botanist; he therefore acted on the suggestion of his future father-in-law and set himself up in Stockholm as a doctor.

Soon and very forcibly young Dr Linnaeus learned that a prophet was, at all events for a time, not without honour save in his own country. 'Celebrated and respected abroad,' wrote Stoever, 'he was now a stranger in his native land, and the sport of obloquy and derision. The winter of 1738 nipt the laurels he had gathered in Holland.' 'I was the laughing-stock of everybody on account of my botany,' Linnaeus told Haller later. 'No one cared how many sleepless nights and weary hours I had passed, as all declared with one voice that Siegesbeck had annihilated me.' Patients showed no inclination to trust themselves to an inexperienced young doctor. 'There was nobody who would put even a servant under my care. I was obliged to live as best I could, in virtuous poverty....' At this moment Haller's letter, offering him his post at Göttingen, would have arrived if its delivery had not been delayed for nine months; had it done so, probably Linnaeus would have accepted, have carried his young bride with him to Germany, and made his career there. Sweden may well owe the retention of Linnaeus to the dilatoriness of an itinerant German priest.

Then, suddenly, Linnaeus's luck changed – and it was the young rakes of Stockholm who were instrumental in changing it. In his *Lachesis Naturalis* (notes on his medical lectures) Linnaeus had drawn up the daily time-table of these 'men about town', comparing and contrasting it with that of a well-to-do mining engineer at Falun:

> Stockholm's cavalier
> gets up at 8 or 9 o'clock, does his hair, dresses;
> 10 o'clock goes to the coffee-house, drinks a couple of cups of coffee, gossips;
> 11 o'clock does his shopping;
> 12 o'clock goes to the Riddarhus market to hear the latest news;
> 1 o'clock lunches, always with a quart or two of wine;
> 3 o'clock goes to the coffee-house for coffee or a glass of ale;
> 4 o'clock pays a few calls;

5 o'clock goes to the Castenhof or some other tavern, for a glass of Rhenish wine; 7 o'clock goes to Lars's Corner House and takes a whore; gambles till late at night, goes off God knows where; finally gets the pox, ague or fever.

Many weeks having passed without a single patient – 'not even a dog' – Linnaeus 'began to frequent public places' in search of clients. In a coffee-house or tavern he made the acquaintance of young *roué* suffering from gonorrhoea. 'His own doctor had failed to cure him in a year, but I cured him in a fortnight. Then several young men approached me complaining of chest trouble which, they said, prevented them from drinking at table; I gave them some medicine, and soon they were drinking like heroes. Their friends were amazed. . . .'

But Linnaeus was well aware that he did not know enough about venereal diseases; he therefore wrote for advice to a doctor at Montpellier, François Boissier de Sauvages de la Croix, with whom he had been in correspondence since 1737. Sauvages generously sent him details of a practical treatment, which of course included the use of mercury ointment ('a night with Venus, a lifetime with Mercury', as it used to be said). Certainly it proved effective, and Linnaeus prospered; within a few months of his arrival in Stockholm he had 'the greater part of the young men in his care, and by these means his reputation began to increase in the small-pox and agues then prevailing; so that as early as the month of March he had acquired a considerable practice'. To an old friend, Carl Mennander, later Bishop of Åbo, he wrote:

From seven in the morning until eight at night I hardly have a moment to snatch even a hasty meal. This fills my purse but so eats up my time that I cannot find a peaceful hour for myself or my dearest friends. . . . For the last two months I have had far too much to do – forty to sixty patients almost every day.

'I became known,' he told Haller. 'I was summoned to the great and . . . soon no invalid could recover without my help. . . . Aha! said I; Aesculapius is the giver of all good things; Flora bestows nothing on me but Siegesbecks! So I took my leave of Flora, a thousand times condemned my too numerous observations to eternal oblivion, and swore never to reply to Siegesbeck. . . .'

It was at this juncture that a stroke of good fortune brought Linnaeus to the notice of the highest in the land. Having been consulted by a senator's wife who had a cough, he effectively recommended gum tragacanth lozenges. This lady passed on the recommendation to Queen Ulrika Eleonora, and soon all the Court was talking of the clever young doctor, who through the influence of Count Carl Tessin was now appointed Physician to the Admiralty.

In following the career of Linnaeus from his childhood in Småland to his return from abroad in 1738 we have neglected to mention what had been taking place during this time in Sweden as a whole. But now that he is coming into contact both with the royal family and with one of the leading political figures of his day, Count Tessin, it is necessary for us to glance at the course of public events over the preceding thirty years.

Queen Ulrika Eleonora, by M. van Mytens, 1730.

Opposite: Count Carl Tessin, by J. A. J. Aved, 1695–1770.

During Linnaeus's boyhood Karl XII had involved his country in the long, foolish and costly Great Northern War. By 1715 Sweden was in open conflict with England, Hanover, Russia, Prussia, Saxony and Denmark, and in the last stages of exhaustion. Three years later Karl was killed in battle and the time had come to pay the bill for his reckless twenty years of fighting – a bill which left Sweden a second-rate power and the country disastrously impoverished. There being no direct heir to the throne, the choice of a successor lay between the late King's only surviving sister, Ulrika Eleonora, and his nephew the young Duke of Holstein. Ulrika, who was married to Prince Friedrich of Hesse, had the stronger claim and was offered the throne; but Karl's misuse of absolute rule had taught the country a sharp lesson, and before she was 'elected' as Queen the Riksdag obliged her to forswear any real say in the government of the country and to disclaim any hereditary rights with regard to the succession. In 1720 the Queen, who still tried to meddle in the country's affairs, was prevailed upon to abdicate in favour of her husband, who ruled, with powers still further shorn, as King Fredrik I until his death in 1751. He was little more than a puppet: the Era of Liberty had been born.

Twenty years of war were followed by twenty years of peace, until 1738 under the firm but cautious control of the Chancellor, Count Arvid Horn, who has sometimes been compared to his English contemporary, Robert Walpole. But gradually an opposition was growing which despised what it considered the timidity, even cowardliness, of Horn's policy and clamoured for war and revenge. This party, led by Count Carl Gyllenborg and Count Carl Tessin, was known, from the tricorns worn by young officers, as the Hats, their allegedly sleepy opponents as the Nightcaps or, more generally, the Caps; the Hats were bellicose and pro-French, while the pacific Caps favoured an alliance with England. In 1738 the Hats carried everything before them and Horn, an old man in his middle seventies, was driven from office; he lived for four more years in retirement – long enough to see his country recklessly involved, on the most frivolous of pretexts, in a new war with Russia. Gyllenborg succeeded Horn as Chancellor while Tessin became 'Landtmarskalk' (Speaker of the House of Nobles) and, later, Gyllenborg's successor.

Tessin was the son of one of Sweden's most famous architects, Nikodemus Tessin, and an ardent patron of science and the arts. He was also a brilliant orator and a polished writer, who as Ambassador Extraordinary to France was soon 'to delight Versailles with his brilliant qualities of *grand seigneur*'. His advent to power at this particular moment was of inestimable value to Linnaeus; not only did Tessin secure for him a well paid post but he also offered him a room in his house and 'a free fork' at his table, of both of which Linnaeus gratefully availed himself until his marriage. Indeed, his gratitude was, and continued to be, unbounded, and Miss Gourlie has drawn attention to flowery letters from him to Tessin which begin, 'To my God and my Tessin I offer my love, honour, praise, and gratitude, so long as I can whisper, and my children shall praise Your Excellency's dust so long as they are on the earth's surface.' When Tessin finally broke with the Court and in 1752 resigned from the premiership, Linnaeus's loyalty and affection remained undiminished.

It may seem strange that Linnaeus, most peace-loving of men, should thus have allied himself with the war party, and, most sea-hating of men, should

have accepted the post of Physician to the Admiralty. But it was Tessin the art-lover and the promoter of science that Linnaeus revered; and as for the sea, Linnaeus had no doubt assured himself that his duties would never require him to leave terra firma.

Another friendship made by Linnaeus at this time was with the distinguished Mårten Triewald, already mentioned in connection with the mines at Dannemora. Triewald urged Linnaeus to apply for a job which he had just relinquished – that of lecturer on assaying and mineralogy at the College of Mines; Tessin backed his application, and after Linnaeus had agreed to give lectures on botany too, he was appointed.

Triewald was planning to establish in Stockholm an Academy of Science whose Transactions would be published in Swedish and for Swedes; the Uppsala Royal Society of Science published in Latin for international circulation. He invited Linnaeus to join his small group of influential supporters, and thus the 'Academy of Science for the investigation of Mathematics, Natural History, Economics, Trade, Useful Arts and Manufactures' was inaugurated. Two years later it was granted a royal charter. The office of President was to be held, in rotation, for a period of six months only; the first President was chosen by lot, and this fell on Linnaeus. Over the years the Royal Academy of Science has played a very important role in the development of science in Sweden; it is the Swedish counterpart of the Royal Society of London.

Less than a year had passed since Linnaeus had settled in Stockholm, but in that short space of time he had won not only a measure of fame but also – and this was no less important to him – he was now earning a regular and very handsome income. The only obstacle in the way of his marriage having thus been removed, on 17 June 1739 he set out for Falun. The wedding took place at Sveden, his father-in-law's country-house about three miles from the town. As was customary, verses were addressed to the bride and bridegroom, one of which

Stockholm in 1693, from *Suecica Antiqua et Hodierna*.

contained reference to a 'monandrian lily' – a single-stamened and therefore 'one husband in marriage' flower.

On 20 January 1741 a son, Carl, was born in Falun. The proud father, too busy to leave Stockholm at that moment, wrote to his Sara Lisa:

My dearest Mother and Wife,

With what impatience I awaited the post, and how excited I was when I received the news I had been longing for – the joyful news that the gracious God had heard my prayer and that my dearest wife had been delivered from so painful and perilous an adventure! . . .

However much it grieves me, dearest Mother, that your labour was so difficult, I nevertheless kiss the gracious hand of God [in gratitude] that it was no worse, that your life was spared and that we have been blessed with a son – a shapely child without deformity. . . . For the sake of God and of all our love let me hear every post-day how you, my dearest Mother, and my son are doing. . . . Dearest Mother, take care to avoid changes of temperature and draughts, for carelessness of that sort might harm you.

I remain, my dearest wife,
your faithful husband
Carl Linnaeus
Greetings to my little Carl.

In his letter to Haller of 12 September 1739 Linnaeus had told him, 'At any moment now both the medical professorships [at Uppsala University] are likely to fall vacant. Professors Rudbeck and Roberg, both very old, are about to resign. If they do, Rosén will probably succeed Roberg and I may get Rudbeck's job. . . .' The reluctance of professors to retire was due, it should be explained, to the fact that normally they received no pension.

In March 1740 Rudbeck died, but it was Rosén, not Linnaeus, who was appointed to succeed him. Linnaeus was indignant that this man, 'who can't even recognize a nettle when he sees one', should have been chosen for the chair which included botany, but in other respects his qualifications were superior to those of Linnaeus. Soon afterwards, however, Roberg was forced to resign, and after a great deal of unpleasant wrangling and a stormy scene at a meeting of the Consistory, Linnaeus was appointed in his place. Among the unsuccessful candidates was Dr Abraham Bäck, a young man who was to become the best friend Linnaeus ever had.

In a letter to Jussieu Linnaeus describes his satisfaction at the way things have worked out:

By God's grace I am now released from the wretched drudgery of a medical practitioner in Stockholm. I have obtained the position I have coveted for so long: the King has appointed me professor of medicine and botany at Uppsala University and so given me back to botany from which I have been sundered all these three years while I was spending my time tending the sick in Stockholm. If life and health are granted to me, you will, I hope, see me accomplish something in botany.

So, in October 1741, Linnaeus moved with his wife and little Carl to Uppsala, where he was to live for the rest of his life.

2.

Öland and Gotland 1741

As early as 1729 Linnaeus's old teacher, Kilian Stobaeus, had sent a group of his students to explore the southern province of Skåne, and Linnaeus's own journeys through Lapland in 1732 and Dalecarlia in 1734 had carried the scientific investigation of the Swedish provinces a stage further. The value to the national economy of such undertakings was becoming increasingly apparent, and in January 1741, while he was still awaiting the outcome of his application for Roberg's vacant chair, Linnaeus, whose highly successful lectures on botany and mineralogy at the College of Mines had not passed unnoticed by the authorities, was approached by the Riksens Ständer (Estates of the Realm) with an invitation to undertake a survey of the two Baltic islands of Öland and Gotland. It was also intended that he should include Västergötland (West Gothland),[1] but in the event lack of time made this impossible. He immediately accepted.

His instructions were to investigate everything of potential value in the three kingdoms of Nature, but he was particularly urged to see whether he could discover a clay suitable for the making of porcelain, at that time an expensive import, and plants for use as dyes. He was also told to try to find out what was the so-called *Manna-blod* (man's-blood), a plant said to grow only near Kalmar 'where it is believed to have sprung from the blood of Swedes and Danes who fell in the battle there'.

On 15 May, just after he had heard the news of his appointment to Uppsala, Linnaeus set out on his journey. With him travelled, at their own expense, 'six capable and intelligent youths' carefully selected from the many who had applied to accompany him; one of those chosen was Sara Lisa's brother, Johan Moraeus. The sun shone on the little party as it rode out through the city gates of Stockholm:

[1] Östergötland and Västergötland are provinces in southern Sweden and must not be confused with the island of Gotland (formerly spelt Gothland). It is perhaps worth mentioning that whereas 'Gotland' is pronounced more or less as an Englishman would expect, 'Götland' is pronounced 'Yertland'.

But the air was somewhat chill. Spring, which should not be measured by the calendar but by the climate and the temperature, had so far arrived that the maples had opened their flowers, but not yet their leaves. The birches were in fresh leaf and flowering splendidly; the alders' stipules had just burst, and on the tips of their branches the firs had small red buds like wild strawberries, which are their still unripe male flowers; the lime, oak and aspen were still wrapped in their winter sleep. . . . The cuckoo had begun to call, and today we saw the first swallow.

The nights, however, continued cold, and at Svalbro, where they could find neither beds nor fresh horses, they 'shivered all night long'. At Norrköping they visited various factories, and Linnaeus mentions without comment that small children were working in the tobacco factory. Following the dusty tracks of East Gothland, on the sixth day they entered the smiling province of Småland, Linnaeus's homeland, where more swallows and a swallow-tail butterfly proclaimed that spring had really arrived in the south. A detour was made to see the gold-mine near Vetlanda, and on the tenth day they came to Växjö where Linnaeus met his old benefactor, Dr Rothman. Finally they reached Kalmar, a coastal town with a fine and picturesque medieval and Renaissance castle, the point of embarkation for the island of Öland.

At Kalmar the famous *Manna-blod* was soon found, but it proved to be nothing more remarkable than *Sambucus ebulus* (danewort or dwarf elder) – a common enough plant in many parts of Europe and known already to Linnaeus. William Turner in 1548 records finding 'Walwurt or Danewurt ... in Cambryge fieldes in great plentie', though possibly it is not a true English native. In fact the legend of the plant seems to have originated in England and to have reached Sweden through John Ray, who wrote that danewort was so named 'because it sprang, so men say, from the blood of the slaughtered Danes'. Linnaeus possessed a copy of this book.

The long and slim island of Öland – its length is about eighty miles and its greatest breadth no more than ten – is clearly visible from Kalmar in fine weather; but now the weather broke and Linnaeus, fearful ever and unlucky almost always where the sea was concerned, preferred to wait for the gales to blow themselves out. Needless to say he did not waste his time, and among other of his activities he describes his visit to the Castle, a part of which served as a prison whose inmates were made to 'haul like horses' all day and every day. 'Their misery made one's hair stand on end ... and they were prisoners for life.' The prison had been constructed below water-level to prevent anyone attempting to tunnel his way out.

For several days the south-west gales continued; but when two of the inmates of the house in which the party lodged developed spotted fever, Linnaeus chose the lesser of two evils and embarked with his companions on the first available ship. After a very rough crossing they landed at Färjestaden, a little harbour some miles to the south of Borgholm, the only town on the island. But the discomforts of the voyage were soon forgotten at the sight of an unfamiliar and thrilling flora, and as at dawn next day they made their way towards Borgholm, collecting at every step under the expert guidance of a Kalmar chemist who had travelled with them, Linnaeus became as excited as a schoolboy. Now the weather began to improve, and by the time they reached Borgholm 'the thrushes were singing, and all Nature seemed to join in the festival that Flora held today in our honour'.

Öland is an island of limestone on which 1,150 species of plants have been recorded, and Linnaeus was particularly struck by the large variety of orchids, some of which he had found during his visit to Fontainebleau; if the whole world had told him that they also grew on Öland he would never, he said, have believed it.[1] During the three weeks that the party spent on the island they explored it thoroughly, noting everything of interest from runic inscriptions to the immense appetites of the Ölanders.

The Old Botanic Garden, Uppsala: Linnaeus's house, and below, the Orangery.

[1] Orchids such as *Cypripedium calceolus*, *Orchis militaris*, *O. ustulata*, *O. mascula*, *Ophrys insectifera* and *Epipactis helleborine* are natives of both central France and the islands of Öland and Gotland.

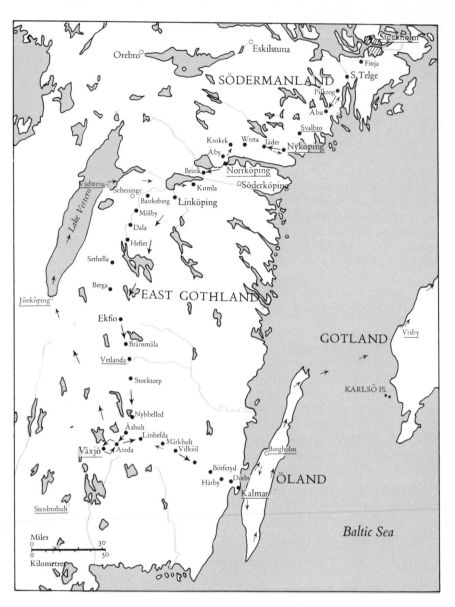

Linnaeus's route to Gotland. Places Linnaeus visited which are mentioned in the text are underlined.

Sweden was now on the brink of war with Russia – in fact it broke out only a month later – and it was understandable that the strange and incomprehensible activities of these inquisitive strangers should arouse suspicion. When 'the man in the black jacket' (Linnaeus) was heard exhorting his friends to 'keep their eyes open', no one could any longer doubt that they were Russian spies; and thereafter they were obliged to take with them a responsible native who was prepared to vouch that though they might be mad they were nevertheless harmless. On 21 June, having seen all there was to see on Öland, the party set sail for Visby, the capital of Gotland.

As early as Neolithic times Gotland had become the emporium of the northern waters and remained such throughout the Bronze and Iron Ages. But

142

the height of its prosperity was reached in the eleventh and twelfth centuries, when owing to the disturbed state of the Middle East a great part of the Eastern trade that had previously passed by way of Egypt and Constantinople was deflected through Russia and the Baltic. Thus Visby, chosen apparently for the advantages provided by its insularity, became the chief distribution centre of the West, and soon so many German merchants had settled there that it was described as being 'almost a German town'. Then, it was said, 'the swine ate out of silver troughs and the women spun with distaffs of gold'; and it is significant that the soil of Gotland has yielded nearly 23,000 oriental coins and some 14,000 English and Irish dating from the eighth to the twelfth century, much of this probably Danegeld. But in 1361 Visby fell to the Danish King Valdemar Atterdag, and thereafter its decline was rapid. Today the splendid medieval town walls and a dozen or so ruined churches are all that remain to tell of its former glory. Gotland was restored to Sweden in 1645.

Linnaeus and his friends sailed eastwards through the night, waking at dawn (two a.m.) to see the Karlsö islands ahead of them:

> The wind dropped and the ship made very slow progress. As we approached the islands the cliffs appeared ever steeper, just like fortification walls. Then the sea became calm and smooth as glass. Duck were swimming here and there, but we saw neither porpoises nor ships. The sailors whiled away the time by telling tales of the two big carbuncles said to have been stolen from the church of St Clement in Visby and to have gone to the bottom when King Valdemar's ship foundered and sank. They alone believed [the legend] that its mast and the glitter of the carbuncles could still be seen when the sea was calm and the sun shining. . . .

Hugging the coast they now sailed slowly northwards until they reached Visby, where they disembarked in the little harbour. Linnaeus was astonished

'Småland waterfall', by Marcus Larson, 1856.

Kalmar castle.

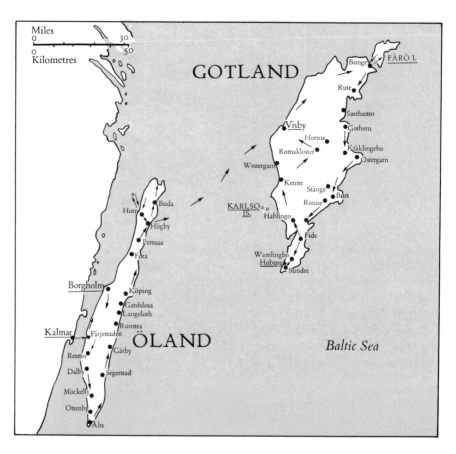

Linnaeus's travels in Öland and Gotland.

at his first sight of Visby, which seemed to him 'like a miniature Rome'. He visited some of the 'large and magnificent' churches and soon discovered that the much revered bones of a virgin giantess, preserved in the Cathedral she was alleged to have built, were whale-bones. 'Alas for legend when science comes along!' he noted. 'It is all swept away.'

About a month was spent on Gotland, and the island explored from end to end. They went first to its northernmost tip and crossed over to the little island of Fårö, the centre of a brisk fishing and sealing industry, where they remained for a couple of days, sleeping by night on the floor of the church. On Gotland almost opposite Fårö was the isolated farm of Hau, where the party spent the night of 27 June:

> I thought it the most charming farm I had seen anywhere in all Sweden. There are no neighbours within three miles, for on one side is the sea, on another a little lake, and on the remaining two a large and barren expanse of limestone flats. Two farmers live here, each of whom has a handsome white house built of stone as well as dwelling-houses made of tarred timber. Inside everything looked clean and pleasant, and the kitchens were full of copper pots, ten or fifteen of various sizes in each.

> The dwelling-houses were surrounded by hop-yards and gardens, and big leafy maples in which had been placed a number of small wooden cylinders, hollowed out at the top, so that starlings and other small birds could lay their eggs in them and from the branches delight the inmates of the house with incessant music.

144

It is interesting to note this early use of nesting-boxes, and also the satisfaction which many people seem to derive from 'background music' – a need so amply catered for today by the wireless. But Linnaeus was charmed. Here, he thought, the well known verses had come true: 'A farmer with eight cows and a horse, living in the forest and not pestered by visitors – he leads the perfect life.'

Linnaeus describes with gusto the rich bird life of Gotland, and gives a full account of the appearance and habits of the razor-bills which flew round their boat in large numbers when they visited the Karlsö islands. 'Even when we fired at a bird,' he noted, 'it did not make off, but continued to fly ever more eagerly over our heads.' He continues:

> The thighs of the razor-bill are situated further back than the centre of gravity of its body. . . . Because of this it swims and fishes well, but it cannot walk as do other birds and has to go upright like a man. With its black coat and white waistcoat, its wrinkled forehead and hooked nose and the effect it gives of wearing spectacles, it looks extremely comical when it walks. It builds its nest in the highest and most inaccessible crevices of the cliffs. . . . If one passes below the cliffs and shouts loudly, 'Come on out!' or something like that, enormous quantities of birds fly out. . . .

At night the party often slept under eiderdowns, and Linnaeus wrote of the birds which provided this luxury:

> There are many eider-duck on the island, but they are persecuted here. They are shot and, what is worse, their eggs are used for making omelettes. In the spring one can see these birds in the fish market in Stockholm. The time will probably come when their valuable down makes them safe from the gun.

There is a delightful description of the grasshopper and the way in which the male produces its characteristic song:

> Grasshoppers were chirping in the meadows, and we caught one. . . . The female draws out her tail like a long sword. The male is entirely green and has four teeth in his tail and two claws between his thighs; in the wings, which lie on top of one another, there is a round hole the size of a vetch-seed and covered with a thin membrane. When the grasshopper serenades his beloved he rubs his wings together and the taut membrane produces the sound; thus his song comes from his wings, not from his mouth. The female has no such instrument in her wings and is obliged to remain silent. . . .
>
> The mouth of both male and female consists of two pairs of jaws, the upper provided with a number of sharp teeth but the lower having none. . . . When the farmers have warts on their hands they take one of these grasshoppers and put the wart to its mouth. The grasshopper bites and injects a black corrosive liquid which removes the wart.

Linnaeus, who had two warts, makes no mention of sampling the local cure.

Plants were his chief interest, and on Öland and Gotland he found no less than a hundred previously unrecorded in Sweden. One that he believed at the time to be new was the garlic-scented ramson,[1] whose spread was encouraged by farmers because it kept other weeds down; he was soon to learn that it was no novelty after all, but well known, even if very local, on the mainland. Many of

[1] *Allium ursinum.* The Old English name is *hramsa*, therefore *hramsan* (giving 'ramson') is the plural and 'ramsons' a double plural. The Swedish is *rams*.

the Gotlanders were, he discovered, well informed about their native flora, and he noted with pleasure the aptly chosen local names of some of the plants.

Linnaeus always liked his friends to enjoy themselves, encouraging games, and even 'romping' in which he himself did not normally join. At När, he tells us, his companions 'amused themselves by playing *pärk* – a very agreeable ball-game often played on Gotland by the farmers, who taught us the rules. It is not known in Sweden, though it is common in Holland and there. It requires both skill and speed.'

Near the southernmost point of the island is the curious bluff, known as the Hoburg, which rises sheer from the water, like the prow of a great ship, to the height of 122 feet – a height which hardly justifies Linnaeus's description of it as 'a very lofty mountain':

> This Hoburg is one of the most remarkable natural phenomena in all Gotland. It is a very lofty mountain, formed like a most beautiful citadel with walls that are vertical on all sides except in one or two places where they actually overhang. The rock is scalable only at a single point, where there is a narrow path. On the top is a field 297 paces by 145, quite bare, and sloping slightly down towards the centre so that it could be made to serve as a reservoir for rain water. The mountain is of limestone, and were anyone to take a few barrels of gunpowder and blast some of the rock near the path it could be rendered inaccessible except by the use of a rope; this would make it a secure refuge in times of war, especially since it is surrounded by open country. . . .
>
> We marvelled that this remarkable spot, where Nature (who never makes anything without a purpose) has created such a masterpiece in such a strategic position at the southernmost tip of the island, should not have been put to any use. There is not even a beacon here, although innumerable ships have been wrecked on these shores – bewildered by storms and darkness and by the currents which always mislead the mariner. It would be a simple matter to install a beacon in a place where there is an unlimited supply of tar and seal blubber.

Today there is a lighthouse, and visitors are shown a cavern known as the Hoburgsgubbens Sängkammare, or Bedroom of the Old Man of Hoburg.

By 17 July the party was back at Visby; but getting away from the island was to prove none too easy:

> Day after day we tried to leave Gotland, but there was no ship ready to sail and we were held there like prisoners. In the end we were obliged to make arrangements to risk our lives in the mail-boat which, like its skipper, was small, frail, ancient and unreliable. I don't know what happened, but the man let us down and sailed without us. If the postal authorities would reorganize this service it would be the greatest boon to the islanders. . . .

Finally, early on the morning of 25 July, they sailed in something more sea-worthy than the mail-boat. And perhaps it was just as well, for (according to Linnaeus) the passage to Öland was dreadful: 'The north wind howled, the waves grew furious and the ship was hurled to and fro between the raging billows. My companions were seasick, the tackle began to break; we were in despair and placed our lives in God's hands.'

At Kalmar the party broke up, leaving Linnaeus to set out alone for Stenbrohult;

Vadstena in 1706, from *Suecica Antiqua et Hodierna*.

but after two strenuous months of travelling, collecting and recording he was so exhausted that on reaching Kråkenäs, near Växjö, he collapsed and had to spend two days in total idleness before he felt strong enough to continue his journey. At last, however, he came to his 'homeland and the flowers amongst which I grew up. Here I saw my beloved birthplace, my grey-haired old father, my brother and all my sisters and relations. . . . And here I found again the very rare plants which I remember gave me such pleasure when I was a boy.'

Linnaeus was now rejoined by three of his companions who had been exploring Skåne, and the four young men set off towards the north. No doubt it was to take as much advantage as possible of travel by water that, after a week of leisurely sightseeing round Växjö, they went to Jönköping, at the southernmost tip of the hundred-mile-long Lake Vettern. Here they visited the building in which the Göta Court of Appeals for southern Sweden met, and were shown

> a large collection of witches' paraphernalia, such as treatises on black magic which we read and found to be full of deceit and vanities, antiquated and false receipts, idolatry, superstitious prayers and invocations of devils. . . . We blew the sacred horn without conjuring up the devil, and milked the milking-sticks without drawing any milk.[1] Here were to be seen sorceries, made neither by witches nor by devils but from the triple stomach of a ruminant animal. Here were eagles' feet with outstretched claws, with which wizards tore the stomachs of those who had colic; I should think that they no more deserved to be burned than do the Chinese who pierce a hole right in the belly, or than doctors who in a case of severe colic burn the stomach with *Moxa* [*Artemisia moxa*]. And here also we were able to see the genuine instruments of wizards: knives, hammers, cudgels and iron bullets by the use of which men have been killed by their enemies.

In Jönköping, two years after Linnaeus's visit, was born a child, Carl Peter Thunberg, who was to become his most distinguished pupil; and a century later the town became famous as the birthplace of that great modern convenience, the safety-match.

The party continued on their way to Vadstena, about seventy miles northwards on the eastern shore of the lake. This town was the birthplace of St Bridget (1302–73), the patron saint of Sweden and mother of another saint, St Katarina of Sweden. After her husband's death in 1344, and encouraged by innumerable visions and celestial promptings, Bridget founded the Order of

[1] 'A bunch of sticks like cows' udders. . . . To milk them filled your pans and made your enemy's cow run dry.' (Gourlie.)

147

Saint Bridget of Vadstena, panel of a retable from Salem church, Södermanland.

Title-page of *Öländska och Gothländska Resa*, 1745.

Bridgittines and set out for Rome, partly to get papal approval and partly 'in pursuance of her self-imposed mission to elevate the moral tone of the age'. It took her twenty years to achieve the first objective of her pilgrimage, and in her second she was never to be more than partially successful. The principal house of the Order, at Vadstena, was richly endowed by King Magnus and his Queen, but was subsequently converted into a lunatic asylum. In England the famous Bridgittine Convent at Syon, Middlesex, was supported by King Henry V and soon became one of the most fashionable nunneries in the country.

What aroused Linnaeus's interest in St Bridget was, however, not so much her piety or her pilgrimage as her famous leek, 'about whose deadly effect on moles there was so much talk in Stockholm and in the Academy of Science. But,' he says, 'I was dumbfounded, for I thought I was going to see a very rare plant; in fact I might just as well have brought back ramsons from Gotland!' Here was another myth for Linnaeus to puncture – but this time by common sense rather than by science: the cloister garden was completely surrounded by a wall with deep foundations, and it was clearly the walls, not the ramsons, that kept the moles away. The following year the Admiralty Chemist sent some ramsons to Linnaeus at Uppsala, recommending their use against rodents. He scattered them around his room but it remained as full of mice as ever, 'and so far as I know it was mice which carried off the ramsons which I had brought back from Vadstena!'

By 28 July Linnaeus was back in Stockholm; his journey, which had taken nearly three months in all, had cost him 536 silver dalers. He was for some time to come far too busy to write up the account of his expedition, but in 1745 *Öländska och Gothländska Resa* finally appeared; an important feature of the book is its index, in which plants are named binomially and with numerical cross-references to the *Flora Suecica*. It was Linnaeus's first full-length published work in Swedish, and he apologizes to his readers for his simple and direct use of his native language which might, he feared, shock 'many Pliny nightingales. But language adorns a science as clothes adorn the body; the body cannot of itself honour the clothes, but must let them honour it. If none but Doctors of Eloquence were allowed to write . . . the world would know less today than in fact it does.'

Though Linnaeus had failed to find china-clay or any important vegetable dyes in Gotland, his expedition had in the main proved rewarding; and in his Preface he lists the most important of his observations. In the field of botany he considered his discovery on Gotland of a new crop-plant, Swedish hay-seed (*Medicago falcata* or sickle medick), of such value that in itself it repaid the cost of his journey. He also reported on the use of marram grass to prevent sand-drifting, and on a sedge employed for thatching. 'In zoology I have described how seals are caught, deer fenced out, eider-duck mismanaged and duck snared; how cod and flounders are taken. . . .' He reported on rock formations, mineral springs and quicksands; on runic inscriptions (of which he gives a number of rough transcripts, there not being time to clear them thoroughly of moss); on methods of farming, and on local remedies for various diseases. 'Superstitions I have noted here and there, but more to entertain my readers than to afford them any practical benefit. . . .' And characteristically he concludes, 'Altogether by this journey I have discovered in the field of natural history more than anyone could have believed possible.'

3.

Professor in Uppsala

n 27 October 1741 Linnaeus gave his inaugural lecture in the Caroline Hall of Uppsala University, speaking in Latin as was ordained for such occasions. His theme was the importance of travelling through one's own country and the economic benefits that could accrue to it from so doing; and he frankly admitted what Sweden already owed to his exploration of Lapland, Dalecarlia, and the two Baltic islands. A brief excerpt may be given from his lecture, in Stillingfleet's pleasant translation:

Good God! how many, ignorant of their own countrey, run eagerly into forreign regions, to search out and admire whatever curiosities are to be found; many of which are much inferior to those, which offer themselves to our eyes at home. I have yet beheld no forreign land, that abounds more with natural curiosities of all kinds, than our own. None which presents so many, so great, so wonderfull works of nature; whether we consider the magazines of snow heaped up for so many ages upon our Alps, and amongst these vast tracks [tracts] of snow green meadows, and delicious vallies here and there peeping forth, or the lofty heads of mountains, the craggy precipices of rocks, or the sun lying concealed from our eyes for so many months, and thence a thick Cimmerian darkness spread over our hemisphere, or else at another season darting his rays continually along the horizon. The like to all which in kind, and degree, neither Holland, nor France, nor Britain, nor Germany, nor lastly any countrey in Europe can shew; yet thither our youth greedy of novelty flock in troops....

(And how, one may venture to ask, was Linnaeus in a position to state categorically that no country in Europe had anything to offer that Sweden had not?)

Then with the customary ceremonial Linnaeus took the oath and joined his colleagues at the professorial table. When, a few months later, permission was given for Rosén and himself to redistribute their spheres of activity, Linnaeus took over botany, dietetics, *materia medica* and the supervision of the Botanic Garden, leaving practical medicine, anatomy and physiology to Rosén; pathology and chemistry they shared between them, each taking that aspect of the subject which he was best qualified to teach.

Linnaeus's first concern was with the Garden and the Professor's residence. The Garden, which had been founded by the elder Olof Rudbeck in 1657, had within thirty years become one of the most important in Europe. Though the

Baron Carl Hårleman.

Right: view of the Uppsala Botanic Garden, as reorganized by Linnaeus, 1745.

house, which stood in the south corner of the Garden, had escaped damage in the great fire of 1702, both it and the Garden had subsequently been allowed to fall into decay. For this there were several reasons: the University had been impoverished by the fire, and the whole country by the wars; and the younger Rudbeck, who had succeeded his father on his death in 1702, had been more concerned with his *Thesaurus* than with his plants. The 1,800 plants cultivated in 1685 had by 1739 dwindled to less than 300, and the house, wrote Linnaeus to the Senate of the University, looked 'more like an owl's nest or a den of thieves than a professor's residence'. However, the Senate proved surprisingly helpful, promptly allotting money for the rebuilding of the house (now provided with the unusual luxury of plaster ceilings) and for the construction of a hot-house or orangery in the Garden. This latter was designed by Linnaeus's friend and patron, the Court Intendant Baron Carl Hårleman.

Fortunately there was no need to search for a good head gardener. Two or three years earlier the post had fallen vacant, and Rudbeck had consulted Linnaeus about a suitable man. Linnaeus had strongly recommended Dietrich Nietzel, Clifford's head gardener at the Hartekamp, if he could be persuaded to come; and tempted by the prospect of very good wages Nietzel had agreed. Linnaeus thus ill repaid the kindness that he had received from his benefactor, and his ingratitude was never forgiven; twenty years later he heard from a friend that Clifford's daughter-in-law was still angry with him for having enticed Nietzel away.

Under Nietzel the Uppsala Garden went ahead again rapidly. It was enlarged; the wages of the staff were doubled, and Nietzel was promoted to the position of Intendant; and by 1748, thanks to innumerable gifts of plants from friends and former pupils, it was possible for Linnaeus to publish a list of some 3,000 species in cultivation. But after the death of Nietzel in 1756, and as Linnaeus grew less active, it once more began to decline. In 1786, when Thunberg was Professor of Botany, it was transferred to a new site near the Castle. In the present century, however, as the result of the initiative of the Swedish Linné

Society (founded in 1917), the old Botanic Garden was piously restored to its original state and the house fitted up as a Museum. The good work was completed in 1955 when the orangery was rebuilt, in a modified form, to serve as a hall, lecture-rooms and offices. To visit the house or walk round the Garden today is to come very close to Linnaeus, and one can almost imagine him still looking from the window of his small study on the first floor, which commands a view of the Garden, in order to observe (as he tells us he did) 'how hard the gardeners are working, and whether any hooligans are damaging or stealing the plants'.

In 1744 Linnaeus admitted in his Autobiography that he was a happy man:

View from Linnaeus's study at Uppsala.

> Linnaeus now had fame, the work for which he had been born, enough money (partly through his marriage), a beloved wife, handsome children and an honoured name. He lived in a fine house that he had built [i.e. rebuilt] for himself near the University, and he had completed the Garden. What more could a man desire, who possessed every satisfaction – even though it could not last for ever? In his collection were innumerable stones, in his herbarium and Garden innumerable plants, in his cabinet innumerable insects that he had assembled and pinned, in his cupboards innumerable fish glued on paper as if they were plants: all these, together with his own library, kept him occupied. . . .

Certainly Linnaeus had every reason to be satisfied with his lot.

In Rudbeck's time a few exotic animals had been kept in the Garden, but they could hardly have been said to constitute a zoo. Under Linnaeus the number was considerably increased, thanks mainly to the generosity of his royal patrons, and during his time as Director the Garden could boast a fine cockatoo and other birds (including peacocks, a cassowary and four different kinds of parrots), a young orang-utan and a number of monkeys, an agouti, a racoon, some goldfish and a variety of other animals. The orang-utan and the goldfish were brought from England in 1759 by Linnaeus's pupil, Pehr Bjerchén, to whom he wrote: 'I am absolutely *longing* to see the orang-utan; every moment of waiting is agony to me. My very dear Doctor, do please send the goldfish tomorrow, so that I can see what I have wanted to all my life but never dared to hope for. . . .' At first Linnaeus himself paid for the maintenance of his zoo; but in the end the cost became so burdensome that he was obliged to ask for, and duly received, a special grant.

His principal favourites were the monkeys and the parrots. One of the parrots used to sit on his shoulder at meal-times and be fed; if lunch chanced to be late it would cry 'Twelve o'clock, Mr Carl!' and persist until the Professor appeared. It had also learned to say 'Come in!' when there was a knock on the door, to the surprise of visitors who entered the room to find it empty, and 'Blow your nose!' to Löfgren, an old gardener whose nasal trumpetings were famous.

The Royal Gardens in Stockholm also had a small zoo, and Linnaeus often advised about purchases for it. In a letter he wrote on 13 July 1753 to Bäck, who had sent him the catalogue of a Dutch animal-dealer, he expresses his amazement at the big sums asked for what were admittedly very desirable animals – civet cats, ant-eaters, and so on: 'My hair stands on end and lice bite at their roots when I look at the prices in the catalogue: 300, 100, 50 gulden – what one has to pay for a pair of riding horses without a coachman. All animals are beautiful, but money is even more beautiful. . . .'

Adolf Fredrik and Lovisa Ulrika on several occasions presented Linnaeus with animals. In 1746 or 1747 Adolf Fredrik, then still Crown Prince, gave him the racoon (*Procyon lotor*, in eighteenth-century Swedish *sjupp*), an American mammal about the size of a badger and a close relation of the now popular panda, commanding him to examine and describe it. This Linnaeus did, and his account of Sjupp was published in 1747 in the *Proceedings* of the Royal Academy of Science. Since Linnaeus's fondness for and understanding of animals is nowhere better illustrated than in this paper, no excuse is needed for quoting extensively from it:

Nature has endowed this animal with a long snout, thereby giving him a remarkable sense of smell. He was completely blind, but this sense served him almost as well as the best pair of eyes. Should there be any cake or sugar on the table or in a cupboard he was on it in a flash, and thoroughly enjoyed himself. If a student came in who happened to have raisins or almonds on him, he at once attacked his pocket and fought until he had captured the spoil. . . . His hearing was certainly poor, and this was probably because his ears were so small. . . . One had to shout quite loud to get through to him. Nature always compensates for a disadvantage by an advantage elsewhere. . . .

He generally ate whatever came his way: bread, meat, porridge, soups, crayfish and bones – especially the bones of birds, which he chewed as if they were meat. But what he liked best were eggs, almonds, raisins, sugared cakes, sugar, and fruit of every kind. . . . On the other hand he couldn't bear anything with vinegar on it, or *sauerkraut*, or raw or boiled fish.

Unless he was hungry or disturbed he slept from midnight to midday – that is to say, he slept when it was night in his native land[1] and did not follow the local custom or the dictates of the sun. In the afternoon our American bear left his den and sunned himself or played about; but from 6 p.m. until midnight he usually paced continuously up and down, even when it was dark or the weather wet or inclement. He loved lying on his stomach with legs outstretched, rarely on his side, because his chest was rather flat . . . but if it was cold he drew his body and feet together and tucked in his head so that his breath would warm his stomach.

This bear had a sense of touch as acute as that of any animal, so that he could find whatever was thrown to him even though he couldn't see it; by patting the ground with his soft hands he could locate the smallest crumb. If anyone threw him a tobacco pipe he would amuse himself for hours on end by rolling it between his hands. He liked to do the same with his food before he ate it, and when he came to eat it he did not carry it to his mouth with one hand only, like an ape, but sat back on his haunches and used both.

He was very fond of water. He used to sit beside his water-bowl, dip his food in it and hold it there in his hands while he ate it. . . . He drank little, and always with his mouth; he never sipped, and if the bowl was too small for him to put his mouth horizontally in the water it was almost impossible for him to drink at all. He walked just like a bear, sauntering on his heels, his long thighs and legs held widely apart, his back bowed and his head lowered; yet when he noticed something that pleased him he could walk quite a long way on two legs, erect like a bear. . . . He became very friendly with people when he got to know them, letting them pat him and play with him (especially if they ingratiated themselves by means of a few raisins) so long

[1] This explanation will not hold, for in the wild the racoon is a nocturnal animal.

as they did not try to pick him up; that was something he simply could not stand. He was remarkably clean, having nearby his little privy place where he unburdened himself of his liquid and ordure.

He was tremendously obstinate. If anyone led him on a rope and tugged at it, he would immediately lie down and throw his arms and legs about defiantly; he would never go for blows, but always for kindness. If someone tried to take hold of him he would defend himself with teeth and claws, growling like a bear. Anyone who had once quarrelled with him found it almost impossible to get back again into his good books. For example, soon after his arrival he happened to meet the gardener, and began climbing up his legs in order to search him. The gardener misunderstood his intention, panicked, and quickly shook him off. From that moment Sjupp developed an irreconcilable hatred of the man; every time he smelt him he began making a noise like a seagull, the sign that he was extremely angry. He was, however, on the friendliest terms with such children and dogs as were known to him, rolling on his back, letting them pull his fur and not spoiling their sport; but in the end, when they grew tired, he overpowered them, became as obstinate as a knife-grinder, hung at their heels and tormented them.

This mulishness of Sjupp's had its drawback, because when he got into any room or cupboard or pocket it was impossible to get him out again. Or if he caught a hen, neither supplications nor blows would make him surrender it. Even if one picked him up by his tail – a thing that he simply loathed – he would lash out with his legs yet never let go of the prey in his mouth. There was, however, one thing which reduced him to a state of abject cowardice: hogs' bristles. . . .

Sjupp (racoon), pen and ink drawing by Laur. Alstrin.

Sjupp came to a tragic end. One night not long ago . . . after everyone had gone to bed, he broke loose, clambered over the fence and into another yard where he encountered a big dog which, to my great sorrow, attacked and killed him. After searching hard for several days we eventually found his body. . . .

There follows a full account of the dissection which then took place, Linnaeus being especially interested in the curious structure of the racoon's sexual organs.

The depth of Linnaeus's knowledge of zoology and branches of natural history other than botany was sometimes criticized. In 1767, when (Sir) Joseph Banks was contemplating going to Uppsala to study under Linnaeus (a project later abandoned), the crusty English naturalist, Thomas Pennant, wrote to him: 'I sincerely wish your tour may answer, but not being greatly smitten with the charms of Linnaeus must be doubtful till I hear from you. As to ornithology he is too superficial to be thought of, in madrepodology [the study of corals] still more deficient. In fossils other judges than myself think him incompetent, his fort is Botany. In that perhaps you may edify from his instruction.' Three weeks later he wrote again, 'I have no very high opinion of Linnaeus's zoological merits', and in his *History of Quadrupeds* (1781) confessed, 'My vanity will not suffer me to rank mankind with Apes, Monkies, Maucaucos and Bats.'

The inclusion by Linnaeus of man among the other animals in his system of nature was, as Stearn has pointed out, unobjectionable at that time from a theological point of view, for man's place in nature was then accepted as being somewhere between the angels and the beasts – though a good deal nearer to the latter. 'Indeed, Linnaeus's methodical disposition and his urge to classify . . . would probably have led to the inclusion of the angels as well had he possessed adequate knowledge based on first hand observation of their characteristics. As things were, he had to stop at man.'

It is inevitable that, particularly in the field of zoology, a comparison should be made between Linnaeus and his great French contemporary, Buffon, author of the superbly illustrated *Histoire Naturelle* (1749–1804) in forty-four volumes, some of them published posthumously. Buffon too has not escaped censure, being accused of making 'excessive and hasty generalisation', of being unmethodical, and of employing at times a 'theatrical and turgid' prose style; his account of the racoon, though abundantly provided with statistics, lacks the charm of Linnaeus's description of Sjupp. Buffon, who had charge of the Jardin du Roy in Paris, was an ardent opponent of Linnaeus, and it must have come as a blow to him when, in 1774, Louis XV issued the order that the Linnaean system was to be adopted in future.

Further examples of Linnaeus's observations of animals will be found in the accounts of his travels through the Swedish provinces, in his *Fauna Suecica* (1746) – described by himself as 'the first Fauna of any value that the world has ever seen' – in a number of dissertations, and in other contributions to the *Proceedings* of the Royal Academy of Science.

On 2 November 1741, a week after his inaugural lecture, Linnaeus gave the first of his public lectures to students. These were held at ten a.m. in the Gustavian building, or in the Garden itself if he wished to have material to hand to illustrate

a botanical subject. Over the next thirty-five years he conscientiously carried out his professorial duties, never missing a lecture unless unavoidably prevented by illness or by necessary absence from Uppsala.

Several of Linnaeus's pupils have left a record of what it was like to sit at his feet. One of these was J. G. Acrel, who on the death of the younger Linnaeus in 1783 handled the sale of the Linnaean collections on behalf of the family. Linnaeus, he wrote,

Sir Joseph Banks, aged about thirty, by Sir Joshua Reynolds; this painting was made after Banks's return from the *Endeavour* voyage with Captain Cook and exhibited at the Royal Academy in 1773.

> had a highly individual style of oratory, and although his voice was neither particularly strong nor particularly attractive, and his Swedish not very correct (at times he lapsed into the Småland dialect), he never failed to captivate his audiences. He knew how to emphasize certain words in his short sentences so expressively that no one could possibly fail to be convinced by his argument. Those who heard him speak about his Introduction to the *Systema Naturae* – about God, Man, the Creation, Nature and so on – were more moved than by the most eloquent sermon. In addition to his powers of persuasion he had the advantage of a clear mind and incomparable memory, so that he could deliver a long oration or a lecture from a few notes scribbled

on a scrap of paper . . . which he would hold between his fingers, marking with his thumb the point he had reached.

Sven Hedin, another pupil, adds that he

combined wit and depth of learning so skilfully that both curiosity and reason were satisfied. . . . If Linnaeus spoke of the power and majesty of the Creator, reverence and wonder showed on every face; . . . if on the rules of diet, he often made his students roar with laughter by his descriptions of the follies of fashion, using a joke and a light touch to teach a valuable lesson about the care and preservation of health.

He was able, it was said, to present natural history as if it were something alto-gether new – and novelty always attracts. His students were amazed to see in Sweden flowers from Asia and the Cape, monkeys and snakes from Africa, and parrots from America. Often his lectures were so crowded out that late-comers were obliged to hear what they could from the entrance hall and corridors; this was especially so during the Seven Years War, when the University was full to bursting-point with young men anxious to dodge military service. Nothing speaks more clearly of Linnaeus's success as a teacher than the fact that no less than twenty-three of his pupils became professors.

Mention has already been made of these lectures on diet, a subject which Lin-naeus understood to cover all aspects of the healthy way of life. His interest in diet can be traced back at least to 1733, when he began to write an essay *Diaeta Naturalis*, which was published by Dr Uggla in 1958. It opens with a list of 136 aphorisms and rules of conduct and health, which are then discussed and illustrated. Many of them today seem trite, but most are still valid. For example:

All excess is harmful.
Brännvin is poison.
Smoking, tobacco-chewing and snuff-taking are poison.
Clothes made from the skins of animals are the best.
Do no evil to your neighbour.
Eat to keep up your strength, not to stuff your belly.
All boiled liquids, even water, are worse for you than unboiled.
Take gentle exercise for upwards of a third of the day.
Cupping, purging, and the like should be resorted to only when all else has failed.

Linnaeus's own lecture notes are mostly in Latin, those of his students in Swedish; and it is a pity that the latter, which are both interesting and entertaining, have never been translated into a more widely read language. 'Nowhere,' writes Miss Gourlie, 'does his dry pointed humour show more clearly.' There is grandeur in the opening words of his first lecture: 'Nothing is more precious than life, nothing more desirable than health, nothing more distressing than sickness, nothing more awful or more terrifying than death.' Our Maker, he says, has not given us a short life – it is we ourselves who make it short; and he warns his students of the dangerous effects of 'worry, sorrow and especially anger'. Yet *lack* of worry makes people fat, like the bears and the wild boar which sleep without a care the whole winter long.

There is much in the lectures about bringing up of young children. Children should be fed often and little at a time. To test the milk of a wet-nurse, put a drop on the finger-nail; if it remains spherical and does not run off, then it is good. Brown cows and brunettes give the best milk. Do not rock babies; this is why they vomit. Babies should not be christened in cold weather or cold water. Young infants should not be tightly swaddled (as was then the custom in Sweden). Wet-nurses pass on illnesses – cross-eyes, for example – to the babies they suckle; in England they think nothing of engaging a wet-nurse who is tubercular. Do not suckle your baby when you are angry; anger turns the milk sour and causes convulsions. Mothers' milk acts as a laxative on adults. And so on.

Here are further random gleanings from the lectures. Mutton is best for people with sedentary jobs, pork for manual workers. Draughts cling to the walls of a room, so place your bed in the middle of it. It is unwise to change too often the clothes and bed-linen of those who have a fever, because they sweat more freely in soiled linen. Butchers should never be judges when a man's life is at stake. The French took to wearing wigs when they went bald as the result of syphilis. One can survive for two weeks without food when one is ill, but not when one is well. God gave men beards for ornament, and to make them distinguishable from women.

Linnaeus mentions the 'kiss of life', and in 1757 he was to save the life of his youngest daughter, Sophia, by mouth-to-mouth resuscitation. He described the circumstances in a letter to his friend Abraham Bäck:

Last Tuesday evening my wife bore me a daughter. She had a very difficult delivery and the girl was stillborn or died at birth, but nevertheless we blew air into her and

Coffee plant, from *Potus Coffeae*, 1761.

used insufflatory medicine. After a quarter of an hour she began to breath a little, then as if drawing her last breath, and finally to give further signs of life. Now she seems fairly well; but my wife is very weak, God help her!

Dr Goerke, who like Miss Gourlie has much of interest to say about Linnaeus as a medical man, quotes two passages which show how advanced were Linnaeus's views on bacteriology; the first is from the *Proceedings* of the Royal Academy of Science (1750), the second from a dissertation, *Mundus invisibilis* (*The Invisible World*, 1767):

It must surely be that smallpox, measles, diarrhoea, syphilis – yes, even the plague – result from the smallest worms.

It is no miracle if these animalcules, a hundred times smaller than the particles of dust that dance in a sunbeam, are disseminated far and wide. The minutest creatures can cause greater devastation than the greatest; yes, they may kill more people than all the wars.

In another passage he seems to anticipate Priestley in his discovery of oxygen:

The air we inhale has electricity; the air we exhale has not.

Both in his lectures and in the dissertations the subject of drink crops up again and again. Though not a teetotaller, Linnaeus denounced the excessive drinking of the Swedes, which gradually reduced them to the level of beasts: of parrots who chattered away without wit or learning, of swine who slobbered over everything within reach, of neighing horses and pugnacious bulls, or of goats who entertained the company with their obscenities. He particularly deplored the giving of *brännvin* to children whose growth is stunted. There are also dissertations on coffee, tea and chocolate. The effects of drinking coffee, he wrote in *Potus Coffeae* (1761) were medical rather than dietetic:

Coffee-drinking promotes wakefulness and destroys the appetite. . . . It is said to prevent flatulence and help digestion after a meal; but there is no doubt that coffee, if not properly roasted, *induces* flatulence and belly-rumblings. . . .
    Most confirmed and regular coffee-drinkers have trembling hands and heads. I remember three distinguished persons (now dead) who from over-indulgence in coffee could scarcely get their shaking hands to their mouths. However, in time and by abstinence they happily were cured. One of these, who could not deny himself the taste, used to hold the coffee in his mouth and then spit it out instead of swallowing it.

Coffee, said Linnaeus, was reputed to be an anti-aphrodisiac, and he quoted in support a story told by the German traveller, Adam Olearius, of a Sultan's wife 'who, finding the operation of castrating a horse revolting, ordered it to be dosed with coffee instead. She had observed the efficacy of this with her husband.' For this reason 'coffee came mockingly to be called "the eunuch's drink"'. Coffee was bad for eyesight, for melancholy and hysterical people, and for hypochondriacs whose acid belchings in a carriage made them intolerable travelling companions. Linnaeus himself, when Physician to the Admiralty in 1740, used to find that by the end of the morning he felt quite sick from the halitosis of his patients; but by drinking at a gulp about a quarter of a pint of black, unsweetened coffee he gained immediate relief. Coffee was not, however, nutritious, and it induced early senility.

Linnaeus, a heavy smoker, praised tobacco as 'a recent and agreeable discovery'. He recommended smoking for soldiers, sailors and fishermen; as a protection against infection, and as a palliative for toothache and severe colic. But he admitted that it loosened the gums, blackened the teeth, left a nasty taste in the mouth and destroyed the appetite, and was to be considered as a medicine rather than a regular diet – advice that he did not put into practice. He also has much to say about expectoration, which smoking encouraged and which he considered beneficial, especially for those who have to visit the sick:

> So one is quite right to hold one's nose when visiting anyone who is very ill, to prevent one's saliva becoming infected and thus, when swallowed, carrying the infection to the stomach. It is therefore a good plan to put something bitter-tasting in one's mouth, so that one spits out the saliva instead of swallowing it.

Linnaeus closes his lecture notes on diet in words as noble as those which opened them: 'Therefore gather on your way imperishable flowers: fear of the Lord, diligence, orderliness, willingness to serve, and the crown imperial – honesty. Now in God's name have I brought my *collegium* to an end.'

Linnaeus, sepia drawing by Jean-Eric Rehn, 1747 or 1750.

4.

Västergötland 1746

In the later forties Linnaeus undertook his last two provincial tours: through West Gothland in 1746, and through Scania in 1749; these he described in his *Wästgöte-Resa* (1747) and *Skånska Resa* (1751) respectively, neither of which has been translated into English.

Linnaeus set out from Uppsala for West Gothland on 12 June 1746, passing to the south of Sweden's largest lake, Lake Vänern, to strike the western sea-coast at Gothenburg. After visiting Bohuslän he turned north-eastwards and so circled the lake, arriving back at Uppsala on 11 August. For most of this journey of about 1,700 miles he had but a single companion, a man named Lidbeck who acted as his amanuensis; but from time to time they seem to have joined forces with other travellers going their way. We need not follow Linnaeus step by step as he examined everything curious or potentially valuable to the Swedish economy that he came across, but one or two adventures and encounters deserve mention and a few extracts from his published account of his travels may be quoted to give the flavour of the book.

Quack doctors seem to have been attracted to West Gothland, and Linnaeus mentions three who had won great reputations in that province. One of these, a man named Sven, lived at Bragnum, and Linnaeus, finding himself on 1 July only a mile or two from his house, decided to call on him:

> Sven had bought himself a little house in which was a small dark room that he had fitted up as his surgery. He was a young peasant of about thirty, but his hair was already turning grey and because of his sedentary way of life he was putting on weight. When we arrived and greeted him he made no move, did not take off his cap or invite us to sit down. He talked freely, yet earnestly. My companions could not refrain from inventing illnesses and asking for his advice. One of them, M.T., pretended that he had been coughing up blood. Sven inquired about his home and what he did and recommended him to buy a certain powder at the chemist's in Gothenburg. He also asked him whether he had been bled. The patient replied No, he was afraid of blood; he was, however, advised to have his arm cupped. . . .

After Lidbeck had received advice about treatment for a blocked ear, M.T. asked whether he might speak to Sven in private. They went together into another room:

The patient pretended that he had been leading a dissolute life and picked up a venereal disease; the peasant promised to help him, gave him a coarse powder made of herbs which he was to take mixed with *brännvin* and white of egg, and charged him sixteen stivers. The patient asked further about his diet, and was told that all that was necessary was to fast for an hour before taking the medicine. . . .

It was at Ållestad, two days later, that Linnaeus came across that remarkable Scots adventurer, Alexander Blackwell, who had established a model farm there. After various adventures Blackwell had come to Sweden in answer to an appeal by Jonas Alström, the famous industrial reformer, for a medical man of enterprise and wide interests to further some of his innumerable projects. An account of his amazing career, which culminated in his execution in Stockholm in 1747 for high treason, may be read in *The Dictionary of National Biography*. Linnaeus was shown all over Blackwell's farm, and it would appear that he did not realize at the time that the man was a charlatan. In his *Nemesis Divina*, however, he wrote a long and gossipy account of the real and alleged crimes of this 'bold ignoramus and atheist' whose fall provided such a fine example of divine retribution. What became of Blackwell's heroic and much wronged wife Elizabeth, who compiled and illustrated *A Curious Herbal*, is not known.

A few days later Linnaeus reached Alingsås, then a flourishing place, where this same Jonas Alström had started various industries including wool-sorting and combing, spinning and weaving, gold-beating and other metal-work,

The West Gothland journey. Places Linnaeus visited which are mentioned in the text are underlined.

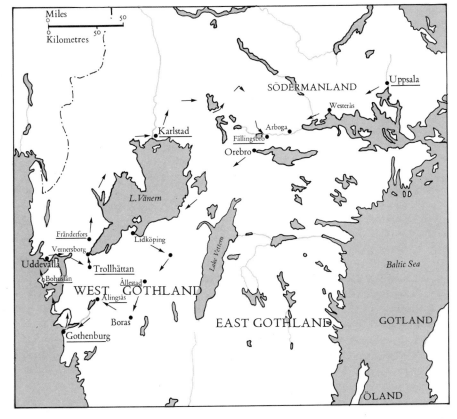

dyeing and pipe-making, and a tobacco factory – all of which Linnaeus describes. Alström was later ennobled, taking the name of Baron Jonas Alströmer, and his son became one of Linnaeus's pupils.

Alingsås was only thirty miles from Gothenburg, where Linnaeus arrived on 9 July. Its inhabitants entertained him very hospitably: Sahlgren, the Director of the East India Company, who over the years was to help a number of Linnaeus's pupils to get passages to distant lands, gave him a bird of paradise, and from other merchants and scholars he received presents of fish, insects, coral, crystals and shells. Linnaeus wrote a full and interesting account of this busy port, which had been largely built by Dutch settlers at the beginning of the seventeenth century and whose architecture reminded him of his years in Holland. He described it as being smaller than Uppsala; today it is seven or eight times larger.

Heading northwards from Gothenburg he reached Bohuslän, a wild district of many islands whose inhabitants, mostly fishermen, are alleged to be descended from the Vikings. On the little island of Marstrand he studied the behaviour of the gulls including skuas:

> Elof is the local name for the blackish gull who cannot himself dive into the sea to catch fish, but who was created to play the robber among gulls. It was very amusing to observe how this Cossack harried the other gulls; the moment one of them had caught a fish, Elof continued pursuing him until he had disgorged the fish he had caught and already half swallowed. For several years I kept a tame gull in the Botanic Garden, and I used to watch with amazement how, even if he had had hardly any food, when anyone chased him he would immediately disgorge what he had eaten. This facility for easily vomiting has been made use of by the Creator to support our Elof family, for the herring gulls often catch more than they need and can therefore afford to give some of their surplus to Blackie. . . .
>
> It must be added that this scavenger is not too particular about what he eats; for sometimes the gulls, if they have caught nothing, are obliged to open the back door and eject tainted food, which Elof makes do with. Blackie is extremely agile and can always catch in mid air the food that the gull throws to him. Nor is he shy, for when the fishermen see him and cry, 'Elof, Elof!' and show him a little fish in an outstretched hand, Elof comes flying towards the boat and catches the fish the moment it is thrown. Elof always hangs about where the prospects seem good, preferring fishing hamlets where every day there are weddings with games and dancing. The Ångermanlanders do not like to see him shot, because he shows by his flight where the herring shoals are.

Turning inland, Linnaeus now came to the once famous Trollhättan Falls of the Göta älv, but only to find them 'a mere toy' after what he had seen in Lapland. In the eighteenth century there were unsuccessful attempts to make a navigable waterway between the North Sea and the Baltic. In 1810, however, the Scots engineer Thomas Telford succeeded in constructing a great stairway of locks, and today the falls are dry except on special occasions when the waters are 'let loose' as a tourist spectacle.

A little above the falls, at the southernmost point of Lake Vänern, lies Vänersborg. From here Linnaeus kept to the west of the lake till he reached Frändefors, a village whose name would not deserve to be remembered had not

its little churchyard inspired Linnaeus to write one of his finest reflective passages, one that has sometimes been called the Swedish equivalent of Hamlet's graveyard soliloquy. He and his companion had begun to discuss whether or not it was proper to remove the fertile soil of a graveyard 'to use as a manure for fields or cabbage-patches'. Linnaeus argued thus:

Trollhätten Falls 1705, from *Suecica Antiqua et Hodierna.*

> Nature teaches us that we should not consume the corpses of our fathers or our children, and I cannot imagine who would have the stomach to do so unless he were an inhuman cannibal. People of all lands have attached great importance to letting the dead rest in their tombs, to laying men of honour honourably in their graves so that they may not serve as food for beasts of prey. The wealthier have coffins made of stone and copper, that their dust may not be scattered abroad. The ancients had themselves and their ashes placed in mounds that could not easily be disturbed, and it is one of God's blessings that the bones, body, dust and ashes of the righteous can rest in peace in their graves; felons of all nations, on the other hand, are exposed to worms and wolves, that the ravens may pluck out their eyes, and the bodies of the ungodly God has thrown to the dogs and wild beasts. . . .
>
> So it happens that when animals die they are converted into mould, the mould into plants. The plants are eaten by animals, thus forming the animals' limbs, so that the earth, transmuted into seed, then enters man's body as seed and is changed there by man's nature into flesh, bones, nerves, etc.; and when after death the body decomposes, the natural forces decay and man again becomes that earth from which he was taken.
>
> Thus when plants chance to sow themselves in this mould they grow luxuriantly, transmuting the human earth to their nature so that the fairest maid's cheeks can become the ugliest henbane, and the arm of the most stalwart Hercules the frailest pondweed. This is eaten by a stinking cimex [bed-bug] and becomes such an animal. This cimex is then eaten by birds and becomes a bird; the bird is eaten by man and thus becomes a part of him. . . .

The theme is indeed the same, wrote Hagberg, as that of Hamlet's soliloquy, 'but the melancholy which characterizes Hamlet's contemplation of the cycle of matter is entirely absent with Linnaeus. He merely states facts; he feels no

163

horror. In the calmest voice he suggests a compromise: since our attitude is what it is, and we feel sick at the thought of eating our forbears, then let us hold the churchyards sacred. . . .'

But not all the narrative passages in the book are in so philosophical a vein, and here and there among its pages are scattered little scraps of miscellaneous information about plants and animals that testify to Linnaeus's insatiable curiosity about everything that came his way. For example:

Toads (*Rana bufo*) love shady places, especially at the foot of mountains where stinking stachys [woundwort] and stinking actaea [baneberry] grow. I don't know why these ugly creatures are so fond of evil-smelling weeds. I have seen how toads invade a house into which this *Stachys foetida* has been brought; in the Ukraine, too, where *Cotula foetida* [*Anthemis cotula*, stinking mayweed] is commoner than else-where, there are such quantities of toads that every house is full of them, but as soon as the mayweed withers the toads also disappear.

I set a dog on a big toad and he bit it. But then he trembled and shook, and after that his mouth was in a very bad state, showing plainly that he had been hurt; nor could he be persuaded to make a further attack. So it is quite possible that what Lister says is true: that if you seize this creature with a pair of tongs, a harmful and poisonous white liquid spurts out of every wart.

There are many ways of getting rid of bugs, but I have never heard a more strongly recommended method than the following. You smear the walls of the room with oil of turpentine and then set fire to it; it flares up quickly and kills the bugs. Although the flames do not very readily scorch or burn, one must always have water handy. Anyone who tries this experiment, which certainly kills bugs, should remember to be careful, especially with an old worm-eaten and moss-stuffed partition; for as Hippocrates said, 'experiment is dangerous'. Others maintain that *Mentha sylvestris* [*M. longifolia*, horse mint] is guaranteed to kill bugs immediately.

Here and there in the book are also to be found descriptive passages which, even if rather 'contrived', are of great poetic beauty. On 30 July, as he completed the last stage of his journey from Karlstad, the capital of the province of Värm-land, to Norum,

night fell with its dense darkness – a darkness in which the fir forests seemed to stand like a wall, twice as high as by day. Summer lightning flickered like ghostly fires, often without any sound of thunder. Sparks flew as the shoes of the horses struck against the stones; owls shrieked like ghosts, and the night-jars churned like spinning-wheels; and Vulcan's shirt-sleeved apprentices thundered and hammered with superhuman strength at their distant forges until, at 11 o'clock and after a journey of an hour and a quarter, we reached Norum.

Nine days later Linnaeus came to Fällingsbro, which he had passed through nearly two months before on his outward journey. Then his *Linnaea borealis* had been in flower in the forests; now its blooms were withered and at any moment would come the first frosts of the winter. He hastened his steps and on 11 August crossed into Uppland; he was now only a day's march from Uppsala. The last entry in his Journal reads:

All the way from Fällingsbro autumn has been ever before our eyes. The woods were still green, but a more sombre green than that of summer. Pastures and meadows were still green also; but now they were flowerless because cattle had stripped the former and the scythe the latter. The fields were filled with golden stooks, and between the yellow corn-stubble green weeds were growing. A wet summer had filled the dikes, which masses of marsh marigolds clothed in yellow. The waysides were covered with persicarias, now turning red and beginning to droop their heads.

Everywhere peasants were abroad and hard at work. Some of the men were cutting corn with sickles while their womenfolk, whose heads and arms were quite white, tied it into bundles. Some were carting home their rye, some threshing, some breaking up the sods, some harrowing the fields, some sowing winter rye, some hoeing down the barley, some levelling the fields with rollers, while the herdsmen's children sang and blew their horns to call home the cattle that were grazing in the more distant pastures. Then as the chill evening wind began to blow and the bright sun to dip below the horizon, we came to the Garden at Uppsala.

Back in Uppsala Linnaeus began at once to prepare his Journal for publication. A group of his admirers now clubbed together to have a gold medal struck in his honour: the obverse showed the head of Linnaeus, and on the reverse was a dedication to Count Tessin and the names of the four donors – Barons Hårleman, Höpken and Palmstierna, and Count Ekeblad. The following year Tessin, 'charmed with the noble example of his patriotic fellow citizens', replied with a large silver medal 'representing on one side the bust of Linnaeus, and on the other three crowns on which the sun cast his beams, with the simple and eloquent motto ILLUSTRAT, "He illumines". . . . In the first crown the heads of an eagle, a lion and a whale are very conspicuous; the two others bear plants and fragments of minerals.'

The same year brought further honours. 'On the 19th of January, 1747,' wrote Linnaeus in his Autobiography, 'His Majesty was pleased, without any application from Linnaeus, and without his even expecting it, to honour him with the rank and title of Archiater [Chief Physician].' A month later he was made a Fellow of the Berlin Scientific Society, one of many similar compliments which were paid to him over the years.

Linnaeus loved honours and recognition, but perhaps he was even more excited by a recent and totally unexpected botanical windfall. He received on loan from a Danish apothecary in Copenhagen the herbarium and set of drawings, acquired in Ceylon between 1670 and 1677 by Paul Hermann, which gave him his first intensive acquaintance with a tropical flora. Linnaeus worked day and night examining these specimens – a task made 'almost herculean', he wrote, 'from the great length of time they had been dried' – and before the end of the year published his *Flora Zeylanica* (*Flora of Ceylon*). The herbarium and drawings were later purchased by Sir Joseph Banks and are now in the British Museum (Natural History). Linnaeus frequently quoted this work in his *Species Plantarum*.

5.

Linnaeus *en pantoufles*

The best accounts of Linnaeus the man, of his relations with his wife and children and with his pupils when he was in their company 'out of school', are principally to be found in the recollections of two of his pupils – Johan Fabricius and Johann Beckmann – both foreigners. Further touches to the 'conversation piece' are given by Linnaeus himself in his letters to his great friend, Abraham Bäck; a discussion of this long and valuable correspondence is reserved for a later chapter. Since both Fabricius and Beckmann did not come to know Linnaeus until the early sixties, in order that their accounts may be intelligibly used at this point certain public events and domestic happenings of the forties and fifties must first be briefly related.

King Fredrik I, by M. van Mytens Junior.

The death in November 1741 of Queen Ulrika Eleonora had reopened the question of the succession. The Empress Elisabeth of Russia, daughter of Peter the Great, favoured her cousin, Duke Adolf Fredrik of Holstein-Gottorp, Prince-Bishop of Lübeck, and offered the return of a large part of Finland to Sweden if he were chosen; the *douceur* was irresistible, and in 1743 this 'altogether insignificant' young man was declared heir apparent with hereditary right to the throne for his male issue. The following year he married the far from insignificant Lovisa Ulrika, sister of Frederick the Great of Prussia. Both Adolf Fredrik and his wife became ardent collectors of objects of natural history (as was then the fashion), and patrons and staunch supporters of Linnaeus; the Crown Prince visited Uppsala University in the spring of 1744, when Linnaeus was presented to him as 'one of the luminaries of the Academy', and later in the same year he was received by the Crown Princess at a private audience. In 1751 on the death of Fredrik I, Adolf Fredrik ascended the throne. During his reign Sweden became involved in the Seven Years War (1756–63), which brought the Caps back into power.

On the domestic front must first be mentioned the additions to the family of Carl and Sara Lisa Linnaeus. In 1743 their first daughter, Elisabeth Christina (Lisa Stina) was born, and the following year a second daughter who died in infancy. A third, Lovisa, followed in 1749 and a fourth, Sara Christina, in 1751. In 1754 came a son, Johannes, who died in 1757, the year that saw the birth of their last child, Sophia.

In 1753 Linnaeus was created a Knight of the Polar Star, and in 1761 (ante-dated 1757) he was ennobled, taking the name of von Linné by which he is still generally known on the Continent.[1] In 1758 he bought the small country estates of Hammarby, Säfja and Edeby, near Uppsala, and four years later added to the very modest living quarters at Hammarby, which became his beloved retreat in the summer months and is today a place of pilgrimage for all who revere him.

Linnaeus has left a verbal self-portrait, various versions of which exist. From them Fries has compiled the following résumé:

Linnaeus was of medium height or rather under, more lean than fat, with fairly muscular limbs and prominent veins from childhood. His head was big, and at the back of it was a transverse depression along the lambdoid suture. His forehead was fairly high, and wrinkled in old age. His hair was neither straight nor curly, flaxen as a child, then brown and reddish about the temples, and finally grey in old age. His face was pallid and his eyebrows brown. So were his eyes, which were very sharp, lively and twinkling; his sight was excellent for even the tiniest object.[2] His nose was straight; he had a mole on the right nostril and a rather larger one on the right cheek. His teeth were bad; he had suffered from acute toothache from his earliest years until he was fifty, and by the time he was sixty he had lost them all. He had no ear for music. His weight was 12 stone 10 lb. His gait was very easy and brisk.

He was no lover of luxury, living moderately and not drinking to excess. He left the running of his house entirely to his wife, and concerned himself with the works of Nature. He was neither rich nor poor, but he had a dread of getting into debt. He wrote his books for honour, not for gain. In winter he slept from 9 p.m. till 7 a.m., in summer from 10 p.m. till 3 a.m.

Linnaeus's son, in a letter to Abraham Bäck, wrote:

My late father never worked unless he was in the mood. He used to get up early, as soon as he woke, light his fire and then start work; but the moment he felt the least tired he stopped and smoked a pipe or rested on his bed; he could always fall asleep at any time (and he snored). A quarter of an hour later he would be up again, wide awake and ready to get back to his table. This recurred at intervals until about 4 p.m., when he felt the need of company to clear his mind of what he had been working on. He loved to joke with friends and pupils, being able, he said, to 'eat a little of anything' and adding, 'The old Romans were quite right in saying that one ought to have a *gula docta* [well-trained palate]; mine is: I can eat anything – and I can also go without.'

Such was a typical day during the vacation. In a letter written in 1761 to the botanist Baron Nikolaus von Jacquin, Linnaeus describes how at that time he occupied himself during the term:

I lecture every day for an hour in public and afterwards give private instruction to a number of pupils. Then comes an hour with some Danes and two Russians. Having thus talked for five hours before lunch, in the afternoon I correct work, prepare my manuscript for the printers and write letters to my botanical friends, visit the Garden and deal with people who want to consult me, and look after my little property – with the result that often I hardly have a moment to eat. If you could see me you

Queen Lovisa Ulrika, by A. Pesne, and below, King Adolf Fredrik, by L. Pasch.

[1] For convenience, however, I in general retain throughout this book the form 'Linnaeus', the name by which he is always known in England. As he himself wrote, 'Linnaeus or Linné is all the same to me; one is Latin, the other Swedish.'

[2] Henry Roscoe, in his *Life of William Roscoe*, mentions that Linnaeus never used a glass, 'even in his minutest enquiries'.

167

Linnaeus's Order of the Polar Star.

Left: Linnaeus as a young man, anonymous drawing.

Right: Linnaeus aged forty-six, pastel by Gustaf Lundberg, 1753.

would pity me, for, surrounded though I am by a large family, I must still make time to attend not only to my own countrymen but also to the foreigners who come here. While my colleagues daily enjoy the pleasures of this existence, I spend days and nights in the exploration of a field of learning that thousands of them will not suffice to bring to completion, not to mention that every day I have to squander time on correspondence with various scholars – all of which will age me prematurely. . . . If the Almighty spares me for a few more years I will free the aging horse from the yoke so that it does not break down and finally become ridiculous. If I can then succeed in growing a few rare plants in my garden I shall be happy.

If Linnaeus was popular when lecturing formally, he was perhaps even more beloved by his pupils when he was in their company on informal occasions. He always tried to make them think for themselves, and not accept 'as gospel' what he or anyone else told them. 'However great your confidence in your teacher,' he said, 'remember that he is capable of making mistakes. He may deceive himself; he may even deliberately try to deceive others.' And he told them how one day, when he was showing his museum to a very naive young lady of the Court who was accompanied by a shaggy-haired dog, he could not resist the temptation to 'pull the leg' of this innocent. He had no difficulty in persuading her that the dog's fur was not its own but had been neatly sewed on, demonstrating as the 'seam' the line where the hairs changed direction.

Linnaeus was seen at his most benign, his most human, and his most paternal, on the botanic forays which were held every Saturday in the summer. One of the students who accompanied him – a seventeen-year-old Dane named Johan Christian Fabricius, who later became a famous entomologist – has described what then took place:

The cheerful party – there were often a hundred and fifty of us of various nationalities – broke up into small groups who had orders to forgather at an agreed hour; Linnaeus kept with him only a handful of the cleverest students. Sometimes the rendezvous

A botanical foray, and left, Linnaeus at Drottningholm.

chosen was the Castle of Säfja, and we would all set out in that direction, not without a lot of hilarity which Linnaeus never attempted to restrain. As soon as everyone had assembled, Linnaeus began to identify the plants which had been collected. A table was spread for twenty, provided with fruit and syllabubs, and those who had found the rarest plants sat with the Master at this table; the rest ate standing up, hoping one day to enjoy the honour all envied and which was enough to stimulate the most lively competition among these young rivals.

Other pupils add further information. The students, we are told, wore light and comfortable linen uniforms, and caps which soon became decorated with flowers. Linnaeus appointed certain 'officials', such as a secretary, a prefect to maintain discipline, and a marksman to shoot birds. Whenever a rarity was discovered a bugle-call was sounded, whereupon everyone ran to Linnaeus to hear him demonstrate. At the end of the day they all marched back to the town, Linnaeus at their head, with banners waving and horns and kettledrums playing. When they reached the Botanic Garden there were repeated cries of 'Vivat Linnaeus!', after which the party broke up. Both the unconventionality of the students' dress and the informality of their behaviour were frowned upon by the staider professors.

Fabricius has left us by far the most valuable sketch of Linnaeus as seen through the eyes of a favoured pupil:

For two whole years – from 1762 to 1764, when Linnaeus was about fifty-six – I was lucky enough to be taught and guided by him and to enjoy his intimate friendship. Not a day passed when I did not attend one of his lectures or, as often happened, spend several hours in friendly conversation with him. In the summer we went to the country with him. There were three of us – Kuhn, Zoega and myself: all foreigners.[1] In winter we lived directly opposite to him, and almost every day he came in his red dressing-gown and green fur cap, his pipe in his hand, to see us. He came for half an

[1] Adam Kuhn was Linnaeus's only American pupil; Johan Zoega, like Fabricius, was a Dane.

hour, but often stayed a full hour or even two; and on these occasions his conversation was extremely lively and agreeable. Sometimes he told us stories about distinguished men of science whom he had known in Sweden or abroad; sometimes he answered our questions or taught us in some other way. And as he did so he would laugh heartily, his smiling face and candid expression showing how much he enjoyed the company of friends.

It was even more delightful when we were in the country. We stayed about three-quarters of a mile from his house at Hammarby, in a farmhouse where we had our own things and fended for ourselves. In summer Linnaeus used to rise very early, usually about 4 o'clock. Because his house was still in the hands of the builders, he would come over towards 6 o'clock and join us for breakfast; then he taught us about the natural orders of plants, staying as long as he pleased and generally until about ten. After that, we would wander until noon among the rocks, where we found plenty to talk about. In the afternoon we went to his garden, and of an evening we almost always played trisett with his wife.

On Sundays the whole family usually spent the day with us, and then we would send for a peasant to come to our barn and play for us, on an instrument like a violin, while we danced. Admittedly these balls of ours were not very brilliant, the company but small, the dances monotonous (always either minuets or Polish dances); but we enjoyed ourselves enormously. While we danced, the old man would smoke his pipe with Zoega, who suffered from very poor health, and watch us; but very occasionally he would join in a Polish dance and prove himself a better performer than any of us youngsters. He was delighted when we got excited and even rowdy, believing that if we did not we might not be enjoying ourselves. I shall never forget those days, those hours, and it makes me happy whenever I recall them.

What made him so especially kind to us was that we were foreigners. With the exception of one or two Russians (who were rather idle) we were the only students who depended entirely on him, who heard and saw no one else, and who remained at Uppsala solely on his account. He realized that we admired his learning and studied zealously, and it pleased him to let his own countrymen see that his work would continue to be appreciated abroad even if it should cease to find favour in Sweden. He also enjoyed talking about natural history, which he had very little opportunity of doing at Uppsala. Natural History was his whole life: he thought of nothing else; and since he was at that time the only naturalist at the University he must often have felt very lonely there. . . .

His mind was wonderfully noble, though I know perfectly well that he was accused of having many faults. His intellect was sharp and piercing: you could see it in his eyes. But his greatest quality was his power of ordered reasoning and logical thought; whatever he said or did was orderly and systematic. When young he had a wonderful memory, but all too soon it began to fail. Even while I was there, there were times when he could not recall the name of someone whom he knew extremely well. I recollect an occasion when he was terribly embarrassed because, having written a letter to his father-in-law,[1] he could not remember his name.

His passions were strong and violent. . . . He could suddenly lose his temper or become very irritable, though such moods passed almost as quickly as they came. You could rely on the constancy of his friendship; it was almost always based on an interest in science, and all the world knows how much he did for his pupils and how devotedly, how fervently, they returned his friendship and became his champions. He was lucky enough never to have had an ungrateful pupil; even Rolander was more to be pitied than blamed.

[1] A slip of the pen; he means 'brother-in-law'.

In writing thus, Fabricius makes it plain that he had never heard of Henri

Linnaeus demonstrating, from a nineteenth-century lithograph.

Missa, a Frenchman who had come to Linnaeus in 1748 on the recommendation of Haller. This was hardly surprising, for after Missa's churlish behaviour towards Linnaeus his name was never allowed to be mentioned. Linnaeus, excited at getting his first (and what proved to be his only) French pupil, had put himself to great trouble and considerable expense to make Missa feel at home. Missa had no money, moderate ability, and an appalling temper; after a few months at Uppsala he suddenly announced that he was sick of botany, and returned home without a word of thanks to Linnaeus, who had 'done more for him than for a brother or a Swede. And now I hear that he goes about slandering me. So I harboured a viper in my bosom unawares.'

Fabricius continues:

Linnaeus's ambition was boundless, and his motto, *Famam extendere factis*[1] was the true mirror of his soul. But this ambition never went beyond his science; it never degenerated into offensive conceit. He did not much mind what people in general thought of him; he was sensitive only to the criticism of scholars. His way of life was modest and thrifty, his dress simple and at times even shabby. The high rank to which his King had raised him pleased him only because he saw in it the recognition of his scientific achievements.

Where his science was concerned he could not brook any opposition. He corrected

[1] '[The task of the brave is] to spread his fame by deeds' (Virgil, *Aeneid*, book 10, line 468).

171

his works at the suggestion of his friends, and was grateful to them; but he scorned the attacks of his enemies. . . . He could not, however, easily forget these attacks, and did everything possible to erase them from the annals of science. He was generous with his praise because he himself loved to be flattered: this was his Achilles' heel. But his ambition was based upon the consciousness of his own greatness and upon the merits he had gained in a science in which he had for so many years wielded the sceptre of sovereignty. Tournefort, as he so often told me, was his model in his youth; he did all he could to equal him, and found at last that he had far outstripped him.

Linnaeus had been particularly charged with avarice. It cannot be denied that his way of life, taking into consideration his good circumstances, was frugal, and that he did not despise gold. When, however, I remember how poor he had long been, I could easily excuse this parsimony. But I cannot say that it ever degenerated into sordid greed; in fact I can from my own experience prove the contrary. After he had lectured to us all through the summer, we had not only to beg him to take the fees we owed him for these lectures, but even to leave the money secretly on his table, because he had firmly refused to accept it.

His family life was not really very happy. His wife was a large, bouncing woman, domineering, selfish, and quite without culture; she often spoiled our parties. Because she could not join in our conversations she did not care for company. So it was inevitable that the children should be poorly educated. Her daughters are all amiable girls, but wholly unsophisticated and without the polish that education might have given them. The son, who succeeded his father in his professorship at Uppsala, certainly lacks his father's vivacity; but the great knowledge he acquired by constantly working at botany, and the many and excellent observations of his father's which he must have found in his manuscripts, combined to make him a very useful teacher. . . .

Linnaeus's services to science were enormous. Not only did he himself enrich it; he also trained a considerable number of very eminent pupils. He found means, partly by his engaging way of lecturing, partly by the expeditions he made with them, to inspire them with a love of natural history which they never lost and which induced them to make long and important journeys and to enrich science by valuable observations at home. Few teachers had the good fortune to make so many disciples who all to some extent contributed to the progress of science, and probably no country has sent so many natural historians abroad as has Sweden. Linnaeus was my teacher too, and I acknowledge with deep emotion my great indebtedness to him for his instruction and for his friendship.

Valuable light is also thrown on Linnaeus and his family by a young German named Johann Beckmann (1739–1811), who taught mathematics, physics and natural history at the Lutheran St Peter's Gymnasium in St Petersburg. In the summer of 1765 Professor J. P. Falck, an old Linnaean pupil who was professor of medicine and botany and in charge of the Botanic Garden there, learned that his colleague was going to Sweden to visit the mines of Falun; he therefore persuaded him to deliver a consignment of plants and seeds to Linnaeus.

Beckmann, best known as the author of that fascinating bedside book *The History of Inventions* (which range from 'speaking-trumpets' to 'secret poisons'), joined forces with another German, Dr Kölpin, in Stockholm, and the two men reached Uppsala at the beginning of September:

As it was the vacation when I arrived, Linnaeus was at his country house at Hammarby; but he was expected back in Uppsala the same day. While waiting for his return I went into a bookshop, where I saw an elderly man of medium height, with dusty shoes and stockings, very unshaven, and wearing an ancient green jacket on which hung an Order. I was not a little taken aback when I was told that this was the famous Linnaeus.

The Order was, of course, that of the Knighthood of the Polar Star, which Linnaeus did not hesitate to wear at all times. Beckmann continues:

I talked with him as he walked to his house – and in Latin, because he did not understand German well. He remembered the letter I had written to him, and was extremely affable. Since he had walked from Hammarby he was sweating a lot. . . . As we were about to go into his house, he pointed to an adjacent building and said, 'Try to get a room there. Everyone who comes to hear me, and all my closest friends, stay there . . . and so does my son. Whenever I have any spare time, that is where I like to spend it – inhaling tobacco smoke and talking with my friends.'

Dr Kölpin, whom Linnaeus already knew, now appeared, and while Linnaeus was being shaved we mentioned our intention of visiting the mines. He told us where we should go and what we ought to see, and also gave us a letter to his brother-in-law, Herr Moraeus, at Falun. In the room there hung the portrait of Linnaeus holding *Linnaea*, portraits of the most famous botanists, and plans of several botanic gardens. We began to talk about insects, and he showed us his own collection; then we went into the splendid Garden, and I cannot describe how eager and excited he was to discover what flowers had come out while he had been away, and to show them to us. It was delightful to see with what pleasure the monkeys greeted him, how caressingly the crested cockatoo called to him, and how affectionately their master responded.

Beckmann was, however, less pleased when the cockatoo seized his hat from his head and bit through two thicknesses of felt. But Linnaeus could apparently take any liberty he liked with his animals. Three years later he received, as a personal gift from the Queen, a monkey (*Simia oedipus*) named Grinn which had been banished from the Court because it had disgraced itself there by teasing the courtiers and snatching the buckles from their shoes; and at the same time the King gave him a handsome oil-painting of Grinn by G. Hesselius, which still hangs in his bedroom at Hammarby. Linnaeus was immensely proud of his royal animal.

Beckmann was ordered to visit Linnaeus again in the afternoon to translate a letter he had received from the English botanist John Ellis. 'He was delighted to find that I could read English, because he himself knew very little of that language.' The German then left Uppsala; but he returned in October and drove out with the younger Linnaeus to Hammarby. The old botanist received him warmly and begged him to stay for a day or two; but the carriage had been hired and he felt obliged to refuse. Of this visit he wrote:

The walls of Linnaeus's rooms at Hammarby were covered with botanical prints taken from the finest volumes of Sloane, Ehret, etc., and pasted on them so that they looked just like wall-paper. . . . Linnaeus's wife . . . is not so friendly towards foreigners as is her husband, and her very bourgeois clothes made her look rather undistinguished. While we were at table Linnaeus said jokingly, 'I have another German here; you must learn German so that you can talk to him.' She replied, 'It wouldn't be worth while learning German for *his* sake.' I replied in my broken

The Museum room, Uppsala.

Swedish that she was right, and that I would learn Swedish for *her* sake. This made Linnaeus laugh, and she then became rather more affable.

Linnaeus had once written to Celsius that he was beginning to grow tired of German students, who were 'full of nothing but titles, requests and questions, and I gain little from them'; but there seem to have been one or two notable exceptions to the general rule. Beckmann mentions several subsequent visits to Linnaeus in the country. On one occasion he stayed for a few days in a farm-house near Hammarby – no doubt the one where Fabricius and his friends had lodged – and botanized with Linnaeus on the rocky knoll above the house. In Uppsala, too, he spent many happy hours in Linnaeus's company and attended some of his lectures. The old botanist now found it hard to lecture formally; he much preferred the informal discussions into which his lectures often declined. This suited Beckmann, who was a trained botanist, but it was less satisfactory for beginners. Linnaeus might, for example, be lecturing on amphibia, but he would soon put frogs and toads aside and send for some plant or other from the Garden and discuss it, the amphibia quite forgotten. When Beckmann visited him in his house, the first question was always, 'Well, what do you want to ask me? What shall we talk about?' Cross-examination never seemed to tire Linnaeus.

Beckmann and Fabricius were agreed in considering Fru Linnaea a crude and tiresome woman, and her husband to be hag-ridden. The pastel portrait of her at Hammarby, made when she was middle-aged, shows only too plainly that any charms that the Fair Flower of Falun may have had in the bud had not survived in the full-blown bloom. She seems to have been a typical *Hausfrau*, a thrifty provider but fond in her early married life of frivolous pleasures and the social round, and especially of card-playing which in time became almost an obsession;

had she lived two centuries later she would no doubt have divided her leisure hours between the bingo halls and the television screen. Linnaeus, his mind on higher things, did not interfere; he could almost have been described as bigamously married, his other wife and true helpmeet being Dame Nature.

It has been said that in the early years of her marriage Sara Lisa gave her husband some cause for jealousy; but it may well have been groundless jealousy that possessed Linnaeus to draw up in the mid-sixties a will by which his wife, 'should she be so foolish as to remarry, which I have reason to believe she intends to do', was to have 'no share in such things as I bought with the money I alone earned by my books, lectures and botanical work'. Whether it was the prospect of losing Hammarby and much else besides that prevented Sara Lisa from a second marriage, we do not know; she cannot in any case have been much of a catch. She died in 1806 at the age of ninety, survived by her three youngest daughters.

Sara Lisa was strict with her servants and with her children. At four in the morning her daughters began to take turns at the spinning-wheel, and over-sleeping was rewarded by boxed ears. But it was her son, Carl, who fared the worst:

Fru Linnaea, pastel by S. N. Höök.

Carl Linnaeus junior, by Jonas Forsslund.

> The son [wrote Beckmann] fears his parents more than he loves them, and his mother has always intensely disliked him. On one occasion, when he was already a professor, she boxed his ears; and when his father told her that she should remember that he was a professor, she replied, 'I'd box his ears, even if he were an archiater.' It was for this reason that the father had taken a room for him in the house where I was living, and why the son was so reluctant to be with his parents.

According to Beckmann, Carl had little genuine interest in natural history, and in other subjects was quite uneducated: 'When need arose he could speak a little Latin, but he was incapable of writing a Latin thesis and knew no other language than Swedish. He has never been abroad and shows no inclination to travel, for which purpose his parents would not in any case have provided the money.' But Linnaeus rashly used his influence to get his son appointed, over the heads of senior and better qualified candidates, Demonstrator at the Botanic Garden at the age of eighteen, an honorary Doctor in the medical faculty at twenty-four, and finally, after the refusal of his pupil Solander to return from England to Sweden, to be designated as his successor. 'The result,' wrote Beckmann, 'is that Professor von Linné [junior] has few friends and things will be worse for him after his father dies.' Stoever, quoting Fabricius rather freely, completes the picture:

> The lady of LINNAEUS was a good housewife, but in no respect a pattern of a sweet and mild mother, or of a tender spouse. Her only son lived under the most slavish restraint and in a continual fear of her. Even when he had attained the age of manhood, and bore an academical dignity, she compelled him to SWEEP HIS OWN ROOM. . . . Galled by these shackles of slavery and constraint, the flower of his mind faded, and he lost that eagerness of zeal which he formerly manifested in his studies. His disgust lessened also the affection of his father. . . . When congratulated by a German friend on being his father's successor, he replied (aged 30): 'POH!

Linnaeus's daughters: Lisa Stina, and below, Lovisa;

A portrait of Carl, painted in the last year (1783) of his short life, shows a good-looking young man with full and sensual lips. He had the reputation of being a ladies' man, and an acquaintance wrote of him in 1770: 'The young gentleman amuses himself daily . . . inquiring less after Flora than after the Nymphs. He holds his head high, dresses and powders himself *à la mode*, and is always to be found in the company of pretty women.' His parents hoped that a sensible marriage might put a stop to his philandering; but Carl demanded beauty and his father stipulated wealth, and it was difficult to find them united. Archbishop Troil's daughter was beautiful and Carl was said to have been very much in love with her; but she was one of a family of ten and his father failed her on the means test. Fröken Asp was indeed both rich and attractive, but she had not had smallpox and might well become disfigured. There was also another very wealthy girl, but she was badly pock-marked. . . . So Carl never married.

Linnaeus wished his daughters to grow up into 'hearty, strong housekeepers, not fashionable dolls'; the four portraits of them at Hammarby and a flowered silk dress preserved in Uppsala show, however, that for special occasions – a royal visit, for example – neither money nor trouble was spared to make them smart and attractive. The elaborate coiffures which were then the mode had to be carried out a day in advance, obliging the unfortunate victims to spend the night bolt upright in a chair.

The silk dresses, together with the fine silver, glass and china still to be seen at Hammarby and in the Uppsala house, testify to the fact that Linnaeus and his family lived in some style. Since Linnaeus himself strongly denounced luxury – he actually once made a list of things that he considered superfluous, and it included almost everything that would make a house comfortable or a meal enjoyable – we may prefer to suppose that it was Fru Linnaea who insisted upon 'keeping up with the Joneses'. Linnaeus did not, however, always practise what he preached, for his list includes wines and spirits, tobacco, tea, coffee, silks, silver, china and paintings.

If Linnaeus did not wish his daughters to become dolls, still less did he want them to become blue-stockings. They were not allowed to learn French; and when Sara Lisa, taking advantage of his absence in Stockholm, placed Sophia in a school, on his return he immediately put a stop to this nonsense. Queen Lovisa Ulrika offered to receive one of the girls at Court, but Linnaeus refused. The Queen, amazed, asked if she was not to be trusted; Linnaeus's reply, though respectfully worded, made it quite plain that he thought she was not.

But though French was forbidden, a mild interest in botany was apparently permitted; and Lisa Stina, the eldest daughter, made some study of the subject. In 1762 she contributed a paper to the *Transactions* of the Royal Academy of Science entitled, 'Remarks on a luminous appearance of the Indian cresses' – these being the flowers the gardener calls nasturtium and the botanist *Tropaeolum*. 'This appearance,' wrote Pulteney, 'which had never been noticed before, is like the sparks that arise from a fulminating powder, and was first observed by this lady when she was walking in her father's garden at Hammarby. She mentions its being visible only in the dusk of evening, and ceasing when total darkness came on.' The 'celebrated electrician, J. C. Wilckes' considered the phenomenon, which was also observed by Goethe and others at a later date, to be 'of an electrical nature'; but modern scientists dismiss it as an optical illusion.

Sophia was the beauty of the family; indeed a young man who saw the four girls together went so far as to say that she did not seem to be 'even of the same genus' as her sisters. She was also, wrote Fries, from her infancy her father's darling:

> When she grew rather bigger he used often to take her with him to his lectures, where, if the fancy took her, she would stand all the time between his knees and listen. She would also accompany him, her neck, arms and head bare, on his walks through the town, and he would tie his handkerchief round her neck to prevent her catching cold.
>
> He tried, too, to protect her from her mother's rough scolding. One day, just as she was about to carry a tray of crockery upstairs, she fell and smashed everything to pieces. In desperation she turned to her father, who told her not to upset herself over such a small matter; he then immediately went out and bought a new set. It is not difficult to picture Fru Linnaea's surprise at dinner, and no doubt she suspected that Sophia had 'done it again'; but on this occasion she had to be content with her husband's explanation that he thought the old set so ugly that he had broken it and bought a new one.

Almost the last happiness that came to Linnaeus, shortly before his death, was the news of Sophia's engagement to a proctor of the University.

Linnaeus, Fabricius had written, 'was accused of having many faults', and perhaps the most conspicuous of these was his undisguised and almost unbelievable self-satisfaction with his own achievements. Single-handed he had created order where formerly chaos reigned. *Deus creavit, Linnaeus disposuit*. 'God saw every thing that He had made, and, behold, it was very good'; Linnaeus saw the confusion that he had inherited and warmly congratulated himself on the successful completion of a half-finished job.

Any author would be well satisfied with reviews such as the following, of three of his books: of *Species Plantarum*, 'The greatest achievement in the realm of science'; of *Systema Naturae*, 'A masterpiece that no one can read too often or admire too much'; of *Clavis Medicinae Duplex*, 'The fairest jewel in medicine.' And who was the generous critic? Why, none other than Linnaeus himself! It was Linnaeus, too, who wrote, 'Many people believe my *Species Plantarum* or my *Systema Naturae* to be the labour of a lifetime for one man', and who informed the Diet, 'I have fundamentally reorganized the whole field of natural history, raising it to the height it has now attained. I doubt whether anyone today could hope, without my help and guidance, to make any advance in this field.' Here are a few extracts from the Autobiography of this modest man:

Sara Stina, and below, Sophia, by S. N. Höök.

No one before him had
    pursued his profession with greater zeal and had more hearers;
    made more observations in natural history;

Glasses engraved with *Linnaea borealis*.

had fuller insight into all the three kingdoms of Nature;
been a greater botanist or zoologist;
so well described the natural history of his own country – its flora, fauna and
  topography;
written more books, more correctly, more methodically, from his own experience;
so completely reformed a whole science and inaugurated a new era;
sent out his disciples to so many parts of the world;
written his name on more plants and insects, indeed on the whole of Nature;
become more famous the whole world over . . .
listed so many animals – yes, as many as all the others put together . . .
been a member of more scientific societies [of which a long list follows].

It has been pleaded in Linnaeus's defence that he was not so much praising
Linnaeus as praising God for his good sense in having chosen him as His
instrument. There is no doubt a grain of truth in this, and in another passage he
attributed his triumphs directly to divine intervention:

GOD Himself has led him with His own almighty hand;
  has caused him to sprout from a stump, transplanted him to a distant and lovely spot
    and made him grow into a goodly tree;
  has inspired him with such an ardent enthusiasm for science that it became his
    greatest objective. . .
  provided him with the largest herbarium in the world, his greatest joy;
  preserved him from fire;
  let him live for more than sixty years. . . .

But the fact remains that Hagberg was being charitable indeed in writing no
more strongly than that Linnaeus was 'not one of those who doubted themselves
or the significance of their achievements'. Linnaeus would have seen nothing
surprizing in this judgment, for he wrote of himself that he was 'in the highest
degree averse from everything that bore the appearance of pride'. Self-deception
could hardly go further. But perhaps the most remarkable thing about Linnaeus's
paean of self-praise is that almost every note it sounds happens to be true.

A confirmed belief in one's own omniscience naturally makes it difficult for a
man to believe that those who disagree with him can possibly be right, though,

as J. E. Smith once said, 'sometimes even a blind hen comes across a grain of corn'. At times Linnaeus behaved like 'an easily wounded and egocentric diva, who did not tolerate criticism' (Sven Lindroth). It was, however, something almost indistinguishable from jealousy that made him resent other botanists naming a plant, and on the flimsiest of excuses he would substitute a name of his own. This sometimes led to trouble, and there were innumerable protests when he changed *Meadia* (so named by Catesby in honour of Dr Richard Mead) to the cumbersome *Dodecatheon*, which it still retains. And may it not also have been jealousy that made Linnaeus attempt to dissuade his pupils from attending lectures other than his own, especially those of his enemy Wallerius?

Linnaeus was certainly a deeply religious man, who would have agreed with the hymnographer that

Johan Christian Fabricius.

> All things bright and beautiful,
> All creatures great and small,
> All things wise and wonderful,
> The Lord God made them all.

But he did in time come to doubt the historical accuracy of certain events recorded in the earlier chapters of the Old Testament. Once he had written, 'I should like to believe that the earth is even older than the Chinese believe it to be, but the Scriptures do not allow this'; later, however, he found that he could no longer accept a universal flood, or that the world was created and equipped in a matter of only six days. He tried to keep these heretical opinions to himself; but though he never aired them in print they became known and led to his being looked upon in certain quarters as a crypto-atheist.

When at Hammarby he went every Sunday to the parish church at Danmark, accompanied by his dog Pompe. If he was prevented by illness from attending, the dog would go without him and sit quietly in the Hammarby pew. Linnaeus considered the local parson long-winded, and after an hour would get up and go, although the sermon might still be in progress. The dog, even when alone, followed his master's example in this, and after an hour would make a solitary, pointed exit.

It was also held against Linnaeus that he found it more blessed, or at all events more agreeable, to receive than to give. Collinson had entertained him hospitably in England and for more than ten years plied him regularly with gifts, but Linnaeus left his generosity unrewarded. Finally Collinson brought himself to speak his mind on the subject:

> I herewith send you some of the early ripe Indian corn. . . . You promised me some books, but none has reached me so far. . . . My good friend, I must tell you frankly . . . you have been in my museum and seen my little collection, and yet you have not sent me a single specimen of either fossil, animal or vegetable. I have sent you seeds and specimens every year, but without the least return. It is a general complaint that Dr Linnaeus receives all, and returns nothing. I tell you this as a friend, and as such I hope you will receive it in great friendship. As I love and admire you, I must tell you honestly what the world says.

179

Then there was Linnaeus's vanity. It is true that he spoke of honours as 'empty nut-shells', but it was no less true that he was delighted when they came his way and indignant when they did not. Finally, we may mention his credulity and his obstinacy. Though the time came when his reason would not allow him to accept as factual all that he read in the Book of Genesis, yet in certain other matters he remained a child of his age, occasionally even lagging behind the more advanced thinking. He still believed, wrote Sven Lindroth, 'that in winter the swallows slept upon the bottom of lakes, that the rattle-snake be-witched the squirrel, that puppies became dwarfed if they were anointed with spirits'.

In this grotesque belief about swallows, which was as old as Aristotle, Linnaeus had at all events the partial support of Dr Johnson and, more sur-prisingly, of Gilbert White. White refers to the matter in a letter which he wrote on 4 November 1767 to Thomas Pennant. 'A Swedish naturalist,' he says, 'is so much persuaded of that fact, that he talks, in his calendar of Flora, as familiarly of the swallow's going under water in the beginning of September, as he would of his poultry going to roost a little before sunset.' After mentioning some young swallows that he had seen hovering over a roof-top in Oxford at the end of October, White continues, 'Now is it likely that these poor little birds (which perhaps had not been hatched but a few weeks) should, at that late season of the year, and from so midland a county, attempt a voyage to Goree or Senegal, almost as far as the equator?' One eighteenth-century naturalist was convinced that swallows wintered on the moon.

Peter Collinson took a sensible view of the matter, suggesting that Linnaeus should make controlled experiments. But he never did, and continued to his dying day to maintain that he was right. Did he, one may ask, really believe this absurdity, or was he too proud to admit his error? Attractive myths die hard, and Alfred Newton, F.R.S., writing in 1909, lamented that there were still 'many who should know better' who gave credence to the old fable.

Of Linnaeus it was written:

> [He is] an egoistic man with an analytical and constructive mind, who sees matters clearly, using intuition and perception, who is very methodical and who has a simplicity of outlook, living and working within a narrow private world. He is rather vain and conceited, knows he is clever and is sure he is right, does not like to be challenged and can be obstinate, although being diplomatic and calculating he will give a point to gain two. He is very secretive and watchful, not really a friendly person, not a born leader, thus very selective about friends, and there is a coldness about him. He was depressed and psychologically exhausted at the time of writing this letter.

This letter? The character sketch of Linnaeus here given is the verbatim report of a handwriting expert, employed to give confidential reports on character as revealed by handwriting, made at the request of Dr Stearn from a letter written in Latin by Linnaeus in 1766. Stearn, who took care not to give the name of the writer or any information about him, confesses that he was 'indeed shocked to find that a view of Linnaeus's character I had obtained only through extensive reading over a long period could be reached by a handwriting expert in about five minutes!'

180

Pub.^d as the Act directs Feby 1789 by Wm Curtis Botanic Garden Lambeth Marsh

Pub. by Wm Curtis St Geo. Crescent Apr. 1. 1798.

J. Curtis del. Pub. by J. Curtis Walworth Augt 1825. Weddell sc.

Pub. Decr 1790 by W. Curtis St Georges Crescent

4026.

W. Fitch Del.t   Pub. by S. Curtis, Glazenwood, Essex, July 1. 1843.   Swan Sc.

6.

The Apostles

It was Linnaeus himself who, in 1750, first named 'apostles' those of his students who went overseas to investigate the plants of distant lands; and how far-flung were the journeys of these disciples can be seen from the map reproduced from *Den Svenska Historien* on page 186. As Stearn has said,

his own admittedly stop-gap 'sexual system', although repugnant to the best botanists of the time like Amman and Haller, enabled specimens to be allocated quickly to groups and provided with names, instead of going unsorted and unnamed into cupboards. The Linnaean method of botanical recording thus made botanical exploration worth while, for this became a means of contributing on a large scale to the world's knowledge. Therein lies the clue to the zeal for travel that animated so many of Linnaeus's students.

The Master eagerly awaited news of his apostles and, still more impatiently, the arrival of plants; but five of these men, Anders Berlin (1746–73), Pehr Forsskål (1736–68), Fredrik Hasselqvist (1722–52), Pehr Löfling (1729–56), and Christopher Tärnström (1703–46), including two of the most brilliant, were never to return. Tärnström's wife angrily upbraided Linnaeus for having made her a widow and her children orphans, and he often reproached himself for sending these young men to their deaths, wondering whether anyone ought to expose himself to such risks and hardships in the pursuit of botany. To the more fortunate, who included Adam Afzelius (1750–1837), Pehr Kalm (1715–79), Johan Gerard König (1728–85), Lars Montin (1723–85), Pehr Osbeck (1723–1805), Daniel Rolander (1725–93), Daniel Carl Solander (1736–82), Anders Sparrman (1748–1820), Carl Peter Thunberg (1743–1828) and Olof Torén (d. 1753), Linnaeus's promotion of scientific travel gave not only the rewarding experience of seeing strange lands, peoples and vegetation but also the satisfaction of making valuable contributions to knowledge and sometimes furthering successfully their own careers. Many specimens gathered by them, representing species previously unknown and given names from this material by Linnaeus, are preserved in the Linnaean Herbarium and remain scientifically important.

One far-reaching effect, through the sailing of his admirer Joseph Banks and his student Daniel Solander on Cook's voyage round the world in the *Endeavour*,

Pehr Kalm.

1768–71, was the establishment of a tradition that exploring ships of the British Royal Navy should carry a naturalist to make biological collections and observations. Thus the travels of the Linnaean apostles in the eighteenth century led to those of Darwin, Huxley and J. D. Hooker in the nineteenth and so to the acceptance of the theory of the evolution of plants and animals.

The adventures of these men deserve fuller treatment than they can receive here. It must suffice to indicate the careers of only a few.

The first to set out and the first to fall by the way was this same Christopher Tärnström, who was in fact several years older than Linnaeus and who had been his companion on many botanical forays round Uppsala. Though a clergyman, married, and with a family, he had begged to be allowed to go, as priest and botanist, to China. He obtained a free passage in one of the Swedish East India Company's ships early in 1746, but he got no further than Cochin-China, where he died of a tropical fever. Linnaeus could do nothing beyond trying to get financial help for the indignant widow and her children, and naming in the dead man's honour the tropical genus *Ternstroemia*. 'Tärnström's death has greatly upset me,' he wrote to Bäck when he heard the news.

'No one in this country can be compared with Tärnström', said Linnaeus, 'except Kalm.' Kalm was sent out to North America to find useful plants which might tolerate the Swedish climate; in particular he was urged to send back the red mulberry, *Morus rubra*, so that the silk industry could be started in Sweden. Money for the expedition was provided by the Universities of Uppsala and Åbo and from industry. After a stormy crossing to England and a long stay there, he and his companions finally reached Philadelphia in the autumn of 1748. In Delaware, which had earlier been a Swedish colony, he found many of his countrymen. Two and a half busy years were spent in the States of Pennsylvania, New Jersey and New York, and in southern Canada, from where Kalm returned to Stockholm with a magnificent collection of pressed plants and seeds. Linnaeus, ill though he was with a sharp attack of gout, waited (he told Bäck) 'as impatiently as a bride awaits one in the morning' for a sight of these treasures; so excited was he that he quite forgot his aches and pains and rose from his sick-bed to welcome his pupil.

Kalm's collection proved to be all that Linnaeus had hoped. Whereas in his *Hortus Cliffortianus* he had described only 170 North American plants, his *Species Plantarum* of 1753 included more than 700, at least 90 of which he owed to Kalm, suitably commemorated in the handsome *Kalmia*. Kalm published an account of his travels, which appeared in an English translation in three volumes in 1770–1: a new edition of his original Swedish *Resejournal* (travel diary) was published in 1966 and 1970.

The next apostle to set out was Fredrik Hasselqvist, 'modest, polite, cheerful and intelligent', but unfortunately also sickly and penniless. Linnaeus in his lectures had often mentioned the Levant, and Palestine in particular, as fruitful, un-explored country for the naturalist, and he fired Hasselqvist with the desire to go there. In vain the Master tried to dissuade him: the boy hadn't the money, he hadn't the stamina (he showed signs of consumption). But Hasselqvist would not listen to reason. The money – just, but only just, enough – was raised by Linnaeus, and a free passage to Izmir (Smyrna) found in one of the ships of the Levant Company. On 7 August 1749 Hasselqvist sailed from Stockholm.

After spending the winter in and around Izmir, in March he made a trip into the interior; then he sailed for Egypt where he remained until, ten months later, his money ran out. Friends in Sweden – Linnaeus, of course, and the younger Olof Celsius – persuaded the Senate to make a grant and also put their hands deep into their own pockets. So Hasselqvist was able to continue on his way through Palestine (part of which he called 'Arabia'), Syria, Cyprus, Rhodes and Chios, to return at last to Izmir with an enormously rich collection in the three kingdoms of Nature. He was, however, already a very sick man and 'on 9 February 1752, at 6 o'clock in the evening and to the grief of all who knew him, our beloved Dr Hasselqvist died like a lamp whose oil is consumed'.

It appeared that Hasselqvist had incurred a debt of 14,000 copper dalers – a great deal of money – and that until it had been settled his collections and manuscripts would not be handed over. The sum was quite beyond Linnaeus's power to pay; but in the end the Queen generously came to the rescue. The manuscripts were handed over to Linnaeus, who wrote to Bäck on 18 July 1755:

> The day before yesterday I received Hasselqvist's papers from Baron Ehrencrona. . . . God bless the peerless Queen for letting me see them! But I had come so near to losing them that when I began to read I couldn't stop before I had reached the end. I swear I have never yet read anything so full of fresh, genuine and precise observations as these; they penetrate me as God's word penetrates a deacon. . . . May God grant that Her Majesty has them published as soon as possible, so that all the world may taste the pleasure I had yesterday. . . . So admirable a travel journal has never before appeared. . . .

Linnaeus published the *Iter Palaestinum* in 1757, and English, French, German and Dutch translations followed in due course.

In 1750 Pehr Osbeck sailed as ship's chaplain from Gothenburg for the Far East, returning to Sweden in June 1752. Linnaeus wrote to his pupil as he was about to leave:

Pehr Osbeck.

> On your return we will make crowns with the flowers you bring back, to adorn the heads of the priests of the temple of Flora and the altars of the goddess. Your name shall be inscribed on substances as durable and indestructible as diamonds, and we will dedicate to you some very rare *Osbeckia* which will be enrolled in Flora's army. So – hoist your sails and row with all your might; but take heed not to return without the choicest spoils, or we shall invoke Neptune to hurl you and all your company into the depths of the Taenarum.

Osbeck spent four or five months in China, on his return presenting the whole of his fine collection to Linnaeus and thus thoroughly deserving to be remembered in so handsome a plant as the *Osbeckia*. He also brought back a china tea-set, commissioned by Linnaeus and decorated with Linnaeus's own flower, *Linnaea borealis*. A part of the set was broken in transit; but replacements were ordered, and in this second set the flowers are red rather than the correct pink.

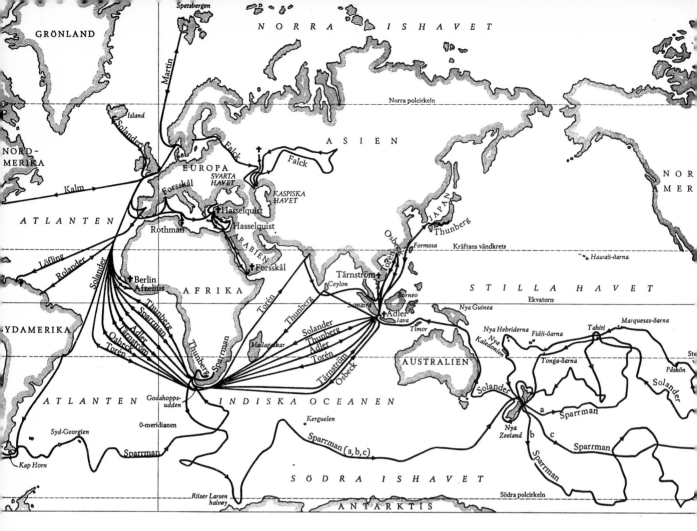

The journeys of the Apostles.

The four attractive Chinese paintings which hang on the walls at Hammarby were probably brought back to Europe either by Osbeck or by Magnus Lagerström, an ardent collector who was of immense service to Linnaeus and a generous benefactor to Uppsala University. It was certainly Lagerström who brought Linnaeus from China the rhinoceros-horn cup which was presented on 11 November 1970 by the President of the Linnean Society to H.M. the King of Sweden in honour of his eighty-eighth birthday. Drinking-vessels made of rhinoceros horn were highly prized in Asia and Africa for their reputed power of revealing the presence of poison, which was said to ferment the liquid until it overflowed. Linnaeus's horn is exquisitely carved with rocks, flowers, fruit and a lizard. Sir James Smith acquired it in 1784 along with the Linnaean collections. On his death it passed to his widow, who in 1869 gave it to the Linnean Society. Perhaps this horn did after all have some magical potency, for Lady Smith lived to the uncommon age of a hundred and four.

In 1750 the Spanish Ambassador in Stockholm asked Linnaeus, on behalf of his King, to recommend a young student to investigate the neglected flora of Spain; he chose the twenty-one-year-old Pehr Löfling.

If Hasselqvist was the St Paul of the Linnaean apostles, then Pehr Löfling, 'his most beloved pupil', was his St John; he gave the boy the strange nickname of 'the Vulture', perhaps because of his keen-sightedness when searching for plants. At Uppsala Löfling formed a close friendship with another student, J. O. Hagström, who thus describes him:

When he first came, as a very young man, to Uppsala, he looked so simple that he gave the impression of being a diffident rustic. In his first year he made friends with no one but me, who like himself had come to the University from the backwoods. When he looked through my bookshelves it was my herbarium that immediately caught his eye. . . . This pleased me enormously, and I at once began to enjoy his company both day and night; thus we both lived and slept together. He shared with me his father's letters, the main theme of all of which was that his son should become a clergyman. He himself had no liking for that profession, and was therefore all the more upset by his father's well-intentioned exhortations. As he lived with me he had nothing to pay for fuel, but he included this in the bill he sent his father and spent the money on paper on which to make a herbarium. His father had no financial resources. . . .

Academically I was several years his senior, and I advised him not to waste his time on Greek, logic and metaphysics – subjects which had made scandalous inroads on mine in my younger days. Löfling changed over to the botanical school, where he made such steady and rapid progress that amongst all the students it was he who was found worthy to become tutor to Linnaeus's son.

So far as Pehr Löfling's character is concerned I can honestly say that his personality was graced with virtue, common sense and uprightness; he was God-fearing, serious, affectionate and loyal, and in addition he had a delightfully quick understanding of Nature's many secrets. In appearance he was like Professor Kalm of Åbo, tall and towering and with a manly and agreeable countenance. He looked the picture of health, and while he was with me he was always very fit and energetic.

Linnaeus, when in 1758 he came to edit the *Iter Hispanicum* (*Spanish Journey*) of his late pupil, wrote:

He attended lectures every day – both public and private, kept company with the brightest of his fellow students, was early and late in the Botanic Garden, and at our midday meals never failed to ply me with astute questions on the subject of Flora. He lived with me in the greatest intimacy, for he had a soul as pure as gold and was without a trace of deceit in word or deed. There was nothing in the least soft or effeminate about him; he took no interest in what he ate or what he wore, and it was a matter of complete indifference to him whether he slept on the hardest boards or in the softest bed; but to find a little plant or scrap of moss the longest road was not too long for him. . . .

In 1749 Löfling created something of a stir by his disputation *De Gemmis Arborum* ('On the buds of trees'), and the following year he found himself in a position to be of help to his devoted teacher. Linnaeus was just starting work on his *Philosophia Botanica* when he was taken ill. In his Autobiography he wrote:

In 1750, when I was beginning my *Philosophia botanica*, I had such a sharp attack of gout that I doubted whether I should survive it. But when I began to recover I got my dear Löfling to write at my dictation while I lay in bed, and thus I was able to finish the book. At first this was heavy work for a young man; but later it became so easy and agreeable to Herr Löfling that he would not have forgone it on any account.

Carved rhinoceros horn cup, brought back to Linnaeus from China.

187

For as I tried in this book to get to the heart of botanical study, and as Herr Löfling never failed to ask me to explain what he had not understood, he finally became so well grounded in botany that I could defy all the false prophets in Flora's realm to turn him into a heretic.

No portrait of Löfling survives, but it is not too difficult to picture this tall and handsome young Swede who made friends and won hearts wherever he went. In Stockholm, while making preparations for his journey to Spain, he was showered with gifts of instruments by various members of the Academy, and the Spanish Ambassador, who had already arranged for the payment of his voyage, insisted upon giving him additional pocket-money 'so that he could undertake the journey pleasurably and advantageously'.

Löfling sailed for Lisbon and so reached Madrid where he remained for two years, overcoming by his personal charm the jealousies of the local botanists, writing with dutiful regularity to his former teacher and sending him much material for his herbarium. Then in 1754 the Spaniards organized an expedition to Spanish South America, and Löfling was invited to accompany it as botanist 'to collect specimens for the Spanish Court, the King of France, the Queen of Sweden, and Linnaeus' – fine company to find oneself in, commented Linnaeus proudly when he heard. One of the objects of the expedition was to settle a boundary dispute between Colombia and Venezuela; but it was principally designed to carry out scientific research, and Löfling had under him two young surgeons and two draughtsmen.

After a short stop in the Canary Islands the party sailed on to the Venezuelan port of Cumaná. At first all went well and Löfling collected as energetically as ever; but the climate was lethal and before the year was out he was down with fever, the first of many attacks which gradually undermined his strength. Finally he was 'laid up in a tertian ague, became dropsical', and on 22 February 1756 died in a Mission Station at Merercuri, in Guiana; he was twenty-seven. 'The great Vulture is dead,' wrote Linnaeus sorrowfully to Bäck; and in his Preface to the *Iter Hispanicum* he paid a poetic tribute to his 'dearest and best' pupil: 'Löfling gave his life for Flora and her lovers; they mourn his loss.'

Unfortunately, nothing could be drearier to the non-botanist than *Loeflingia hispanica* – a little Spanish weed with almost invisible flowers, named by Linnaeus in 1753 before Löfling had had an opportunity to collect more splendid tropical plants.

The now popular *Alstroemeria* commemorates the very modest journeys through Spain and other European countries, between 1760 and 1764, of Baron Clas Alström, son of the more famous Jonas Alström whom Linnaeus had visited at Alingsås.

Alstroemeria pelegrina reached Europe many years before the now more commonly grown *A. aurantiaca*. 'From Peru [*sic*], as might be expected, [*Alstroemeria pelegrina*] found its way into Spain, from whence by the means of his beloved friend, ALSTROEMER, LINNAEUS first received seeds of it; the value he set on the acquisition is evident from the great care he took of the seedling plants, preserving them through the winter in his bed-chamber' (*Botanical Magazine*, 1795). Alström first came upon the plant in 1760 in the garden of

Baron Clas Alström, engraved after a portrait by P. Krafft.

the Swedish Consul in Cadiz, but it had already reached Kew seven years earlier; it is figured on two china plates now in the Linnaeus Museum in Uppsala.

Alstroemeria is familarly known as 'the Lily of the Incas' or 'the Peruvian lily'. Since it is not a lily, and does not come from Peru, the names are unfortunate. 'Chilean daffodil' would be more appropriate. As Miss Alice Coats has pointed out, 'the alstroemeria has the distinction of being the only garden plant to wear its leaves upside-down, every leaf-stalk having a twist in it that brings what should have been the underside of the leaf uppermost'.

Linnaeus used often to associate some peculiarity of a plant he named, with some quality or characteristic of the man whom it honoured. 'It is commonly believed,' he wrote in his *Critica Botanica*, that the name of a plant which is derived from that of a botanist shows no connection between the two. But anyone who has but slight knowledge of the history of letters will easily discover a link by which to connect the name with the plant. . . .' He gives a few examples, such as: '*Commelina* has flowers with three petals, two of which are showy, while the third is not conspicuous; from the two botanists called Commelin, for the third died before accomplishing anything in botany.' What, one may wonder, did he see in Alströmer to associate him with a plant whose peculiarity seems to be a desire to stand on its head?

Solander, and below, Banks.

Daniel Solander was one of the greatest travellers of all the apostles. Linnaeus appears to have taken a special interest in this young man, the son of a Norrland pastor; he 'brought him up under his own roof and cherished him as a son', hoped for him as a son-in-law, and marked him down as his successor. In 1760, at the age of twenty-four, Solander visited England on Linnaeus's recommendation. Here 'the connection he was known to bear as the favourite pupil of the great master . . . his perfect acquaintance with the whole scheme [i.e. the sexual system] and the urbanity of his manners' did much to further the advance of the system in England.

In 1762 Linnaeus obtained for him the offer of the professorship of botany at St Petersburg and invited him to succeed him in due course in Uppsala. He was far from pleased when Solander, after delaying four or five months before replying, informed him that he intended to settle permanently in England. The usual messages of love to 'my sweetest mademoiselle' (Linnaeus's eldest daughter, Lisa Stina) faded from Solander's letters to Linnaeus, and soon afterwards the girl was married – very unhappily, as it turned out – to a Swedish officer, Carl Bergencrantz, a grandson of the younger Olof Rudbeck. There was now something of a breach between master and pupil, who never met again.

In 1763 Solander became Assistant Librarian at the British Museum, and at a later date Keeper of its Natural History department. In 1768 he sailed with Banks (and at his expense) on Cook's famous voyage in the *Endeavour*, and after his return visited Iceland with Banks, whose secretary and librarian he became. Solander 'had, as it were, caught his preceptor's mantle and imbibed, by a sort of inspiration, a peculiar talent for concise and clear definition', so that 'no one ever came so near his great teacher in the specific discrimination of plants'; it was thus a great loss to science that his excellent descriptions of the many new plants which came into his hands, the fruit of great industry and

189

accurate observation, were not published in his lifetime or immediately after his death.

On board the *Endeavour*, at anchor off Rio de Janiero in 1768, Solander wrote a last letter to Linnaeus; it concludes with greetings to Linnaeus's family and to 'your eldest daughter, whom I had hoped would make me happy'. From his three-year voyage round the world Solander sent no specimens to Linnaeus, who was angry and indignant; but these belonged not to him but to Banks. In his later years Linnaeus was often heard to complain of 'the ungrateful Solander', but in fact he was far from ungrateful; when Linnaeus's son visited England in 1781 and 1782 it was Solander who acted as his cicerone and who also nursed him through a serious illness. Solander died suddenly of apoplexy in 1782; probably his name is now known rather by the Solander case which he invented than by the handsome genus *Solandra* or by the cape, north of Sydney, which bears his name.

On 20 December 1771 Linnaeus wrote to his old friend John Ellis:

> My pupil Sparrman has just sailed for the Cape of Good Hope, and another of my pupils, Thunberg, is to accompany a Dutch embassy to Japan; both of them are competent naturalists. The younger Gmelin is still in Persia, and my friend Falck is in Tartary. Mutis is making splendid botanical discoveries in Mexico. Koenig has found a lot of new things in Tranquebar. Professor Friis Rottböll of Copenhagen is publishing the plants found in Surinam by Rolander. The Arabian discoveries of Forsskål will soon be sent to the press in Copenhagen. . . .

The majority of these travellers were his pupils, and he had good reason to be proud of what they were achieving.

Anders Sparrman, when he became Linnaeus's pupil, had already at the age of seventeen travelled to China as surgeon in one of the Swedish East India Company's ships, returning two years later with a rich harvest of plants. In December 1771, when he was twenty-three, he sailed for the Cape where he became tutor to the Resident's children and botanized energetically in his leisure moments. A year later Captain Cook, at the beginning of his second voyage round the world, called at the Cape, and Sparrman was invited to join the crew of the *Resolution*, supplementing by his botanical knowledge the zoological knowledge of the Forsters. More than two years and 6,000 nautical miles later he landed again at the Cape, and after eight further months of collecting in South Africa returned in 1776 to Sweden, worn out by his exertions. In 1787 he was again in Africa, this time in Senegal and elsewhere on the west coast with an expedition searching for territory suitable for colonization. After his return to Sweden he was appointed professor of natural history in Stockholm and later assessor to the Medical College. He died in 1820.

The *Sparmannia* (so spelt by the caprice of botanists) is a large shrub belonging to the lime family. *S. africana*, sometimes seen in English greenhouses, has big, white-petalled flowers whose clustered stamens, when gently blown upon, open like the unfolding tentacles of a sea-anemone.

After the death of Linnaeus in 1778 and of Solander in 1782, the Linnaean mantle fell upon Carl Peter Thunberg. A Smålander like his teacher, he came

Anders Sparrman.

to Uppsala at the age of eighteen and in 1770, after taking a doctorate in medicine, went with a travelling scholarship to Paris. In Amsterdam on his way home he met Linnaeus's old friend Johan Burman, and his son who like himself was a Linnaean pupil; through their influence Thunberg entered the service of the Dutch East India Company as a surgeon and sailed first to the Cape of Good Hope, with the intention of ultimately reaching Japan under Dutch protection. The money for this project was advanced by wealthy Dutchmen eager to enrich their gardens with plants from Japan, which was at that time closed to all but the Dutch, and the Germans and Scandinavians employed by them.

Carl Peter Thunberg, engraved after a painting by P. Krafft, 1808.

'Don't be afraid of exposing yourself to some degree of danger,' wrote Linnaeus from the comfort and safety of his armchair in Uppsala; 'anyone who hopes to reach a glorious goal must take many risks. . . . This voyage is not as perilous as some people here would have us believe. The Norwegian coast is the most dangerous part of the journey; following winds will carry you from Sweden to China, and there is less to fear after you pass the Dutch coast.'

Thunberg reached the Cape in April 1772 and remained in South Africa for nearly three years. Here he collected some 300 new species and dispatched many herbarium specimens to the delighted Linnaeus, who wrote to him in 1773 when he heard that Thunberg was about to set out on one of his big expeditions into the interior:

> Let me know the route you propose to take on your long journey. I am most anxious to live until you get back; what a joy it would be for me to be present on that great day, and to touch with my hands the laurels that will crown your brow. Lay for me a wreath of flowers on the altar of African Flora. . . . I gather that you intend going to the Indies next spring. May God grant you a prosperous voyage. Think of me as often as I think of you, which is whenever I touch your plants; when I study them it is as if I were talking to you.

In 1775 Thunberg sailed to Java, from where, like the German naturalist and scholar Engelbert Kaempfer nearly a century earlier, he was able to continue his journey to Japan to become one of the Company's staff at its trading post in Nagasaki harbour. Thunberg remained in Japan for fifteen months, for most of the time kept virtually a prisoner (as were all foreigners) on the tiny island of Deshima – it was 236 paces by 82 paces and linked to the mainland by a guarded causeway – and unable until February 1776 even to set foot in the town of Nagasaki. Desperate to learn about the Japanese flora he used to go daily through the fodder brought by Japanese servants to feed the swine and cattle penned on Deshima and pick out specimens for his herbarium. He also encouraged Japanese interpreters to bring him plants, many of which must have come from local gardens. His one opportunity to gather a few for himself on the mainland came on the annual visit of homage to the Shogun at Yedo (Tokyo).

Thunberg returned to Sweden by way of Java, Ceylon (where he spent six months), Holland, England and Germany, reaching Uppsala after nine years of absence to find that his teacher had died the year before. In 1784, on the death of the younger Linnaeus, Thunberg was appointed Professor of Botany at Uppsala, a post which he held with great distinction until his own death, at the age of eighty-five, in 1828.

Thunberg's classic *Flora Japonica* was published in 1784, his *Prodromus Plantarum Capensium* between 1794 and 1800, and his *Flora Capensis* in 1823. An account of his travels (the cost of which had been in part paid for by the sale of faked unicorn's horn to credulous Orientals) appeared in four volumes between 1788 and 1793, and was immediately translated into German, French, and English. Of these books Goerke writes, 'A striking feature of Thunberg's works is their cold objectivity. His interest in nature was purely scientific. He never sought adventure, nor does it seem that the beauty of a foreign scene, the strangeness of new plants or the circumstances of their discovery particularly moved him. His principal concern was the practical value of what he found. . . .' Comte A. de Fortia de Piles, who was in Sweden in 1791, has left an interesting account of Thunberg's cabinet of curios at Uppsala; it may be read in Pinkerton's *Voyages*, vol. vi, pp. 478–9.

'As long as in our paradise of flowers there wanders a single botanist,' wrote the South African botanist, Verduyn den Boer, 'so long will the name of Thunberg be held in honoured remembrance'; and gardeners who grow in their greenhouses the delightful *Thunbergia alata* ('Black-eyed Susan'[1]) may care, as they tend it, to remember the great traveller whose name it bears.

Such were some of the men whom Linnaeus sent out to distant and dangerous lands in order that man's knowledge of the world's flora and fauna might be extended. When he learned of the perils to which they had been exposed, and the hardships that they had endured, when he remembered those who had died or who had returned with broken health, he may well have recalled what he had written in 1737 in his *Critica botanica* while reviewing the lives of earlier botanical travellers: 'Good God! When I observe the fate of botanists, upon my word I doubt whether to call them sane or mad in their devotion to plants.'

[1] Curiously enough this name is also sometimes given to *Rudbeckia hirta*, another plant with Linnaean associations.

One of four Chinese paintings brought back to Linnaeus from China.

7.

Skåne 1749

In the autumn of 1747 Linnaeus was invited to make a journey through Skåne (Scania) in the following summer.

He was none too enthusiastic. He had been overworking for years past and the strain was telling on him; he felt that the time had come when he might reasonably be allowed to sit back and leave the rough and tumble of travel to his pupils; at forty he was already almost an old man. He therefore wrote to Elvius, the Secretary of the Royal Academy of Science:

> I have always wanted to make a careful survey of Skåne, because it is the part of Sweden that I like best. But when I think of the long distances to be travelled and the labour that this will involve, my head reels. I am wearing myself out before my time, and there will be no one to look after my children. . . . Things get more difficult each day, and one has to feed oneself and one's family decently and adequately.
>
>   If I go,
>
> | | |
> |---|---:|
> | I shall wear out a carriage | 400 dalers |
> | I shall wear out a whole suit of clothes | 400 dalers |
> | I shall have to forgo my private coaching, which in the summer might earn me | 800 dalers |
> | I might even have a couple of presidencies | 200 dalers |
> | | 1,800 dalers |
>
> In addition to all this I shall have to pay a secretary, with the result that I shall not make a penny out of it but merely lose 1,800 dalers and wear myself out – when all the time I might have been sitting comfortably in my room. . . . Finally I shall have to publish an account of my travels, which will mean a lot of hard work, the risk of being misunderstood, and so on. . . . I am ready to work to train competent successors – men who can travel until they have travelled as far and worked as hard as I have and who will then have an excuse for being weary.

But the King wanted the survey made, and the only concession that Linnaeus could get was to have the journey postponed until 1749.

As things turned out, the year 1748 was to prove one of the unhappiest of Linnaeus's whole life. In May came the death, at the age of seventy-four, of Nils

Linnaeus. His elder son was unable to be at his bedside, and almost the last words his father spoke were, 'Carl is not here. Carl has brought me much happiness.' He was succeeded at the Rectory by his younger son, the 'Bee King' Samuel.

His father's death affected Carl deeply, and by ill chance there followed hot upon it a number of petty irritations which at any other time might have been seen in their true perspective. First came friction with an old friend, Dr Halenius, Professor of Divinity at Uppsala, who attacked a disputation promoted by Linnaeus. Even more disturbing was the quite unexpected hostility of a yet dearer friend, Baron Carl Hårleman, who criticized the unconventional dress and behaviour of Linnaeus's students when they took part in botanical forays. Linnaeus was, he said, antagonizing many of their closest friends among the professors at Uppsala, whose staider methods of instruction were no longer attracting the best students; and he warned Linnaeus of the great danger of 'setting oneself too far ahead'. It was, of course, the familiar story of old, un-imaginative, and probably idle dons resenting the success of a cleverer and younger man; and what wounded Linnaeus so deeply – 'almost killed him', he wrote in his Autobiography, and 'left him for two months unable to sleep' – was that his trusted friend and supposed ally should have sided with the powers of darkness.

Another cause of annoyance was the publication by the brilliant but unstable French doctor, Julien Offray de la Mettrie, a former pupil of Boerhaave, of an article entitled 'L'Homme Plante' in which the Linnaean sexual system was parodied and held up to ridicule. In it mankind was classified as *Dioecia* (male and female flowers on different plants), the male being of the order *Monandria* (one stamen) and the female *Monogynia* (one pistil). The calix was missing, its place being taken by clothes. The petals of the corolla were the limbs, the nectaries the breasts, and so on. The article first appeared in Potsdam, where La Mettrie had taken refuge after being hounded out of France and Holland, and was soon after included in his *L'Homme Machine*, copies of which were publicly burnt in Leyden.[1]

Linnaeus, who at the time of his marriage had apparently seen no harm in a little jesting about monandrian lilies, would have spared himself much un-happiness had he been able to take La Mettrie's squib less seriously and dismiss it from his thoughts; instead he let it rankle, telling Sauvages that he cursed the day when he first began to publish his works, that when *Materia Medica* was finished he would never print another word, and that unless God or man punished La Mettrie as he deserved he would burn what he had so far written of his *Species Plantarum*.

A further pinprick was the sudden enforcement of certain lapsed regulations designed to keep university professors up to the mark. Though Linnaeus, conscientious always, had in his day been a victim of professorial idleness, he now resented various petty restrictions which he could not evade. For example, no professor might go further than seven miles from Uppsala in term-time without informing the Chancellor; and it irked him that, even when he was summoned by the King, he had to apply for leave of absence. The salaries of those who arrived a day late for the start of the term were sharply docked, and there was a new regulation by which a heavy fine was imposed on any professor

[1] Voltaire, a great admirer of Lin-naeus, on being told that La Mettrie accused the latter of classing man 'along with horses and pigs', replied, 'Oui, mais vous conviendrez que, si M. Lin-naeus est un cheval, c'est le premier de tous les chevaux.' ('Yes, but you must agree that if M. Linnaeus is a horse, then he is the first of all horses.')

who published a book abroad – something which Linnaeus believed to be aimed entirely at himself 'since no one else had done so'. Had he been a bachelor, he told Bäck, he would have left Sweden for ever and accepted an offer to succeed Dillenius at Oxford – 'little though I like that nation'; in Sweden people only laughed at him, saying that he would never be content until he had found a fly with one more hair on its body than had ever been seen before. Then Linnaeus was once again bickering with Haller, and there was also a disappointment over a scheme to interest the Swedish government in the production of artificial pearls.

The result of these accumulated troubles and grievances was that in the autumn of 1748 Linnaeus came very near to a nervous breakdown, and for the rest of his life was to be periodically prostrated by fits of morbid depression which happily alternated with long stretches when he was gay and full of zest for work. So it was really all for the best that *force majeure* was about to make him leave Uppsala for several months; the trip might prove exhausting, but at least it would take his mind off troubles at home.

The Skåne journey. Places Linnaeus visited which are mentioned in the text are underlined.

195

Samuel Linnaeus.

On 29 April 1749 Linnaeus left Uppsala with an amanuensis, an under-graduate named Olof Söderberg, and headed for the south on his last provincial tour; he had never before set out so early in the season, but the spring was forward that year and he was going to the southernmost province in the country, one whose climate he describes as being 'almost as mild as Holland's'.

It took Linnaeus a fortnight to reach Vrigstad, in Småland, where he spent his birthday, 13 May (Old Style), with his sister, Fru Höök, and several other members of his family, including his brother Samuel who had come over from Stenbrohult. Two days later he was in Stenbrohult, where he wrote sadly that he 'found the birds flown, the nest burnt and the brood scattered, so that I hardly recognized the place where I had been reared. . . . The very uncommon wild flowers which used to grow here, and which had been the delight of my childhood, had not survived. Twenty years ago I had known everyone in the parish; now I found hardly a score of them left.'

On 19 May, shortly before reaching Kristianstad, Linnaeus saw by the road-side a big recently felled oak. By studying the distances between the various rings, and later consulting the meteorological records, he was able to establish that growth was in general greater in warm summers than in cool ones; thus he was a pioneer in dendrochronology (dating by tree-rings). The following day he set off for Åhus, the port of Kristianstad:

> Many people told us that in summer, between Kristianstad and Åhus . . . there were some deliciously scented sandy tracts, and that this scent was at its strongest at midsummer and particularly in the morning and the evening. They also thought that both rosemary and lavender grew there, as they do in the fields in Spain, and we were curious to discover what it was that pleased their senses. When we reached the place we found that all the scent came from the flowers of a pink [*Dianthus arenarius*] which we had never seen further north; but from now on we came across it here in Skåne on every sand-field – and, strangely enough, even on drifting sand – in such quantities as to make it a common weed. . . .

Here and elsewhere in Linnaeus's writings we find a strange similarity to the prose and poetry of the Far East. Even more Oriental in feeling is the following passage from his introduction to the *Skånska Resa*, which reads almost like one of Arthur Waley's translations of Chinese poetry; how fresh, how revolutionary, must such writing have seemed in an age of artificiality!

> BROWN with Sorrel are whole fields lying fallow.
> BLUE of the brightest are sloping fields covered with *Echium*, surpassing in splendour anything that can be imagined.
> YELLOW and brightly gleaming are the fields of *Chrysanthemum*, former ploughed fields of *Hypericum* and sand-fields of *Stoechas citrina*.
> RED as blood are often whole slopes of *Viscaria*.
> WHITE as snow are sand-fields of the sweet-smelling *Dianthus*.
> DAPPLED are the waysides with *Echium*, *Cichorium*, *Anchusa* and *Malva*. . . .

In so glorious and fertile a land, Linnaeus continues, the animals are no less wonderful than the flowers. Scanian cattle are bigger than those in the north; such splendid horses, such sheep and such swine, are not to be found elsewhere

196

in Sweden. And as he comes to the subject of his beloved birds he once more waxes lyrical:

GEESE gleam white on every hand, flying, snapping and crying in the big fields; and oats being so abundant, you can hardly find an old woman hereabouts who does not keep geese.

Linnaeus often mentioned frogs, and when, on 30 May, he reached Andrarum he wrote of the 'corn-frogs' there – so named because their cry is first heard when it is time to sow the corn:

The corn-frogs croak towards evening, making a sound like big bells rung three or four miles away although they are undoubtedly in the nearby marshes. It seems to me very extraordinary that the call of this creature should give the impression of coming from a great distance. If, in summer, one puts a bucket upside down on one's head, goes beneath the surface of a lake and then calls into the bucket, that too sounds like a cry from a long way off.

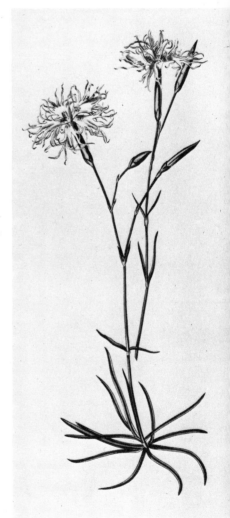

Dianthus arenarius, from the *Botanical Magazine*, 1829.

The reader of Linnaeus's travel books snatches eagerly at any little episode which throws light on his character or behaviour. One such is the story of the divining-rod at Tunbyholm, where Baron Esbiörn Reuterholm had an estate; in Skåne there were many big estates, and Linnaeus was frequently entertained by their owners and shown their gardens and collections:

A divining-rod is a curious piece of trickery which purports to persuade people that it can reveal where metals are hidden, and every now and then my secretary would pick a hazel-twig, split it into two equal parts and entertain the company with them. The same thing happened again here, one person hiding his silver tobacco-box and another his watch in the bushes, both of which my secretary was fairly successful in finding. I had never believed in the rod and had not wanted it mentioned, for I thought that my companions and my secretary were in league to hoax the company; so I went off to a large field to the north of the cow-shed, removed a small piece of turf, buried my purse and replaced the sod so carefully that there was no trace of the ground having been disturbed. I marked the spot by a big buttercup which was growing there – the only tall plant in the whole field. Then I rejoined the party, told them what I had done and invited my secretary to find the ducats with his rod. . . .

My secretary was delighted to have the chance of making me take a more sympathetic view of his rod, at which I had always jeered, and the company was curious to see it vindicate itself. My secretary searched for a good hour, while I, who remained with my hosts, had the satisfaction of seeing the rod used in vain; because since the purse could not be found the rod became an object of ridicule. Later I went myself to recover the purse; but when I got to the field I found that our diviners had so trampled down the grass that there remained not the slightest trace of my buttercup, and I was obliged to look for my ducats as hopelessly as had the rod.

I had no desire to lose a hundred ducats on a wager with the rod, so we all started a tiresome and ridiculous search which proved fruitless. At last I had to admit defeat. Then the Baron and my secretary asked me to point out where I thought I had buried the purse, and this I did; however, the wretched rod would not point, but drew us in a completely different direction. Finally, when we were all tired of the rod and I was feeling pretty miserable, my secretary, who was standing on the other side of the field, announced that if the purse was not there he had no idea where it could be. I did not even bother to join him, because he was nowhere near the place where I thought I had hidden it; but Baron Oxenstierna got down on his knees and began searching, and very soon lifted with one finger the sod under which the ducats were lying.

So on that occasion the rod did work. . . . If I witness one or two more successful experiments I suppose I shall be obliged to believe in something that I do not in the least want to believe in. . . . But I never again want to risk so many ducats putting it to the test.

On 10 June Linnaeus reached Lund, the little university town where he had studied in 1727. He found that big changes had taken place, many of the improvements being due to the energy and generosity of the Chancellor, Count Carl Gyllenborg. Even the flora was no longer the same:

I now went to examine the local wild flowers on the ruined town-walls of Lund – flowers which twenty years ago had given me such pleasure – and found how great a change had taken place in so short a time. *Pulicaria* [*P. vulgaris*, marsh fleabane] in my day grew in one or two places only; now it is to be found on every wall. *Carduus nutans* [musk thistle], which I had not seen outside Gotland, was also as common on the walls as the former. *Anagallis* [pimpernel], which is never to be found further north, grew there too and in the fallow fields; it opens all its flowers at 8 a.m. and closes them at midday. . . .

While in Skåne Linnaeus made a special study of the time of day at which various flowers opened and shut. He wanted the information for a floral clock on which he had long been working – 'a clock by which one could tell the time, even in cloudy weather, as accurately as by a watch'. Two of the plants he observed were a *Crepis* (hawk's-beard) and a *Leontodon* (hawkbit):

The *Crepis* began to open its flowers at 6 a.m. and they were fully open by 6.30. The *Leontodon* opened all its flowers between 6 and 7 a.m. In the evening the *Crepis* began to close its flowers at 6.30, and by 7 all were closed; but the *Leontodon* shut all its flowers between 5 and 6 p.m. Experiment was then made with the same flowers indoors in a vase of water. The *Crepis* now opened at 6.30 a.m. but the *Leontodon* not before 7 a.m. The *Crepis* closed at 7 p.m. and the *Leontodon* at 6 p.m.

One of his correspondents, when he was told about the floral clock, wrote that Linnaeus would soon put all the watchmakers in Sweden out of business and thus make himself highly unpopular.

While at Lund Linnaeus also noted:

Every morning early, in every village and town on the plain, the shepherds blew their horns and shook their rattles. Then the girls let out the cows, which were collected from all the houses at the same time and led by the herdsmen to their pasturage – and in such an orderly way that it was a pleasure to see. It would be a good idea to do the same in many towns further north in the country.

But of Scanian agricultural methods in general, Linnaeus had a very low opinion:

The practice of agriculture in Skåne seems, to us who live near Stockholm, for the most part as incompetent as the ploughs there are long. You see a farmer harness eight

to twelve men to draw a plough which as far as weight is concerned could be drawn by two horses. You see how the farm labourers shout and sing to herd their sheep, often from a couple of miles away; how they sow their rye long before Christmas and, though the climate is splendid, finally harvest from it only a few ears of corn.

But the Scanian farmer holds as obstinately to the ways of his forefathers as our young people clamour to change them. They rely as much on traditional methods as we on new ideas and projects. They are as sure of their ground as we are uncertain of ours. A serious illness is never cured, except by sheer good luck, unless the doctor is properly trained in medicine. I have taken on myself to diagnose the illness; I must now see if I can suggest the cure.

On reaching Malmö Linnaeus was laid low by one of his recurrent attacks of migraine, which on this occasion resulted from drinking a glass of sloe gin. Sometimes it was alcohol – sour wine in particular – which brought them on, sometimes cold weather or strong winds. Or even a sharp disappointment: a few years later he recorded in his Autobiography an occasion when an attack was induced by annoyance at the loss, through a gardener's stupidity, of some long desired cochineal insects brought back for him by a pupil, Daniel Rolander, from Surinam:

Rolander . . sent to Linnaeus (who was lecturing just at that time) a cactus with cochineals in a jar. The gardener opened the jar, took out the plant, cleansed it from the dirt (and of course from the insects) and replaced it in the jar, so that the insects, though they arrived alive, were destroyed before Linnaeus could even get a sight of them; and thus vanished all his hopes of rearing them with advantage in the orangery. This grieved him so much that he had the most dreadful fits of migraine he ever felt.

On 23 June Linnaeus was at Skanör and Falsterbo – villages once famous for their herring-fisheries but today little seaside resorts, their ancient churches partly buried in the drifting sands. Of Skanör he wrote:

It was Midsummer's Eve, and young farm hands and girls had gathered in the market-place. The men had brought poles, the girls flowers. The poles were joined together to form a very high mast with cross-beams, and within a few minutes these were all covered with flowers and wreaths. . . . The specially prepared maypole, which was very splendid, was raised with much shouting and cheering, and although it was raining the young people danced round it all night.
June 24th: Midsummer's Day
Games played by the old Romans were still played here. In Lent the young men take a barrel, bore holes in it through which they pass a rope, and after they have put one or two live cats into it they suspend it above the street between two houses; then with poles in their hands they ride past the barrel, and the one who succeeds in smashing the barrel to bits, though he may not be much of a hero, is called king, is adorned with many garlands, and may choose any of the company of girls as his queen. Then come dancing and other gay pastimes.

It seems strange to us today that Linnaeus should describe this cruel sport without adverse comment, but the sight of a criminal hanging by the roadside left him equally unmoved.

Kalmia angustifolia, acquatint and stipple engraving after Reinagle, from the *Temple of Flora*. 'High rise the cloud-capp'd hills where KALMIA <u>glows</u> with <u>dazzling beauty</u>, 'mid a <u>waste of snows</u>. . . .' (Shaw).

201

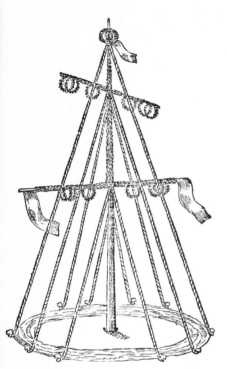

Maypole in Scania, from *Skånska Resa*, 1751.

From Ramlöse, where he arrived on 11 July, Linnaeus could see the island of Ven (or Hven) on which the astronomer Tycho Brahe had built his famous observatory; but he makes no mention of visiting the island, or of crossing to Copenhagen while he was at Malmö. At Helsingborg he looked across the Sound to Elsinore, remembering no doubt the day, fourteen years earlier, when he had set out from there with Sohlberg for Holland. Continuing along the coast he came to the promontory of Kullen, with its dramatic granite cliffs. At Ängelholm he turned inland, heading east and visiting so many grand country-houses that, as Mrs Caddy says, this part of his tour 'reads like a royal progress'. On 27 July he was again at Kristianstad and eager to get back to Uppsala and his Garden because 'it can happen in Uppland that in August one gets a frost three nights running, and with the first frost the tenderest plants suffer'.

But he could not pass through Stenbrohult without breaking his journey, and he also spent a night or two at near-by Ryssby to see his sister Sophia whose husband, Johan Collin, was Rector there. At Ryssby he had the satisfaction of finding a plant never before recorded in Sweden, one which he had missed on his youthful botanical rambles in the neighbourhood; this was *Isoëtes lacustris*, or quillwort – an aquatic perennial, more interesting than beautiful, which is sometimes used in aquaria. After taking leave of his brother and sister he travelled so swiftly that by 13 August he was back at Uppsala. He found on arrival that there had been no frost, and that even his very rare little Indian plants were safe.

The preparation for the press of Linnaeus's *Philosophia botanica*, his term of office in 1750 as Rector of the University, and a very sharp attack of gout, combined to delay the publication of the *Skånska Resa* until 1751. This was the gout attack mentioned in the previous chapter, when Löfling acted as his amanuensis; and in a letter to Giseke Linnaeus describes how he accidentally discovered a cure for it:

> In 1750 I suffered such torture from sciatic gout that I could hardly walk. The pain became so intolerable that after seven sleepless nights I wanted to take opium; but a friend who came to see me in the evening prevented me. My wife asked me if I would like some wild strawberries. 'Very much,' I said; it was the beginning of their season and they were delicious. An hour later I fell asleep, and did not wake until 2 a.m., amazed to find that I had slept in spite of the pain. . . . I asked if there were any more strawberries, and was given what were left; I ate them and slept till morning. The pain had settled near my ankles; the following day I ate as many strawberries as I could, and a day later the pain had completely gone. I feared at first that there might be gangrene; but the flesh was perfectly healthy. Feeble though I was, I was able to get up.
>
> The disease returned the following year and also the year after, but in an ever milder form and the wild strawberries always cured me. Unfortunately I cannot grow strawberries in the winter, and I have wholly failed to preserve them.

However, the Queen came to the rescue and ordered that wild strawberries should be grown for his special use in the royal hot-houses. It is amusing to learn that when the news of Linnaeus's miraculous remedy became generally known, so great was the sudden demand for strawberries that their price rose to ten times the normal figure.

The publication of *Skånska Resa* was not only delayed; it also ran into trouble. As every author knows to his cost, it is difficult to write a book without giving offence in some quarter or other, and Linnaeus had had a foreboding that something he wrote might be 'misunderstood'. The little row that he had had with his friend Baron Hårleman three years earlier had been forgiven and forgotten, and the Baron had in fact joined Linnaeus for a few days in Scania; now he chanced to see the proofs of the *Skånska Resa*, where he read with indignation that Linnaeus gave his blessing to the old Swedish custom of cleaning the ground by setting fire to the stubble – a practice that he himself had condemned in print. This led to the exchange of bitter letters and to a good deal of unpleasantness.

In a long letter to the Secretary of the Royal Academy of Science Linnaeus poured out his grievances, complaining that trouble-makers had been at work and lamenting that with him-industry always seemed to provoke hatred and jealousy. He cared as little, he said, whether or not a farmer burnt his land as whether or not he smoked a pipe. But he had now decided to print a new leaf in which the offending passage would be replaced by some innocuous observations on manure; a few copies with the unexpurgated text have, however, survived. Hårleman appreciated the gesture, and soon the two men were once more reconciled.

Skånska Resa was dedicated to Count Claes Ekeblad, Tessin's right-hand man. Linnaeus's accounts of his travels to the two Baltic islands and through West Gothland had been dedicated to Crown Prince Adolf Fredrik and Crown Princess Lovisa Ulrika respectively, and in the formal prose that was fitting; the dedication to Ekeblad, on the other hand, is unconventional and poetical, and the trouble that Linnaeus took over its composition is proved by three rough drafts which have survived. After listing the various honours of the illustrious Count, Linnaeus proceeds:

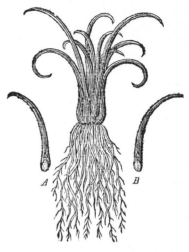

The peasant rejoices in his green field,
The Hottentot delights in his ugly brats,
Authors hug themselves self-complacently over their works;
   But
No fruits reward the tiller's labours
   Unless God sends favourable weather;
The success of youth is vain
   Unless He who is above all shows grace;
The sciences are pursued in vain
   Unless the Patron favours the cause;
    And therefore
Ploughmen invoke the Heavens for blessings,
Parents invite a worthy Godfather for their child,
Authors dedicate their works to a Noble Patron. . . .

Isoëtes lacustris (quillwort) from *Skånska Resa*, 1751, and below, title-page of *Skånska Resa*, 1751.

The book was well received and Linnaeus was urged to make further journeys; but he had had enough. As he told the Secretary of the Royal Academy of Science, 'Many a time have I set sail to bring back gold from Ophir, only to come home a broken man, my ship disabled and her sails in tatters. Another voyage might well be the end of me.'

8.

Friends and books

It was to Abraham Bäck that Linnaeus turned, again and again in the latter part of his life, for consolation and the kind of sympathetic understanding that his wife could not provide, and that even Bäck's marriage in 1755 did not interrupt.

Bäck, after he had failed to win the professorship of medicine at Uppsala, had gone abroad for several years, returning to Sweden in 1745. It was now that the intimate and lasting friendship between himself and Linnaeus was sealed – a friendship that is recorded in more than 500 letters written to him by Linnaeus. These serve almost as a skeleton autobiography of the last thirty years of Linnaeus's life, and it is much to be regretted that scarcely any of the other half of the correspondence has survived. Bäck, who was six years younger than Linnaeus, settled in Stockholm, where in 1748, after failing to get appointed State Physician, he bought a Court practice for what Linnaeus considered the absurdly large sum of 14,000 dalers. Four years later he founded the still extant Seraphim Hospital, and in the same year became President of the College of Medicine and an Archiater; for many years he was also Physician in Ordinary to the King. He died in 1795 at the age of eighty-two.

Linnaeus and Bäck were close as brothers; indeed Linnaeus commonly addressed him as 'Min Kiäreste Broder' ('My dearest Brother') – abbreviated as 'M.K.B.' – as was customary in Sweden between intimate friends. It was taken for granted that when Bäck came to Uppsala he would stay with Linnaeus, and that when Linnaeus had to visit Stockholm he would lodge with Bäck. There was nothing that the two men enjoyed more than a long and cosy evening together after the womenfolk had been packed off to bed, when for hours on end they could gossip over their pipes or discuss the state of medicine in Sweden. Every man who is married to a Fru Linnaea should find himself a Herr Bäck.

Going to stay with Bäck, especially if he could contrive to leave his wife behind, always revived Linnaeus. 'Ever since my visit to Stockholm,' he wrote in June 1751, 'I have felt cheerful, brisk, able to work, whereas before I was depressed, melancholy, and incapable of doing anything.' Bäck's disappointments and successes affected him almost as deeply as did his own. Disappointments – for example, Bäck's failure to be appointed State Physician in Stockholm – were soothed by lengthy letters full of Biblical quotations; successes were celebrated by the drinking of many toasts, and when Bäck became President of the

College of Medicine Linnaeus declared that he was going to 'break the necks of some bottles of wine, even if it brings on a migraine'.

During 1754 almost all the Linnaeus family and household fell ill in turn, and once again it was the solicitude of Bäck which sustained Linnaeus in these dark days. In February his third daughter, Sara Stina, a child of three, very nearly died. Then on Christmas Eve his wife was struck down by the dreaded Uppsala fever, and for nearly a month, while her life hung in the balance, he hardly left her bedside. It was, he lamented to Bäck, a great burden being a married man with a lot of children.

But it was a warning that went unheeded, for Bäck, who had shown every sign of being a confirmed bachelor, had just got engaged – and to a girl less than half his age. For some reason or other Linnaeus did not go to Stockholm for the wedding in March, but he celebrated it in Uppsala at a dinner given by Böttiger, the University Apothecary; 'We drank your healths in formal toasts,' he told Bäck, 'and I quite let myself go – because I hadn't been so delighted for ages. I swore that I wouldn't leave the house before the [hour when the] bride-groom left with his bride. My wife thought I would not return home that night; but in fact I did – at 1 o'clock.' Linnaeus welcomed Fru Bäck as a 'sister'. He became in due course godfather to the first child – a girl – and grew much attached to one of the sons, christened Carl in his honour, who died of con-sumption before he was seventeen.

Abraham Bäck, engraved after a painting by Gustav Lundberg, 1763.

In 1756 the royal family unsuccessfully attempted a *coup d'état*. Lovisa Ulrika had long resented that her husband was no more than a puppet king, dancing to the strings controlled by the Diet. She forced him to assert himself by refusing to sign certain documents submitted to him by his ministers; the ministers replied by rubber-stamping them. The Queen counted upon the support of the army, but her conspiracy was discovered; many heads fell, and many Court officials were unsaddled. Neither Bäck nor Linnaeus openly concerned himself with politics, but both were perhaps fortunate to come unscathed through a crisis which had for its only result a yet further diminution of the power of the monarch.

The year 1756 was a bad one for Sweden. A disastrous harvest in the previous summer had brought the country, already torn by internal strife, very close to famine, and set Linnaeus investigating what substitutes if any could be found for wheat in the making of bread. Then in the summer came the start of the Seven Years War.

One of Linnaeus's occupations at this time and later was the cataloguing of the royal collections and that of his friend and patron, Count Tessin.

In the twentieth century the rich man achieves, or attempts to achieve, a reputation for culture by collecting Rembrandts or Cézannes or Picassos, as the fashion of the moment dictates; in the eighteenth century, and especially if he lived north of the Alps, he was just as likely to invest his money in objects of natural history as in *objets d'art*. For this cult of the 'cabinet of curios' in Sweden Linnaeus was largely responsible: 'Linnaeus [wrote Linnaeus] had brought natural history in Sweden from the lowest place to the very highest, because it was loved and cultivated by the great in the land and even by royalty. This is what industry can achieve!'

205

Illustration from Seba's *Thesaurus*, Plate CXI. In May 1753 Linnaeus wrote to Bäck: 'I am delighted that the little elephant has arrived safely. He may be expensive, but he is much admired and as rare as a diamond.'

Below: Crystal from Linnaeus's *Museum Tessinianum*, 1753.

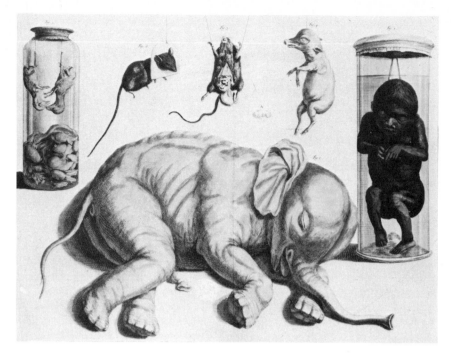

A typical collector was Count Tessin, who specialized in minerals and snails while his Countess showed a preference for the vegetable kingdom. Linnaeus published a catalogue of the Count's collection – *Museum Tessinianum* (1753), a handsome folio with twelve engraved plates – receiving in return 'a gold watch and a copy of Rumphius's *Herbarium Amboinense*, together worth 100 plåtar'. But the greatest Swedish collectors of the day were King Adolf Fredrik and his consort, Lovisa Ulrika.

The King had begun collecting while still Crown Prince, and in 1746

Linnaeus had written a short dissertation on his cabinet; but five years later he began work on full-length accounts of the royal collections, which were housed in the castles of Ulriksdal and Drottningholm – a task that brought him into frequent contact with the King and Queen. The King's collection at Ulriksdal was mainly zoological – 'a splendid cabinet of various animals preserved in alcohol, innumerable stuffed birds, and an unbelievable quantity of pinned insects and shells in little boxes'. It contained a number of human embryos, including the foetus from a miscarriage of Lovisa Ulrika, and an elephant's embryo purchased from Seba in Amsterdam; many of the objects had been bought abroad, some of them for enormous sums. The embryos were kept hidden behind a silk curtain so that no female visitor might come upon them unawares. To Bäck Linnaeus wrote in December 1752: 'I have been working day and night at the description of His Majesty's natural history cabinet, and my eyes are so sore that I can hardly close them.'

It was at Drottningholm, the charming royal palace which lies about six miles to the west of Stockholm, that the Queen kept her 'magnificent collection of shells and insects from India – a collection unrivalled anywhere in the world'. In 1751, wrote Pulteney, 'Linnaeus was commanded to go to Drottningholm to describe them. For the shells, where no one had prepared the way, he unexpectedly found himself obliged to create a new system of classification. He had the honour of conversing every day with this great and excellent Queen and with his gracious Sovereign; thus, contrary to his inclination, he found himself a courtier.'

The courtier *malgré lui* proved, however, a considerable success. The Queen wrote to her mother while Linnaeus was cataloguing her collection of butterflies and other insects: 'Je m'amuse à le ranger avec un professeur d'Upsal, qui est très grand connaisseur et physicien. C'est un homme fort amusant, qui a tout l'esprit du monde sans en avoirs les manières, et qui m'amuse infiniment par

Drottningholm Palace 1692, from *Suecica Antiqua et Hodierna*.

207

Dodecatheon meadia, the American cowslip, aquatint and stipple engraving after Henderson, from the *Temple of Flora*.

Overleaf: Seba's *Thesaurus*, plate XXXVIII: Fig. 1: 'four-eyed' opossum, presumably *Philander opossum* (L.), *Didelphys opossum* L. with young. Figs. 2 and 3: three-banded armadillo, *Tolypeutes tricinctus* (L.) cited by Linnaeus under *Dasypus tricinctus* L. Fig. 4: black-capped lory, *Domicilla lory* (L.), *Psittacus lory* L. Fig. 5: king bird-of-paradise, *Cicinnurus regius* (L.), cited by Linnaeus under *Paradisaea regia* L. Fig. 6: unidentified bird. Figs. 7 and 8: leaves of *Belila Orientalis* or Stavadi, and *Valli Cari capoeli*. The parrot used to say 'Good Sir, good-morning, a glass of wine' in Dutch, but when it changed owners it pined and died, and was pickled by Seba.

ces deux raisons. Les soirs, il est obligé de se promener avec le Roi, et il ne se passe point de jour qu'il ne trouve moyen de mettre tout le monde en bonne humeur.'[1]

Linnaeus was shown many marks of the royal favour and was among those privileged to play blind-man's-buff with the Queen and the courtiers. On such occasions it was a serious breach of etiquette for anyone to catch the Queen; but Linnaeus, when he became blindman, 'continued to see a little', and deliberately caught her. 'It is *I*!' cried the Queen indignantly. Linnaeus took no notice of the reproof and clapped her on the head: 'Those who play a game,' he said, 'must abide by its rules!'

The catalogue of the King's Collection, *Museum S.R.M. Adolphi Friderici*, the first zoological work in which the binomial nomenclature was employed, was published in 1754 in a splendid folio volume with thirty-three plates – two of monkeys, nine of fishes and twenty-two of snakes; a slim octavo unillustrated second volume appeared ten years later. In the Preface to the first volume, which has been delightfully translated by Sir J. E. Smith under the title *Reflections on the Study of Nature* (1785), Linnaeus surveys the mineral, vegetable and animal kingdoms (in that order) and praises their Creator in almost Biblical prose:

Here the ponderous and shining *metals* are constantly forming; the ductile *gold*, which eludes the violence of fire, and which can be extended in length and breadth to an almost incredible degree. . . .

The Vegetable Kingdom. . . . Of all its productions, the first covering of the earth was furnished by the wintry *mosses*; of such variety in their forms, that they scarcely yield to herbs in number; and although extremely minute, yet of so admirable a structure, that they undoubtedly excel the stately palms of India. . . .

The dumb *fishes* which glitter at the bottom of the waters, and which surpass birds in number, find an ample repast prepared for them in the numberless worms which have their dwellings there. . . .

The winged inhabitants of the air, which excel all other animals in the beauty of their forms, find in the loftiest trees a rich provision of insects for their sustenance: here they modulate their harmonious throats to the tender melody of love, preparatory to their producing new tributes for the ornament of future seasons. . . .

Quadrupeds, which wander and sport in the fields, convert all other things to their use: by their joint endeavours they purge the earth from putrefying carcases; by their voracious appetites they fix bounds to the number of living creatures; and they join in the contracts of love; and, when urged by hunger, unite in pursuit of their prey. . . .

The Author of nature has frequently decorated even the minutest insects, and worms themselves, which inhabit the bottom of the sea, in so exquisite a manner, that the most polished metal looks dull beside them. The Great Golden Beetle (*Buprestis gigantea*) of the Indies has its head studded with ornaments like precious stones, brilliant as the finest gold; and the *Aphrodita aculeata*, reflecting the sun-beams from the depth of the sea, exhibits as vivid colours as the Peacock itself, spreading its jewelled train. . . .

The less sumptuous but far more substantial catalogue of the Queen's collection, *Museum S.R.M. Ludovicae Ulricae*, also appeared in 1764; about two-thirds of its 720 pages are devoted to insects – a subject to which Linnaeus had given

[1] 'I have been amusing myself by arranging it with an Uppsala professor, a very great connoisseur and doctor, and a very witty man though he doesn't look it; for both these reasons I find him most entertaining. He has to walk each evening with the King, and not a day passes when he does not contrive to put us all in a good temper.'

Fig. 8.

Fig. 5.

Fig. 8.

Fig. 6.

Fig. 1.

Fig. 8.

A

Fig. 3.

TAB. XXXVI

Fig. 4.

Fig. 7.

Fig. 2.

Pæonia communis
vel fœmina
C. B. Pin. 323.

Pæonia femina. (Lin:)

much thought – and the remainder to shells. Lovisa Ulrika rewarded the author with 'a fine gold ring set with an oriental ruby. . . . But what gave Linnaeus most pleasure was that the Queen asked him how his son was getting on, and whether he showed an interest in natural history. On hearing that he did, she promised to send him, when he was grown up, to travel through Europe at her own expense.'

It might be imagined that, for a university professor who was conscientiously carrying out his academic duties, who was often far from well, and who now had a sizable family which made many demands on his time, little leisure could be found for writing. In fact, Linnaeus's literary output during his years at Uppsala was prodigious and it is impossible, in the space available, even to list his lesser publications.

The dissertations of which he was really the author, and the papers which he contributed to the *Transactions* of the Royal Academy of Science and other learned journals, range over every aspect of Nature's three kingdoms. He wrote of lemmings and ants, of the three-toed woodpecker, the phosphorescent Chinese grasshopper and the mud-iguana of Carolina; of Siberian buckwheat, bear-berries and rhubarb; of peacock-stones, fossils and crystals. He investigated the causes of leprosy, intermittent fever, the stone and epilepsy in Skåne, and the value of electrical treatment in medicine. He described how to set about creating a museum, and how to make a plaster cast of a flower. To take but a single example to show the labour that a dissertation might involve, in *Pan Suecicus* (1749) he examined information, assembled by himself over many years, on nearly 900 plants, in order to find out which were eaten, and which rejected, by cattle, goats, sheep, horses and pigs. The dissertations – there were about 170 of them – were collected and published in seven volumes entitled *Amoenitates Academicae* (Stockholm, 1749–69), and three further volumes appeared after Linnaeus's death.

Another dissertation was the *Calendarium Florae* or 'Calendar of Flora' (1756), in which Linnaeus, basing his observations upon Uppsala, provided a timetable of the four seasons; it was reprinted by Benjamin Stillingfleet in an English translation in 1762. Many of the Latin names given by Linnaeus to the months closely resemble those coined later for the French Revolutionary Calendar – e.g. *Brumalis* (month of fog – *Brumaire*); *Germinationis* (month of buds – *Germinal*); *Messis* (month of reaping – *Messidor*), and so on. This similarity seems too great to be coincidental.

In addition to these *opuscula* there are major publications. In 1749 came *Materia Medica* – 'literature's classic work on pharmacology', and in its day an invaluable reference book for doctors. It contained, in tabulated form, the names and synonyms of a large number of medicinal plants, together with full information about their countries of origin and their pharmaceutical effect, the illnesses in which they might prove helpful and the doses to administer. Taste and smell dictated their appropriate use – for example, strong-smelling plants affected the nervous system. Linnaeus recommended the choice, so far as was possible, of native plants, not only as being cheaper but also because they were more likely to be fresh and unadulterated. He also included advice on the collection, preservation and preparation of herbs. The much shorter *Clavis Medicinae Duplex*

Peony *(Paeonia officinalis)*, by Claude Aubriet.

THE

CALENDAR of FLORA.

I. REVIVING WINTER MONTH.
From the winter solstice to the vernal æquinox.

Dec. XII.
xxii. *Butter shrinks and separates from the sides of the tub.*
xxiii. *Asp flower buds begin to open.*
Jan. I. i. *Ice on lakes begins to crack.*
ii. *Wooden walls snap in the night. Cold frequently extreme at this time, the greatest observed was 55.7.*
iv. **Horse dung spirts.*
viii. *Epiphany rains.*
xxvi. *St. Paul's rains,*
Feb. II.
xxii. *Very cold nights often between Feb. 20 and 28, called* STEEL NIGHTS.

* Note. This was explained to me by Mr. Solander, an ingenious and learned disciple of Linnæus, now in England, who says, that horse dung, in very severe frost, throws out particles near a foot high, and that no other dung does the like.

S 3   II. THAW-

Page from the English translation of Linnaeus's *Calendarium Florae*.

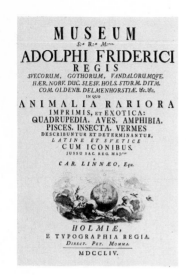

MUSEUM
S.æ R.æ M.ᵗⁱⁱ.
ADOLPHI FRIDERICI
REGIS
SVECORUM, GOTHORUM, VANDALORUMQVE.
HÆR. NORV. DUC. SLESV. HOLS. STORM. DITM.
COM. OLDENB. DELMENHORSTIÆ. &c. &c.
IN QUO
ANIMALIA RARIORA
IMPRIMIS, ET EXOTICA:
QUADRUPEDIA, AVES, AMPHIBIA,
PISCES, INSECTA, VERMES
DESCRIBUNTUR ET DETERMINANTUR,
LATINE ET SVETICE
CUM ICONIBUS
JUSSU SAC. REG. MAJ.ⁱⁱⁱ
A
CAR. LINNÆO, Eqᵘ.

HOLMIÆ,
E TYPOGRAPHIA REGIA.
DIRECT. PET. MOMMA.
MDCCLIV.

Title-page of Linnaeus's catalogue of King Adolf Frederik's collection, 1754.

(*Double Key to Medicine*) – the work which Linnaeus had described as 'the fairest jewel in medicine' – followed in 1766.

In 1751 came *Philosophia botanica*. 'Linnaeus's correspondents [wrote Linnaeus in his Autobiography] had every year requested him to publish his *Philosophia botanica*, in order that the terms and principles [of his system] might be explained in one work, which Linnaeus considered as a matter of importance, not only to the learned world, but also to his pupils; wherefore this work was concluded.' The book is a complete survey of the Linnaean system, and contains in condensed form a good deal of material that had been dealt with more fully in *Critica botanica*, *Bibliotheca botanica* and other works. At the end are ten explanatory plates illustrating leaf forms, roots, flowers, and so on, some of which had already appeared in *Hortus Cliffortianus*, and short notes on practical matters such as how to organize botanical forays, how to lay out a botanic garden and how to keep a journal when travelling.

Both Rousseau and Goethe were considerably influenced by *Philosophia botanica*. The former, who considered that it contained 'more knowledge than the largest folios', wrote to the delighted Linnaeus on 21 September 1771: 'Alone with Nature and with you I spend happy hours walking in the countryside, and from your *Philosophia botanica* I get more real profit than from all other books on ethics. . . . I read your works, study them and reflect on them; and I revere you and love you with all my heart.' Goethe, who was only two years old when the book first appeared, took a copy of it on his Italian journey in 1786. 'I carried my Linnaeus with me,' he wrote from the Brenner, 'and had his terminology [i.e. system of classification] firmly stamped on my mind.' Towards the end of his life he told Zelter: 'I have recently been re-reading Linnaeus, and was amazed by this extraordinary man. I have learned an enormous amount from him, and not only in botany. With the exception of Shakespeare and Spinoza, I do not know anyone among those no longer living who has so strongly influenced me.'

But Linnaeus's most enduring work, the crowning achievement of the many years he had devoted to his beloved Flora, was his *Species Plantarum* (1753); he himself called it 'the greatest in botany', and all that he had previously written on the subject was, as it were, a preparation for it. Its two volumes run to 1,200 pages, and in them, arranged of course according to the sexual system, are to be found every plant known to him, with its generic and specific name and the synonyms used by previous botanists. No less than 5,900 species are listed, placed in 1,098 genera.

As early as 1733 Linnaeus had mentioned, in a letter to Gustaf Cronhielm, his intention of one day producing such a work, and the two notebooks now in the possession of the Linnean Society show that he was already collecting material for it. In the middle forties he began to attack the book seriously, periods of intense activity alternating with periods of listlessness and exhaustion or of preoccupation with other activities. By 1748 more than half of it was written; then came a whole year when he was either too busy or too worn out to add anything. But on 13 February 1750 he told Johann Gessner that 'when my Scanian journey is finished and printed, I shall, God willing, devote myself entirely to the *Species Plantarum*'. The year saw, however, little progress with his *magnum opus*: it was his turn to be Rector of the University; he was busy with his *Philosophia botanica*; and all too frequently he was ill. In June 1751 his pupil Kalm returned from North America with new material which forced him to revise everything that he had already written. But now all went rapidly ahead, and a year later he was able to write triumphantly to Bäck, 'I have finished my *Species*!' The first volume, which was dedicated to the King and Queen, appeared in May 1753, the second three months later.

Sir William Watson, reviewing *Species Plantarum* in the *Gentleman's Magazine* of December 1754, described it as 'the masterpiece of the most compleat naturalist the world has seen'. But at first not everyone thought the same, and Linnaeus can hardly have been pleased when Collinson wrote to him: 'A celebrated

Emerald tree-boa, *Corallus caninus* (L.), *Boa canina* L.; capuchin monkey, or organ-grinder's monkey, *Cebus capucinus* (L.), *Simia capucina* L.; Sterlet, *Acipenser ruthenus* L. and smaller fish, with two eel-like skinks, from Linnaeus's catalogue of King Adolf Frederik's collection.

botanist desired me to lend him your *Species Plantarum*. He returned me the books with the following observations: "I have very carefully examined Dr Linnaeus's *Species Plantarum*, and do find this to be the most careless of his performances; and through the whole work he seems so vain as to imagine he can prescribe to all the world."' But Linnaeans triumphed. By international agreement the work has now been accepted as the starting-point of modern botanical nomenclature, while zoologists similarly refer back to the publication in 1758 of the first volume of the tenth edition of *Systema Naturae*.

Linnaeus was all his life interested in the problems of divine retribution on earth, and it was probably soon after he had settled in Uppsala that he began to jot down any examples of it that came his way. Fée suggests that the idea may have been in his mind even as far back as the time of his quarrels with Rosén, when his thoughts were full of 'fearful plans of vengeance which finally yielded to the more moderate and rational decision to leave vengeance to God'. At some later, but unascertainable, date Linnaeus collected and gave shape to these rough notes, adding to them various moralizings and reflections on the subject of life and death, together with quotations from the Bible and tags from Latin authors. This bundle of loose sheets, which he entitled *Nemesis Divina*, was intended for no eyes but those of his son, for whom it was to serve as a guide to conduct after his own death. In 1844 these pages, which are now in the Uppsala University Library, were discovered in complete disorder in a private library in Kalmar, and more recently some of the earlier jottings came to light among Linnaeus's papers in London. Various editions of *Nemesis Divina* have been published at one time or another, the latest and most complete being that edited by Bishop Elis Malmeström and Dr Telemak Fredbärj (Stockholm, 1968).

To the average English reader most of *Nemesis Divina* appears as little more than a rag-bag of trite and gossipy anecdotes illustrating the simple, time-worn lessons that 'pride comes before a fall' and 'crime does not pay'; but Swedish scholars are inclined to treat it as a serious philosophical work, and Knut Hagberg devotes a whole chapter of his biography of Linnaeus to a discussion of it. Those who wish to study *Nemesis Divina* in greater detail should turn to this interesting book.

Nemesis Divina is dedicated 'To my only Son' in a curious poem, full of admonitions, which begins:

> You have come into a world that you know not.
> You see it not, but you marvel at its glory.
> You see confusion everywhere, the like of which no one has seen or heard.
> You see the fairest lilies choked by weeds.
> But here there dwells a just God who sets everything right.
> *Innocue vivito, numen adest!*[1]

The entries in the book are listed by subjects: 'Death', 'Avarice', 'Ghosts', 'Friendship', etc., or under the names of the persons concerned: 'Julius Caesar', 'Admiral Byng', 'The Duke of Marlborough', 'Stobaeus', 'Blackwell', etc. A typical story is that of Madame N.N.:

[1] 'Live blamelessly; God is present' – Linnaeus's motto, which he inscribed over the door leading into his bedroom at Hammarby.

Madame N.N. had a maid who, as she was carrying a china bowl upstairs, fell and broke it. Madame was furious, struck the girl a severe blow and stopped her wages to cover the cost of its replacement.

That same evening as she was coming downstairs, Madame slipped and broke her leg.

Sometimes the Nemesis aspect of the tale is far from clear – for example, of that entitled Avarice:

Lohe, a nobleman who had inherited wealth from his father, having fallen ill in Stockholm, reduced by one half the quantity of medicine prescribed for him, because it was too expensive. His only son, a student at Uppsala, died, and was left unburied for a year because of the cost. A woman who lived in the same house used to put out milk every morning for her kittens; he drank it, and the kittens faded away.

Some of the anecdotes are of an erotic nature and were therefore omitted from the earlier editions of *Nemesis Divina*; one or two of these might, indeed, have come straight from the *Decamerone*. There is, for example, the familiar story of the wife who agrees to take the place of the unwilling maidservant with whom the husband has arranged to spend the night, but who finds out too late that at the last moment her husband has consented to stand down in favour of a lecherous old friend. Another story deals with 'the wife who is a whore'. Linnaeus begins in Swedish:

She dislikes being at home, especially when her husband is there.
She longs for him to go away, and hates it when he returns.
In order to stop him from coming to her she often pretends to be *menstruans*.

Then, continuing in Latin, he describes in every clinical detail the tricks that she indulges in in order to make coition, when she can no longer avoid it, as unenjoyable as possible for her unfortunate husband.

Linnaeus has sometimes been blamed for the erotic tone of a part of *Nemesis Divina*; but the charge is unfair, and in our present permissive climate it sounds ludicrous. He never intended that his manuscript should see the light of day, and in writing as freely as he did of adultery, incest and masturbation he was merely telling his apparently highly sexed son the 'facts of life' and warning him against sowing wild oats that he would later come to regret.

9.

The man of property

At the beginning of 1758 Linnaeus suffered from a severe fit of depression, and on 10 February he poured out his unhappiness to Bäck:

I cannot write more today; my hand is too weary to hold a pen. I am the child of misfortune. Had I a rope and English courage I would long since have hanged myself. I fear that my wife is again pregnant.[1] I am old and grey and worn out, and my house is already full of children; who is to feed them? It was in an unhappy hour that I accepted the professorship; if only I had remained in my lucrative practice, all would now be well. Farewell, and may you be more fortunate.

It is hard to remember that this exhausted, embittered old man was not yet fifty-one.

But before the year was out he took an important step which, hazardous though it undoubtedly was, must have cheered not only himself but also the whole family: he decided to buy the two small country estates of Hammarby (including a part of Edeby) about six miles from Uppsala, and Sävja which was only about half that distance. The purchase was exciting because it would at long last enable him and his family to pass a large area of the summer in the country, away from the unhealthy part of the town in which the Garden was situated and where the dreaded Uppsala fever so often struck. It would also provide him with properties to bequeath to Sara Lisa and the children on his death. But to find the 80,000 dalers for the purchase he had to raise a loan, and nothing worried him so much as being in debt.

It was Hammarby, rather than Sävja, which particularly caught Linnaeus's fancy, and it soon became so important a part of his life that the pilgrimage there is obligatory upon all his admirers. Today the journey from Uppsala across the featureless, shadeless plain (once a part of the sea-bed) is tedious enough even by car – and Linnaeus must have made it innumerable times on foot; there are few flowers and fewer birds to be seen in that monotonous landscape. It is, indeed, difficult to picture those nature rambles of Linnaeus and his pupils producing much more than a crow and a dandelion, till one remembers that the elaborate draining of the plain in the last hundred years has put paid to its once rich flora and fauna. But the little manor-house, which stands on the skirts of rising and

---

[1] She had no more children; the last, Sophia, was born in 1757. It may have been a miscarriage.

218

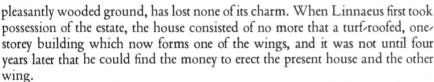

pleasantly wooded ground, has lost none of its charm. When Linnaeus first took possession of the estate, the house consisted of no more that a turf-roofed, one-storey building which now forms one of the wings, and it was not until four years later that he could find the money to erect the present house and the other wing.

In April 1766 a disastrous conflagration in Uppsala, of which Beckmann gives a graphic eyewitness account, destroyed about a third of the town and at one moment seriously threatened Linnaeus's house there and the treasures it contained. This so alarmed Linnaeus that he decided to construct at Hammarby, on the rocky knoll above the manor, a small unheated building in which to keep his books and collections safe from fire, though, as time was to show, far from safe from damp and vermin. The museum – which Linnaeus used affectionately to call 'my little back-room', 'the pleasure pavilion on my hill', 'my castle in the air' or 'my museum *in altis*' – is laughably small: less than sixteen foot square; it would just make a two-car garage. Yet in it space was found for Linnaeus's herbarium and more precious books; for his shells, insects and minerals; for the lecture-stool he used when teaching his students and the benches on which they sat to listen to him – though in fine weather instruction was often given *al fresco*. To this humble sanctuary men of science came from all over Europe to pay homage to the greatest naturalist of his day.

The house itself, like all Swedish provincial architecture, is charming and un-pretentious, its woodwork agreeably free from stains and gloomy varnishes. In 1879, after its purchase by the State from Linnaeus's descendants, it was piously restored, so far as was possible, to its original condition. On its walls hang portraits of Linnaeus's parents, of himself and his wife at the time of their marriage, of their daughters, other members of the family, and family friends. Linnaeus's study and bedroom are on the first floor, and above the door leading into the bedroom there hangs a drawing of a whale and its offspring, joined by the umbilical cord which had convinced Linnaeus that the whale was not to be classified as a fish but as a mammal.

The same piety has been extended to the garden, in which are grown the flowers that he knew and loved, and to the near-by grove which he planted and

Hammarby, aquatint engraving by Akrell, 1820, and right, from a film about Linnaeus made in 1957.

Below: drawing of whales showing the umbilical cord.

219

Hammarby, the house and garden – the original house is on the right.

where he enjoyed taking his meals out of doors in the summer. 'Keep my grove as I planted it,' he wrote in a letter to be read by his wife after his death. 'If a tree dies, then plant another in its place.' Below the museum is a slope which he called 'Siberia', where he naturalized *Corydalis nobilis* and other Russian natives; and not far from here still stands a stone which proudly records, in runic letters, the bold purchase of Hammarby and Sävja by the 'Knight' Carl Linné.[1]

Since the day when he had watched pearl mussels being fished at Purkijaur Linnaeus had given much thought as to how pearls might be produced artificially, and experiments carried out in the River Fyris at Uppsala finally proved successful. The invention was not, however, altogether new, something similar having being achieved by Red Sea fishermen in the first centuries of the Christian era and by the Chinese at least as early as the thirteenth century. The method employed by Linnaeus was as follows. He bored a small hole in the shell of the mussel and then introduced a little globule of plaster of Paris or uncalcined limestone attached to a silver wire which was tied to the shell. After five or six years a true pearl was formed, about the size of a pea.

In 1748, as has already been mentioned, Linnaeus had made an attempt to interest the Swedish Government in his secret. 'I am afraid you will be spoiled for a gardener,' Collinson had then written to him, 'for you will grow so rich with the breeding of oriental pearls.' At the time nothing came of his project; it was, however, revived thirteen years later, when the State Chamber of Commerce sent for him and invited him, under a promise of secrecy, to disclose his method. This he did, producing at the same time a handful of pearls of his own manufacture[2] which had been vetted by a jeweller and pronounced to be of very high quality. Eventually it was agreed that in exchange for his patent Linnaeus should receive the very considerable sum of 3,000 plåtar, together with the promise that he might in due course pass on his professorship at Uppsala to the successor of his choice. His friend Bishop Mennander had worked hard behind the scenes to get him these favourable terms, and when the Bishop wrote to tell him Linnaeus replied at once in an ecstatic letter of gratitude.

> Can what my Brother writes really be possible – that I have been awarded 3,000 plåtar? . . . If I get this I am the luckiest man in the world, free from all my debts – and my child provided for: what more could I or anyone want! . . . Now I am content, and ready to sail when my time comes. Thank you, dearest Brother, for all your faith in me since I was a boy. . . . I feel quite dizzy; I can hardly believe what my dear Brother writes; to receive this double gift: money and provision for my son! Either was reward enough; I had never thought, would never have dared, to ask for both at the same time. Please confirm it by the next post; it seems too good to be true.

The debts to which Linnaeus here refers were of course those incurred over the purchase of Hammarby and his other properties.

The generosity of the State was, however, a great deal less than appeared at first sight; in fact it was less than nothing. Linnaeus's secret was sold to a Gothenburg merchant in return for 3,000 plåtar and a half share in all future profits; thus at no cost to the country Linnaeus was paid off and a regular if small annual revenue assured. Fabricius alleges that it was largely on account of these pearls that Linnaeus was ennobled, and the honour might well appear a fit

---

[1] 'RIDDAR KARL LINNÉ KOPTE HAMMARBY-SÄFJA 1758.' Curiously enough it contains several wrong runes, including the misspelling of his own name as 'LILLE'.

[2] A few of these pearls may still be seen at the premises of the Linnean Society, London.

reward for his patriotic gesture in refusing to let his secret be sold abroad, where he would probably have got a better price for it. In fact the award of the peerage came first, and if anyone was expressing gratitude it must have been Linnaeus.

He was of course overjoyed when he learned of his ennoblement, and immediately set out designing a coat of arms for himself. His idea was to have 'my little Linnaea in the helmet, with the shield divided into three fields: black, green and red – the three kingdoms of Nature – superimposed an egg cut in two, or half-egg, to denote Nature, which is continued and perpetuated *in ovo*'. To his disgust the State Herald turned down his design (in which the yolk of egg looks more like a turnip), producing an alternative which Linnaeus considered to be 'full of absurdities'; but after a mild attempt at protest he acquiesced and eventually came so far as to admit that it was 'more truly honourable and beautiful than I deserved'.

With his passionate interest in the improvement of the Swedish economy, Linnaeus had long been irked to see the vast sums of money that flowed out of the country to China for the purchase of tea, and 'looked upon nothing to be of more importance than to shut that gate through which all this silver leaves Europe'. He therefore made strenuous attempts to introduce the tea plant (*Camellia sinensis*) into Sweden or, alternatively, to discover a native substitute.

For many years all his efforts failed. Proposed substitutes proved worthless, and plants alleged to be tea turned out to be nothing of the kind: one was in fact the creeping willow (*Salix repens*) – something 'as different from the tea bush', he said, 'as a peacock from a crow' – and a plant imported from China in 1757, though indeed a *Camellia*, was the wrong species. Then in 1763 came the exciting news that Captain Carl Ekeberg, taking Linnaeus's advice to sow seeds on board when his ship sailed from China, had arrived at Gothenburg with a number of flourishing seedlings. 'If this *really* is tea,' Linnaeus wrote excitedly to Ekeberg, 'then I will make it my business to see that your name outlives that of Alexander the Great.' Tea it certainly was; but the *Ekebergia*, by which Linnaeus hoped to immortalize the gallant Captain, is now sadly less familiar than the name of the great conqueror.

It is said that Fru Ekeberg herself delivered some of the tea plants to Linnaeus in Uppsala, holding them on her knees in the coach throughout the 330-mile journey. For a while the seedlings seemed to thrive, and several even flowered; then, one by one, they succumbed to the uncongenial Swedish climate. By 1765 only two plants remained; and soon there was none.

In May 1764 Linnaeus had a severe attack of Uppsala fever, from which he recovered thanks to the devoted administrations of his former enemy, Rosén. This forgiving act brought about a complete reconciliation, and two years later Linnaeus was able to return it in kind when Rosén succumbed to the same disease. He also attended Rosén in 1773 during his last illness – an attack of dysentery – though he was not able to be with him when he died. In that same summer of 1764 Linnaeus and his wife celebrated their silver wedding.

One of the most curious of all surviving Linnaean documents is the draft of a letter written in Latin by Linnaeus that year to Lady Anne Monson, asking if

Hammarby: Linnaeus's study, and below, bedroom.

223

Bishop Carl Mennander, 1712–86,
engraved after a portrait by P. Krafft.

he might name a plant in her honour. Lady Anne, a great-granddaughter of King Charles II and *en secondes noces* wife of Colonel George Monson, Warren Hastings's famous opponent, had a shady past and spent some years of her married life in India, being renowned in Calcutta as 'a very superior whist-player'. But she was also a keen botanist, collecting in India and with Thunberg and Masson in 1774 at the Cape. She was in England when she received – if it was ever dispatched, for it is known only from the draft among the Linnaean papers at Burlington House – the following whimsical letter:

I have long been trying to smother a passion which proved unquenchable and which now has burst into flame. This is not the first time that I have been fired with love for one of the fair sex, and your husband may well forgive me so long as I do no injury to his honour. Who can look at so fair a flower without falling in love with it, though in all innocence? Unhappy is the husband whose wife pleases no one but himself. I have never seen your face, but in my sleep I often dream of you. So far as I am aware, Nature has never produced a woman who is your equal – you who are a phoenix among women. . . .

Those who fall in love are wont to ingratiate themselves by precious gifts. I follow the accepted custom and enclose a few rare and genuine pearls which I have recently collected. Sow them in a flower-pot and place it in your window where it will get the sun; then you will see them germinate in February, and in early summer produce the most beautiful flowers: flowers of the *Alströmeria*, which no one in England has ever seen. . . .

But should I be so happy as to find my love for you reciprocated, then I ask but one favour of you: that I may be permitted to join with you in the procreation of just one little daughter to bear witness of our love – a little Monsonia, through which your fame would live for ever in the Kingdom of Flora. . . .

The *Monsonias* are South African plants belonging to the Geranium family, whose flushed petals would seem to suggest that they take after the mother rather than the father. As for the *Alstroemeria* – this must have been *A. pelegrina*, which had been grown at Kew since 1753. Mention has already been made of the care with which Linnaeus tended his own seedlings 'through the winter', but it is almost impossible that seeds germinating in February could flower in the summer of the same year.

In March 1767 Linnaeus received the sad news that Fru Bäck had died at the age of only thirty. He wrote at once an enormously long and not very original, though none the less deeply felt, letter of sympathy to his old friend. We brought nothing into the world, he said, for all we had in life was a loan from God. With the gift of life came also the gift of death. Measured against eternity, life is but a moment of time, and so on. 'We suffer so many thousand tribulations, dangers, miseries, cares and vexations,' he continued, 'that I can say with Seneca, "truly no one would accept life if it were not thrust upon him unawares". . . . Life is but a dream: shall we mourn for one whose dream was shorter, who has escaped the sorrows and tribulations of old age?' Linnaeus was sixty; he could never now forget that senility lay in wait for him round the corner.

Bäck never remarried, and no doubt after his wife's death he valued more than ever the friendship of his Brother. From time to time they exchanged visits, and

Bäck's children often passed a part of the summer enjoying the country air and the company of other children at Hammarby: but both Bäck and Linnaeus were very busy men, and the forty miles that separated Uppsala and Stockholm meant in those days quite a considerable journey. Three letters from Linnaeus to Bäck, written in the latter half of 1769, show how anxious Linnaeus was that they should meet soon and how difficult it was for a meeting to be effected; he was at the time endlessly busy examining a large collection of South African plants:

> I regret nothing so much as the fact that I so rarely manage to see you,[1] and all the more so now that I have got my museum in order. . . . I shall have to go to Stockholm in the autumn, whether I want to or not. . . . [15 August]

> All this summer I have been intending to go to Stockholm to see you once more before I die; but day after day pressure of business has prevented me. Now the term is about to start, and then it will be impossible. So I have made up my mind to come to Stockholm today week, Tuesday morning next, unless something unforeseen occurs and provided that you are going to be there – for I have little else to attend to. So may I stay two nights with you, or three at the most? I can't stay longer than that, because I have to be back in Uppsala on the Friday evening. First my wife said she wanted to come too, and then an hour later said she did not; I shall try to discourage her from making the journey. . . . [19 September]

> I well know that you are not afraid to give me a meal, and that you can afford it; but I shall spare you that, so long as we can talk together in the evening. . . . I had persuaded my wife to remain at home; but she snatched your letter out of my hand, and then said that as you had so kindly invited her she would come after all. . . . My wife and I always get along together in one bed; but in the evening we will talk without her. . . . [22 September]

Whenever Linnaeus needed commissions executing in Stockholm he would appeal to Bäck or his '*Mademoiselle*' (Fröken Bäck) to see to them. That same autumn the girl purchased four caps for Linnaeus to present to his wife when she returned from a visit to her brother in Falun, and Linnaeus gives his 'word of honour as a gentleman' that he will refund on the first possible occasion the thirty-five dalers that she has paid for them.

The building of Linnaeus's little museum at Hammarby had been completed in the spring of 1769, and in June Crown Prince Gustaf came to see it. Every foreigner visiting Stockholm also made the pilgrimage to Uppsala to meet the great naturalist. Among these was Joseph Marshall, describing himself as 'a mere English gentleman, travelling in Sweden through curiosity', who in that same summer paid his respects to 'Sir Charles' and was courteously received although he came with no letter of introduction and was no botanist. He discussed agriculture with his host and informed himself about the Swedish turnip, talking apparently in French – a language in which Linnaeus was very far from proficient.

In August of the following year a real English 'milord' made the journey to Sweden expressly to meet Linnaeus. Frederick Calvert, sixth and (fortunately) last Lord Baltimore (1731–71), was an ardent admirer, and had recently

Linnaeus's coat of arms and his original sketch for it.

[1] Linnaeus, as was then the custom, writes 'My Dearest Brother' instead of 'you'. I have here preferred throughout to use the second person, as sounding less affected in English.

A gold snuff-box, Lord Baltimore's gift to Linnaeus.

dedicated a volume of Latin poetry and translations, *Gaudia Poetica*, to his hero. He was described by Winckelmann as 'one of those worn-out beings, a hipped [crazy] Englishman, who had lost all moral and physical taste'; and Lord Orford declared of another of his works, *Select Pieces of Oriental Wit, Poetry and Wisdom*, that it 'no more deserved to be published than his bills on the road for post-horses'. Two years before his visit to Sweden Baltimore had been tried, but acquitted, on a charge of 'rape on the body of S. Woodcock and of E. Griffinburg, etc.' But Linnaeus was so flattered by the hero-worship accorded him that he praised Baltimore's verses exaggeratedly as 'immortal work'.

Baltimore, who was enormously wealthy (he owned Maryland, in America), arrived in his own coach which he had brought with him from England – a vehicle of such size that, in order for it to reach Hammarby, all the gate-posts in the lanes had to be dismantled. Linnaeus gave his guest a lesson in natural history, which was rewarded by the gift of a superb gold snuff-box, a dressing-case valued at 12,000 crowns, and a hundred ducats; whatever his faults, Baltimore was not lacking in generosity. It is said that Linnaeus asked him why he had not stopped at Stockholm to see the King. 'Why should I?' he replied. 'I've never seen my own.'

Gaudia Poetica was sumptuously produced (in Leipzig) in an edition of only ten copies, Linnaeus's being now in the Library of the Linnean Society in London. The book contains an extraordinary and apparently irrelevant yard-long folding plate showing a scenic railway of the kind seen today in fairgrounds. In the following passage (in which printers' and other errors have been retained), the author, translating his own Latin verses, praises his hero in flowery language:

> Upsal, formerly the glory of the northern Empire, then directed the long reigns of government. . . . Nature was miserable buried in darkness, and mourneful science lay prostrate in eternal night. Linnaeus brought her forth from obscurity, and unveild her, illustrating with his knowledge and with labours the whole world. O Linneus! I send the most trifling and wretched works to a Lucretius. O most venerable Man! Pardon I beseech you, these verses which I composed whilst I was surrounded by your profound thinking Doctors. May the flowers, the birds, the fish, and the beasts of Sweden remain famous by yours means!

'The Flying Mountains', detail, from Lord Baltimore's *Gaudia Poetica*, 1770.

Flattering though it was to Linnaeus to be wooed by a member of the English aristocracy, he was still more gratified when in the spring of 1771 he received the

following letter from Count Carl Scheffer, who was in France with the Crown Prince:

> While I was at Versailles the King of France [Louis XV] asked several times after the Archiater's health. Besides this, he wanted to know the state of the Botanic Garden [at Uppsala]. That was not all: His Majesty having with his own hands collected various seeds, commanded me to send them to Uppsala, saying 'I think that will please the Archiater.'

Seeds of 130 different species duly reached Uppsala, together with a number of live plants.

It was at this very moment that news reached Paris of the sudden death (from over-eating) of Adolf Fredrik, and Scheffer hastened back to Sweden with the new King, a young man of twenty-five.

Adolf Fredrik had been 'little more than a state decoration' who 'would have made a model country parson'; his son was of very different clay. Carlyle described him as 'a *shining* sort of man'. A brilliant and attractive boy, his education had at first been described by Tessin, and after Tessin's fall from favour, by Count Scheffer, who also had a passion for France and French culture. 'I am persuaded that this Prince would please you,' Madame du Deffand had written to Horace Walpole. 'One cannot imagine greater ease, gaiety, tact, and politeness.' With his charm and good looks, and his enthusiasm for the stage, Gustaf, the first Swedish King to be born on Swedish soil for more than fifty years, was to make something of the same immediate impact on his countrymen as did Ludwig II when he ascended the Bavarian throne in 1864. But unlike Ludwig he was a king who knew how to rule, restoring the power of the monarchy that had been usurped by the Riksdag under his two predecessors; he was undoubtedly one of the greatest sovereigns of the eighteenth century, and like his father he was to befriend Linnaeus. He met his death by assassination in the Stockholm Opera House in 1792.

227

10.

The closing years
1772–8

In 1772 the Prince of Botanists was sixty-five, and there was hardly a scientific society in Europe of which he had not been elected an honorary member. 'I am weary,' he told Bäck, 'of corresponding with so many.'

Though he had by no means declined into 'second childishness', yet he was often ailing and very conscious that he had reached that 'last scene of all' in the tragi-comedy of life. From his letters to Bäck we learn the thoughts that were in his mind as he prepared himself to make the final, the inescapable exit. On 28 February he wrote:

> Many things have happened to warn me that my time is nearly up and that my fate will be a stroke; I get giddy, especially when I bend down, and stumble like a drunken man. . . . There is nothing surprising in this, for I have come to an age which not nine people in a hundred reach. I have exerted my body and my mind to their uttermost limits – and I am worn out. Perhaps God will take me in time to spare me the misery that must inevitably lie ahead. . . .

Bäck replied by return, presumably advising his friend to take better care of himself, to watch what he ate and drank and to have himself cupped, for on 3 March Linnaeus wrote again:

> Last night, just as I was going to bed, came your letter, so full of tenderness and indescribable affection for me. . . . God seems to be postponing the execution this time, but I feel that my doom is 'deferred, not annulled'. When the sand is run out in the hour-glass, it must stop. . . . It is work, not only the years, that has consumed me.
> You can rest assured that there is nothing wrong with my diet. I never touch *brännvin* unless I have guests, and even then I only take a dram, very diluted. I often go without it for a whole month. . . . But I take three cups of tea every morning, and two cups of coffee every afternoon which since this attack I have cut down to one. The coffee may be to blame. . . . I never drink wine except with Archiater Bäck; I take the line that I never drink other people's wine because I will not offer wine to others.
> You are right in saying that I ought not to work so hard. Latterly I have overtaxed my brain, and now, on Monday next, I have to begin my lecture course. I tried for one term letting my son lecture; but I was like the old cart-horse whose legs grew stiff

before it had been a month in the stall, like a gentleman's horse. I grew so absent-minded that term, and so muddled, that I became frightened; and if it had gone on for another term I would have forgotten my own name. . . .

A fortnight later he confessed to Bäck:

I have smoked a lot – too much, perhaps – and now I am cutting it down. I have always smoked because of my toothache, which has plagued me all my life.

The coronation of the new King, Gustaf III, was to take place in May, and Bäck wrote warmly inviting Linnaeus, his wife and daughters to be his guests in Stockholm for the occasion. Linnaeus replied that he had rashly read Bäck's letter out loud to his family, who forced him to accept on their behalf and could now think and talk of nothing else. His wife and the three younger girls would be coming; he himself would gladly have accompanied them, but he simply cannot get away. It was his third term of office as Rector and he had to make preparations to preside at a graduation ceremony; he also had three disputations, several private lectures, and 'six hundred other things' which made it impossible for him to leave Uppsala at the moment. 'I go about Uppsala with my *pedanterie*, like the ant with its pine-needle,' he wrote obscurely. 'Enjoy yourself,' he added, 'and bear your cross with patience when you discover what a lot of trouble a bevy of women can create.'

King Gustaf III, by A. Roslin.

Two visitors to Hammarby in 1772 have left their impressions of Linnaeus at this time. One was his distinguished old pupil J. A. Murray, son of a chaplain to the German colony in Stockholm and now professor of medicine at Göttingen University. Murray found 'in this great man the same warmth, vivacity and enthusiasm for collecting rare objects of natural history that I had admired in him in the old days when I attended his lectures . . . .' He felt that those who criticized him would have been completely won over could they have heard how warmly he spoke of them. While he was with Linnaeus, Murray noticed an interleaved copy of the twelfth edition of *Systema Naturae*; with Linnaeus's permission he carried this away with him, and later produced in Germany an augmented edition of that part of the book which dealt with plants. For this Linnaeus received handsome payment.

The other visitor was an Icelander named Hannes Finnson, who was taken out to Hammarby by one of Linnaeus's pupils. Finnson wrote of Linnaeus: 'His fire, people say, still burns brightly, and you can see it in his eyes. He is a short man with a powerful bone structure, and not particularly good-looking. His way of speaking is rather chilly and aloof, yet agreeable, and he is somewhat obstinate; in short, he is like a Dutchman.'

In December Linnaeus's term of office as Rector came to an end and he delivered the customary valedictory Latin oration, choosing for his subject *Deliciae Naturae* – the Delights of Nature. It was a moving occasion and he rose to it, speaking lovingly of the lasting pleasures to be derived from the study of natural history. In words reminiscent of the *Song of David* of his exact contemporary, Christopher Smart, he spoke of what was strange and marvellous in the animal kingdom: of

Linnaeus, by P. Krafft the Elder, 1774.

Vampires, which suck the blood of sleepers.

The Polecat, which defends itself with its foul stench.

The Opossum, which conceals its young in its belly. . . .

And so on.

Hagberg quotes two well turned phrases from it: birds are described as 'cavalry, light, nimble, resplendently clad', the amphibians as 'an ugly, horrible, naked pack, on foot'. At the close of his address Linnaeus thanked the students for their excellent behaviour during his months of office; there had apparently been none of the rioting which was almost as prevalent in those days as it is in ours, and which had been particularly bad in the previous spring. (Fries gives an amusing account of the misbehaviour of students under previous Rectors, one student with a bad record being finally sent down for calling a fire watchman a 'sausage' and going through the motions of eating him.)

Next morning a deputation of students arrived at Linnaeus's house to express their gratitude to him in the name of the University and to ask him to publish a Swedish translation of his oration – something for which there was no precedent, he noted proudly. That Christmas he was more light-hearted than he had been for many months past.

In 1773 Linnaeus suffered first from angina and later in the year from sciatica 'from the hip to the knee'; for the last years of his life he was never to be long free from illness. But in spite of his disabilities he managed to get to Stockholm to sit on a Commission which had been set up to revise the translation of the Bible. He stayed of course with Bäck, but as soon as he was able to get away he hurried back to his beloved Garden – absent-mindedly leaving his sword behind in Bäck's study; the journey, he confessed, had taken more out of him than the whole of his Lapland tour. In March 1774 came a further session of the Commission, from which he returned home with a pair of his host's white silk stockings; 'I almost fainted from shame when I found them,' he wrote penitently. 'Heaven alone knows how they got into my box. They must be sent back by the first messenger, or else dropped into the post. Dear friend, please don't imagine that I *stole* them!'

It was probably during this latter visit to Stockholm that Linnaeus sat to Per Krafft the Elder for a portrait commissioned by the Royal Academy of Science, and the following year Alexander Roslin painted him in a more serious mood. Roslin usually charged his sitters high fees, but insisted upon painting the great naturalist for nothing. Linnaeus considered both pictures to be good likenesses, but from an artistic point of view Roslin's is certainly the more accomplished; it is now at Versailles, but there are two replicas in Sweden and a copy at the Linnean Society's rooms in London.

In May came what Linnaeus described as his 'first visit from the Messenger of Death'. He was lecturing to private pupils in the Garden when he had a stroke which left him for a time partly paralysed and from which he was never fully to recover. It has been suggested that the publication by Haller of a volume of letters addressed to him by various eminent contemporaries may have been in part responsible for this attack. Linnaeus had received a copy and was indignant to find included in it, and without his permission, an intimate letter from himself in which he had discussed his engagement and the treachery of B[rowallius].

230

Linnaeus, by A. Roslin, 1775.

But as if to compensate him for these misfortunes came good news also. First was the engagement of his youngest daughter, Sophia, to Samuel Christoffer Duse, a proctor of the University. Then he learned with great satisfaction of the progress that his system was making all over Europe. To his pupil Thunberg he wrote on 29 October:

The King of England has established a very large garden containing every obtainable plant, and beside each plant is a wooden label bearing its generic and specific name according to my system. The King of France did the same, more than two years ago, at the Trianon near Versailles. A new chair of zoology has been founded in Edinburgh, and the instruction given there follows the plan laid down in my *Systema Animalium*. About fifteen years ago the Pope [Clement XIII] ordered the burning of all my works entering the Papal States; now he [Clement XIV] has dismissed a professor of botany who did not understand my system and replaced him by another professor. The latter has orders to adopt my new system in his public lectures. . . .

231

Well might Linnaeus have cried, 'Eppur si muove!' ('But it moves all the same.')

From the Spanish naturalist José Celestino Mutis he now received a valuable collection of Colombian birds, plants, and drawings of plants, and at the end of the year a still more splendid gift from the King which served better than any medicine to improve his health and revive his spirits. On New Year's Day 1775 he told Bäck:

> Never in my life have I spent a pleasanter Christmas. His Majesty was so wonderfully gracious as to give me sixteen great chests containing plants preserved in spirits of wine – just as they grow, with their flowers and fruit. There they were, so well preserved that they looked as though they had just been gathered. . . . There is all the difference in the world between seeing plants pressed and dried and seeing them as they grow. Only today have I finished going through them. They are all from South America, and include a whole lot of new genera and species. . . .

These he described in a short paper entitled *Plantae Surinamenses* (1775), and at the same time named a genus of tropical American shrubs *Gustavia* in honour of his royal patron.

Wedgwood portrait medallion of Linnaeus based on a medallion by Carl Fredrik Inlander, 1773.

In August 1775 the young King graciously came to pay his respects in person to Linnaeus in Uppsala. It was a day of pouring rain, but the royal escort had to remain, as was the etiquette, mounted on their horses in the yard. Fru Linnaea's heart went out to the wretched men, who were soon soaked to the skin; therefore when the King asked her if she had any wish that he could fulfil, she begged that they might be allowed to come into the house, dry their clothes, and have something to eat and drink. The King was taken aback, but gave the necessary permission. The episode is in itself trivial; but it deserves to be recorded because it shows Fru Linnaea, who in general received a bad press from visitors to her house, in a more amiable light.

Linnaeus had recently won a new and influential royal admirer – Princess Caroline Luise of Hesse-Darmstadt, Margravine of Baden. With the rash enthusiasm of youth – she was only twenty-four – the Margravine was proposing to produce an edition of the *Species Plantarum* illustrated with engravings of 10,000 drawings made by herself. In August she sent him for criticism a specimen plate, a *Veronica*, which she had coloured by hand, together with an expression of her gratitude to him for naming a Surinam tree *Carolinea* in her honour.[1] A little later came a letter from her secretary inviting him to visit her. 'She promises you,' he wrote, 'a fine and spacious house, as handsomely furnished as yours at Hammarby; for I had told her Highness about the beautiful flower-prints you had been sent from England, and how you had decorated your walls with them.'

It was out of the question for Linnaeus to go to Baden. Indeed he had just obtained the Rector's permission to be relieved of the strain of public lecturing because 'I am old and decrepit, and find the autumn cold almost unbearable. My teeth are gone and I can hardly talk.' The Margravine's great book made slow progress, and at the time of her death in 1783 only 138 plates had been made; they were never published and their present whereabouts is not known.

¹ Now *Pachira* – a name which had been given to it earlier by Aublet.

In October 1775, at the suggestion of the King, a Hamburg mineralogist named Schultz came to Uppsala to show Linnaeus a very remarkable opal, known as *oculus mundi*, and a brilliant rainbow-coloured agate. Schultz heard the younger Linnaeus lecture in the Botanic Garden; he found his delivery fluent, 'but mixed with a certain cold indifference' as if he were merely performing a duty, whereas when old Linnaeus spoke of flowers his tired eyes still lit up.

In the opening months of the following year Linnaeus seemed to be rather better and was even coaching students, though more often than not they could hardly understand a word he said. On 22 June he presided, for what proved to be the last time, at a disputation; but the autumn found him 'very decrepit and broken', though putting a brave face on his infirmities. There were days when he could hardly write. A foreign student called upon him and produced, as was the custom, his autograph album, asking him to put something in it. Linnaeus laboriously inscribed his name and then added, in a hotchpotch of Greek and Roman letters, the word Ρροφhessor (Professor).

It was the avaricious Fru Linnaea who had driven her husband to take pupils in the spring; now, for the sake of the trifling emolument, she persuaded him to act as dean and examiner in the medical faculty for the autumn term, and to take his turn as a member of the committee which looked after the University's finances. The work was beyond Linnaeus, and eventually the matter was tactfully settled by the Rector, who arranged for another professor to replace him when he was unable to carry out his duties – which was, of course, almost all the time.

But there were further charges against Fru Linnaea. 'It was also alleged,' says Fries, 'that she did not give the patient proper care and attention. For example, almost every day when he tried to get up from his armchair he fell and was left lying on the ground. "Nobody seems to remember," people complained, "that it was *he* who had given lustre to the family name."' According to Fries, the younger Linnaeus behaved almost as badly as his mother, 'making use of his father's feebleness to advance his own interests, by requesting the King to appoint him "ordinary professor". This was granted on 27 October 1777. . . .' His promotion aroused general indignation in academic circles, where he was denounced not merely as incompetent but also as 'en lathund i superlativo gradu' – 'a bone-idle fellow of the highest order'. No one wanted him to succeed his father, and many people hoped that Murray might come from Göttingen; but it was soon learned that Murray was happy where he was.

Such was the accepted view of the younger Linnaeus sixty or seventy years ago; it seems probable, however, that he was to some extent maligned, and that a part of his unpopularity stemmed from jealousy. His correspondence and his unpublished manuscripts reveal him as a capable botanist. In London he worked happily with Banks and Solander, both very able men. To quote Stearn, 'he evidently possessed many of the elder Linnaeus's gifts but was too long thwarted in their expression, being overshadowed by his father's greatness like an oak sapling coming up too near the parental tree'. He could not have worked so long and so closely with his father without acquiring a store of knowledge that other students whose paper qualifications were better may well have lacked.

The death in December of Bäck's sixteen-year-old son, to whom Linnaeus had been so attached, affected him deeply, and he sent Bäck a pathetic letter of sympathy. Three days later he wrote again – an almost incoherent little scrawl which was never posted and which was found among his papers after his death. The short note ends: 'Farewell. I am Brother's; Brother's is mine. I am my My Brother's always until death.' It was dated, in error, 5 December 1756, and would hardly have reached its destination since it was addressed: 'ar Monsiurs M:sr Abrah, Brách, Stockholm'.

In the winter of 1776–7 came another stroke. 'Although he is now more dead than alive,' wrote J. G. Acrel, 'one could see his face light up when he caught sight of one of his beloved pupils or when the conversation turned to natural history.' One of these pupils was Sparrman, just returned from his eight years in South Africa and with Cook in the *Resolution*. But sometimes for an hour or two his power of thought would return, as for instance 'when he found lying near him a book on botany or zoology, even one of his own. Then he would turn the pages with evident pleasure, making it clear that he would consider himself a happy man if he could have written anything so useful.'

In May 1777 Linnaeus reached his allotted span of three score years and ten, and soon afterwards he left Uppsala for his customary *villeggiatura* at Hammarby. The country air, the little house and the homely garden he so much loved, strengthened his body and revived his spirits. On fine and sunny days he was well enough to be carried out to sit among his flowers, or up to the little museum above the house to be left there for a while to take pleasure, however uncomprehendingly, from the sight of his books and his collections. When autumn came to call him back to town he found himself once more able to walk a few steps with assistance; he could even enjoy his pipe again. Though all his life he had dreaded the cold above everything, it began to look as though he might survive yet another Swedish winter.

His doctor had ordered him to get out as much as possible into the fresh air, but his coachman had been instructed never to take him beyond the town. One December day, when he was out in his little sleigh, Linnaeus told the man to drive him to his house at Sävja, three or four miles from Uppsala, and would take no refusal. Long after the usual hour for his return a search party eventually discovered him, still in his sleigh which had been dragged into the kitchen; he was sitting there before the fire, contentedly puffing away at his pipe.

The drive home in the rain and the slush resulting from a sudden thaw can have done him no good, and it proved to be the last time he was ever to leave the house. Soon he was ill again, with pain that nothing but large tankards of beer, drained at a single pull, could relieve. On 30 December came a severe seizure, and on 10 January, at eight o'clock in the morning, Linnaeus died. With him at the last were only Christoffer Duse, his youngest daughter's fiancé, and an English pupil named John Rotheram who was later to become professor of physics at St Andrew's University.

Some years earlier Linnaeus had written, and placed in a sealed envelope, instructions for his burial:

Lay me in a coffin unshaven, unwashed, unclothed, wrapped only in a sheet. Nail down the coffin forthwith, that none may see my wretchedness. Let the great bell of the Cathedral be tolled, but not those in other churches in the town or in the Hospital, and in the countryside only the bell in Danmark's church. Let thanksgiving services to God, who granted me so long a life and so many blessings, be held in the Cathedral and in Danmark's church. Let men from my homeland carry me to the grave, and give to each of them one of the little medals bearing my portrait. Entertain nobody at my funeral, and accept no condolences.

The funeral took place on 22 January, and Afzelius, who was present, wrote some years later:

> Linnaeus's funeral in Uppsala Cathedral was the most stately ceremony that I had ever seen, and it made a deep impression on me which has lasted to this very day. It was a still and gloomy evening, the darkness relieved only by the torches and lanterns carried by the mourners, the silence broken only by the murmur of the large crowds lining the streets and the heavy tolling of the great bell – the bell which had so annoyed Linnaeus in his lifetime. . . .

Among the mourners were a number of doctors of medicine who had been Linnaeus's pupils. One of these, Jonas Hallenberg, mentions in a letter to a friend that the service was conducted by Dean Hydrén, 'and everyone was amazed at the moving way in which the old man – he was eighty-three – performed his task. . . . About twenty of those who had taken part in the procession stayed to supper, and next day the whole of the Småland Nation was invited to a luncheon.' Thus were Linnaeus's strict injunctions about funeral feasts deliberately disobeyed by his widow.

Linnaeus's ashes lie under a flat stone near the entrance door of the Cathedral. He had left instructions that near by there should be a bronze medallion inscribed with his name, the dates of his birth and death, and the words *Princeps Botanicorum* – Prince of Botanists. In 1798 a monument of Älvdal porphyry was erected by *amici et discipuli* in a side chapel in the north aisle; it bears a bronze medallion by Johan Sergel. In October 1778, in his address from the throne at the opening of the Estates, the King paid a tribute to Linnaeus, and at the end of the year a funeral oration was delivered by Bäck in the round saloon of the old castle, in the presence of the King.

But no more charming epitaph can be found than the following words, written to Linnaeus from America in 1761 by Alexander Garden (after whom the gardenia was named) – that 'thorough-going Linnaean', as J. E. Smith called him:

Monument to Linnaeus, and gravestone of Linnaeus, his wife and his son, in Uppsala Cathedral. 'A simple entablature of stone . . . now covers the mouldering reliques of this illustrious man.' (E. D. Clarke, *Travels*, vol. II.)

> If seas and mountains can keep us asunder here, yet surely the Father of Wisdom and Science will take away that veil and these obstacles when this curtain of mortality drops; and probably I may find myself on the skirts of a meadow, where Linnaeus is explaining the wonders of the world to legions of white candid spirits, glorifying their Maker for the amazing enlargement of their mental faculties.

The Linnaean
collections

The fate of the Linnaean libraries and collections has been described in great detail by Fries and Jackson; here it must be told very briefly.

Linnaeus had left his widow and children very modestly provided for, their most valuable inheritance being the books and collections. Among the documents left by Linnaeus to be opened and read after his death was the following letter to his wife, written on 2 March 1776 and seemingly at a moment when he was feeling particularly bitter about his son:

Voice from the grave to her who was my dear wife:

1. *The two herbaria in the Museum.* Let neither rats nor moths damage them. Let no naturalist steal a single plant. Take great care who is shown them. Valuable though they already are, they will be worth still more as time goes on. They are the greatest collection the world has ever seen. Do not sell them for less than a thousand ducats. My son is not to have them because he never helped me in botany and does not love the subject; keep them for some son-in-law who may prove to be a botanist.

2. *The shell cabinet* is worth at least 12,000 dalers.

3. *The insect cabinet* cannot be kept for long, because of moth.

4. *The mineral cabinet* contains things of great value.

5. *The library in my museum,* with all my books, is worth at least 3,000 copper dalers. Do not sell it, but give it to the Uppsala library. But my son may have my library in Uppsala at a valuation.

Carl Linné

Hardly was the funeral over when the family started quarrelling. Or perhaps it would be more accurate to say that the smouldering discord of many years now burst into flame. After a good deal of unseemly family bickering – 'the moment I suggest anything, my mother and my sisters grow suspicious,' Carl wrote angrily to Bäck – it was finally agreed that Carl should have all the books and specimens in exchange for his share of the Hubby property – a little farm near Hammarby which Linnaeus had been given by the University in 1776 – and a fairly substantial sum of money. Fru Linnaea also applied for, and obtained, a small pension from the King for herself and her unmarried daughter.

Whether or not Linnaeus had been just in accusing his son of never helping him in his botanical work, it is hard to say with any certainty; there can, however, be no doubt that Carl now did all in his power to save the collections, which had already suffered from moth, vermin and damp, from further deterioration. He removed them from the museum at Hammarby to the Uppsala house, where he worked on their preservation with such energy that each night he went to bed 'as tired as a common labourer'. He also rejected what he called a 'cruel' offer of £1,100 or £1,200 made for them by Sir Joseph Banks, thus saving them for the time being from leaving the country.

Then on 1 November 1783 Carl died suddenly of a stroke, and everything reverted to his mother and sisters. Since the house in Uppsala, where the books and collections were stored, would have to be surrendered to Carl's successor, Fru Linnaea not unnaturally wanted to dispose of these as soon as possible and for as much as possible. She invited an old family friend and Linnaean pupil, J. G. Acrel, to act for her, and Acrel at once approached Banks through an intermediary. It so happened that Banks was giving a breakfast party when news of Fru Linnaea's proposal reached him, and that among his guests was the ardent young naturalist, the twenty-four-year-old James Edward Smith. Banks, feeling that his own collection had now grown to such a size that he could not contemplate adding to it so substantially, urged Smith to make a bid for the great treasure; this he did, offering a thousand guineas if a detailed inventory came up to his expectations.

Meanwhile other feelers were being extended: Baron Alströmer was a possible purchaser; the Empress Catherine II was interested and so too were Dr John Sibthorp and a rich Gothenburg merchant. From the students at Uppsala came a cry that the collections should at all costs remain in Sweden, and Carl's successor, Thunberg, felt the same. The Secretary of State proposed that the King should step in and acquire them; but Gustaf was in Italy, and before he could take any action Smith had approved the inventory and clinched the deal. On 17 September 1784 the libraries and collections left Stockholm in an English brig, the *Appearance*, and within a few weeks they were safely in England.

The story that the Swedes, suddenly realizing their folly in allowing this great national heritage to leave the country, sent a ship in unavailing pursuit, is without foundation, although an engraving of the alleged chase is to be found in Thornton's *New Illustration of the Sexual System of Linnaeus* (1799–1810). But there was considerable indignation in academic circles when the news became known, and the inevitable attempt to make scapegoats. The action of Acrel, and the inaction of Bäck, Mennander and Thunberg, were criticized, but these men were not wholly to blame. The real misfortune was the absence of the King, who, had he been on the spot, would almost certainly have stepped in and saved the collections for Sweden.

And how great was the loss! Smith, when he eagerly unpacked the twenty-six large chests, found even more than he had been led to expect. In all there were about 19,000 sheets of pressed plants, 3,200 insects, 1,500 shells, between 700 and 800 pieces of coral, and 2,500 mineral specimens; 2,500 books; and the whole of Linnaeus's correspondence, consisting of some 3,000 letters, together with a great many manuscripts from the hand of Linnaeus, his son, and other contemporary scientists. In 1788 the Linnean Society of London was founded, its aim being 'the Cultivation of the Science of Natural History in all its

Sir James Edward Smith and the alleged pursuit of the *Appearance*, from Thornton's *New Illustration of the Sexual System of Linnaeus*, 1799–1810.

branches and more especially of the Natural History of Great Britain and Ireland'; in this it differs from the Svenska Linné-Sällskapet (Swedish Linné Society), which is directly concerned with Linnaeus. Smith, who became the Linnean Society's first President, was knighted in 1814, and on his death fourteen years later the library and what remained of the collections – for the minerals had been sold and much of the zoological material had either perished or been dispersed – were purchased by the Society for 3,000 guineas from Smith's widow. Since 1857 they have been preserved in the Society's headquarters in Burlington House, London, and are now being placed in a specially designed room there.

The sale of the Linnaean collections to a foreigner, a calamity comparable only to that of the sale of the Elgin marbles a few years later, has remained a matter of regret, even of shame, to the Swedish people; it is therefore more than generous of Dr Hagberg, a Swede, to write:

> If at first one feels sad because all this has not found a lasting home in a Swedish institution, and slightly bitter against those who were to blame for such neglect, on second thoughts one realizes that a much worse fate might easily have overtaken the collections. . . . Made accessible in a cosmopolitan city and scientific centre such as London, they have been of untold importance to Linné's international renown. Sweden owes an ineffaceable debt of gratitude to the Linnean Society for the reverence with which it has administered and cared for its priceless possession.

And in so writing he expresses the feelings of all his countrymen.

In April 1939 the collections were removed for safety to Woburn Abbey, Bedfordshire. In 1940, the Carnegie Corporation made a grant of £2,000 for preparing a photographic record of this priceless heritage; and it is amusing to recall that while doing this the photographer, Miss Gladys Brown, was stung on the arm by one of the specimens of stinging-nettle dried and mounted nearly 200 years earlier. 'The arm showed a definite blister apparently similar to one produced by a fresh specimen.'

238

BIBLIOGRAPHY

The standard biography of Linnaeus is *Linné: Lefnadsteckning* by T. M. Fries, 2 volumes, Stockholm 1903. For a condensed version of this in English see below under Jackson. By far the larger part of Linnaeus's own works and most of the literature dealing with him is not available in English; the following (listed chronologically) may, however, be consulted:

STILLINGFLEET, B. 1759. *Miscellaneous Tracts*, London.

LINNAEUS, Carl 1792. *Lachesis Lapponica*, translated by Carl Troilius and edited by J. E. Smith, 2 vols, London.

STOEVER, D. H. 1794. *The Life of Sir Charles Linnaeus . . . and of his Son*, translated by Joseph Trapp, London.

PULTENEY, R. 1805. *A General View of the Writings of Linnaeus* (2nd edition) (including the Life of Linnaeus), London.

SMITH, Sir J. E. (editor) 1821. *A Selection of the Correspondence of Linnaeus*, 2 vols, London.

CARR, D. C. 1837. *The Life of Linnaeus*, Holt.

BRIGHTWELL, Miss C. L. 1858. *The Life of Linnaeus*, London.

CADDY, Mrs Florence 1887. *Through the Fields with Linnaeus*, 2 vols, London.

ALBERG, A. 1888. *The Floral King; a Life of Linnaeus*, London.

JACKSON, B. D. 1923. *Linnaeus* (adapted from the Swedish of Theodor Magnus Fries), London.

LINNAEUS, Carl 1938. *The 'Critica botanica' of Linnaeus*, translated by Sir Arthur Hort, London.

HAGBERG, Knut 1952. *Carl Linnaeus*, translated from the Swedish by Alan Blair, London.

BOERMAN, A. J. 1953. 'Carolus Linnaeus, a psychological study' *Taxon* 2:145–56.

GOURLIE, Norah 1953. *The Prince of Botanists*, London.

STEARN, William T. 1957. An Introduction to the '*Species Plantarum*'. Prefixed to the Ray Society's edition of Linnaeus's *Species Plantarum*, London.

UGGLA, Arvid Hj. 1957. *Linnaeus* (a short essay), Swedish Institute, Stockholm.

BLUNT, W. 1971 (Feb.). 'Linnaeus and Botany' in *History Today*. (This contains an account, intended for non-botanists,

of Linnaeus's systems of botanical classification and nomenclature).

Miss Gourlie's and Dr Hagberg's books, to which I am much indebted, are the most recent biographies in English, and Dr Stearn's Introduction is a mine of valuable information. Mrs Caddy's sentimental book has value in that she gives a fairly full account of Linnaeus's Swedish journeys, none of which (except the Lapland journey) is elsewhere available in print in English; but in the Library of the Linnean Society there is the typescript of an English translation by Dr Asberg of the *Gothländska Resa*. It is much to be regretted that Hagberg's biography has no index, and that of Jackson only an inadequate one; a much needed index to Fries was provided in 1956.

The numbers of *Svenska Linné-Sällskapets Årsskrift*, the yearbook of the Swedish Linné Society (1918–), have occasional articles in English and an English summary of most of those in Swedish. The *Transactions* and *Proceedings* of the Linnean Society of London may also be consulted. Stewart Oakley's *The Story of Sweden* (Faber, London 1966) gives a useful survey of Swedish history. Readers of German will find Heinz Goerke's *Carl von Linné* (Stuttgart 1966) very valuable, particularly on account of its medical emphasis, and A. Fee's *Vie de Linné* (Paris 1832) is still of interest to those who read French. For children there is *Carl Linnaeus: the Man who Put the World of Life in Order*, by Alvin and Virginia Silverstein (John Day, New York 1969).

For works by Linnaeus, Dr Stearn gives, on pages 18 to 23 of his introduction, a list of his principal botanical writings, and on pages 56 to 61 his dissertations. There is a useful brief bibliography in this book (pages 164 to 167) and also in the biographies of Jackson and Gourlie. B. H. Soulsby's *A Catalogue of the Works of Linnaeus . . .* (2nd ed., London 1933) and the *Catalogue of the Library of the Linnean Society of London* (new ed., 1925) contain full bibliographies for the periods they cover. Some idea of the quantity of material available can be gauged from the fact that Soulsby lists more than four thousand items published before 1933.

Wilfrid Blunt
15 April 1970

APPENDIX

LINNAEAN CLASSIFICATION, NOMENCLATURE, AND METHOD

William T. Stearn

Although Linnaeus has been declared a pioneer ecologist, a pioneer plant-geographer, a pioneer dendrochronologist, a pioneer evolutionist, a botanical pornographer and sexualist, and much else, the most influential and useful of his contributions to biology undoubtedly is his successful introduction of consistent binomial specific nomenclature for plants and animals, even though this achievement was but an incidental by-product of his vast encyclopaedic task of providing in a concise convenient form the means of recognizing and recording their genera and species. Use of two-word names (binomials) for individual kinds, with one word applicable to a whole group of objects but the other word limiting the name to a single member of the group, is a very old and almost universal manner of naming, rooted in the need to distinguish the general and the particular, but Linnaeus was the first deliberately to apply binomials to plants and animals uniformly. In all he coined Latin or Latin-form internationally usable names for roughly 4,400 species of animals and 7,700 species of plants, linking these names with descriptions, diagnoses, or illustrations which made evident and stabilized their application. His *Species Plantarum* (1753), together with his *Genera Plantarum* (5th ed., 1754), has consequently been accepted by international agreement among botanists as the starting-point for botanical nomenclature in general. Hence botanical names published before 1753 have no standing in modern nomenclature unless they were adopted by Linnaeus in 1753 or later or by subsequent authors and such names are designated as 'pre-Linnaean', including those published by Linnaeus himself before 1753! His *Systema Naturae*, vol. 1 (10th ed., 1758) has similarly been internationally accepted by zoologists as the starting-point for the modern scientific naming of animals. But for these works and their lasting nomenclatural status Linnaeus would not now be remembered and receive so much biographical attention when his contemporaries of equal if not higher intellectual powers, though of less self-sacrificing industry, are mostly forgotten. Taxonomic botanists and zoologists, especially those concerned with European, North American, and Indian plants and animals, have continually to refer back to the works of Linnaeus when checking names. Unless, however, Linnaean methods and the aims and history, the procedures and terminology of these Linnaean works are understood, they are likely to be misinterpreted and Linnaeus's scientific names may be misapplied

through erroneous typification, as indeed some have been. The following notes, mostly brought together from more detailed publications of mine listed in the bibliography, are intended as an introduction to these technical Linnaean matters.

The basis of Linnaeus's achievement was his strong sense of order. It is evident in all his publications and it much impressed his students. Thus the entomologist J. C. Fabricius, who attended Linnaeus's lectures on natural classification in 1764, wrote in 1780 that 'his greatest asset was the co-ordinated arrangement which his thoughts took. Everything which he said and did was orderly, was systematic, and I can hardly believe that Europe will produce a more systematical genius'. In the creation of the methods he used, his ill-fated friend Peter Artedi seemingly contributed as much as Linnaeus himself, but after Artedi's death in 1735 their application to the three kingdoms of Nature fell upon Linnaeus alone. Reared in a pious atmosphere, spared from death on his travels, always strongly egoistic, Linnaeus could excusably believe himself God's chosen instrument for revealing in an orderly way the divinely ordered works of Creation, and he did not spare himself in that task. The first part of it was the classification of organisms into major groups.

NATURAL AND ARTIFICIAL CLASSIFICATION

Linnaeus's mind was essentially practical and realistic, not much at home in abstract and philosophical generalities but perceptive and diligent in concrete visually evident matters of detail. He recognized that organisms could be classified into major groups by two main methods, one using the *natural characters*, i.e. a large number of characters in association, and one using only *artificial characters*, i.e. a few selected for convenience in dividing a mass of objects somehow into groups. A comprehensive *natural classification*, in Bather's words 'a summarizing of knowledge by classing together the things that possess in common the greatest number of attributes' (cf. Bather, 1927), expressive of God's plan in creation, represented for him the desirable but the unattainable. The needs of his time, particularly in botany and horticulture, could, however, be met by an *artificial classification*, i.e. in Bather's words one 'based on superficial and obvious characters, selected and arranged in an arbitrary manner' and thus bringing together organisms which agreed in at least a single character easily observed though they differed in almost everything else. An example of an artificial classification is one based on flower colour. Such a method, adopted, for example, in Carey and Fitchew's *Wild Flowers at a Glance*, may be more convenient than a natural one for quick identification, even though it necessitates the wide separation of closely allied plants, sometimes forms of the same species. Linnaeus's major groups for plants are frankly artificial, being based primarily on the number of floral parts, but his arrangement of the genera within these artificial major groups is often quite natural, bringing together genera which most resemble one another by the sum of their characters. As Bremekamp (1962:50) has emphasized, it is apparently impossible to draw a sharp line between artificial and natural systems. Linnaeus's major divisions of the animal kingdom are somewhat less artificial than those of the plant kingdom. It is therefore convenient to treat them separately.

LINNAEUS'S BOTANICAL CLASSIFICATION

Long before Linnaeus, botanists had been formulating classifications of plants, perceiving resemblances in habit and general character which led to associating those most similar and trying to find logical justification for this by reference to principles not wholly applicable (cf. Bremekamp, 1962). A pioneer was Andrea Cesalpino (c. 1524–1603), who gave particular attention to the seed and seedling and who has been described by Stafleu (1969) as 'the first in a series of systematists who struggled between speculative, preconceived notions and direct observation of nature, or, stated in other terms, between the "artificial" and the "natural", between logical division and natural affinity, between thinking about facts and the facts themselves, between theory and practice'. Linnaeus's work, particularly the occasional disagreement between his description of a genus and the characters of some species he placed in that genus, betrays just such a conflict or lack of harmony in his mind between the scholastic and the empirical approach to classification; this is relevant for the typification of Linnaean generic names because it points to his manner of working. In his *Classes Plantarum* (1738) and *Philosophia botanica* (1751) Linnaeus briefly outlined the systems of his predecessors. The most important of these for him were the Englishman John Ray (1628–1705) and the Frenchman Joseph Pitton de Tournefort (1656–1708). Ray's was the most natural system then and indeed into the second half of the eighteenth century, because it was based on a diversity of characters, including the nature of the fruit and the number of cotyledons in the seed, but it was for that very reason the most difficult to use. An inexperienced person confronted with an unknown plant could not easily find its place within Ray's system and ascertain whether it was already somewhere recorded. Tournefort based his system primarily upon forms of the corolla which, being easy and pleasant to study, 'frappent plus vivement l'imagination', as he said.

The imagination of the adolescent Carl Linnaeus was more vividly struck by the sexuality of plants. From a local doctor

Rothman he learned the essentials of Vaillant's dissertation *Sermo de Structura Florum* (1718), which boldly expounded the sexual functions of the stamens and pistil (cf. Stearn, 1970). This revelation caused Linnaeus to examine every flower he could find and count their genital organs. As he frankly said many years later, 'the singular structure and remarkable office of the stamens and pistil enticed my mind, to inquire what Nature had concealed in them. They commended themselves by the function they perform'. The great diversity in the number of these organs led him to base upon them his so-called 'sexual system'. This was first published in his *Systema Naturae* (1735) and adopted as the basic arrangement of all his botanical works. He divided all flowering plants (angiosperms or phanerogams) into twenty-three *classes* based on the male organs, i.e. according to the number, relative lengths, etc. of the stamens, as *Monandria* with one stamen (exemplified by *Canna* and *Salicornia*), *Diandria* with two stamens (exemplified by *Salvia* and *Veronica*), *Triandria* with three stamens (exemplified by *Cyperus* and *Iris*), and so on. His twenty-fourth class, the *Cryptogamia*, included plants which seemed to be flowerless, such as the mosses. These classes were in turn divided into *Orders* based on the female organs, as *Monogynia* with one style or sessile stigma (exemplified by *Lilium* and *Campanula*), *Digynia* with two styles or sessile stigmas (exemplified by *Bromus* and *Gentiana*), *Trigynia* with three styles or sessile stigmas (exemplified by *Euphorbia* and *Viburnum*), and so on. He coined the names of these classes and orders from the Greek words *adelphos* (brother), *aner*, *andros* (man, male), *dynamis* (power), *gamos* (marriage), *genesis* (birth), *gyne* (woman, female), *oikos* (*oecos*, house, home), and the Greek suffixes *mono-* (1-), *di-* (2-), *tri-* (3-), etc. Thus a lily (*Lilium*) and a snowdrop (*Galanthus*), both having six stamens and one style, would be placed in the class *Hexandria* order *Monogynia*, a meadow-saffron (*Colchicum*) with six stamens and three styles in the *Hexandria Trigynia*, a saffron crocus (*Crocus*) with three stamens and one style in the *Triandria Monogynia*.

This so-called 'sexual system' (*systema sexuale*) was thus basically arithmetical and, despite its alluring name, was founded, as has been often observed, on exactly those characters of the androecium, the male organs, and the gynoecium, the female organs, least important as regards their sexual function. Linnaeus's mind dwelled in a world of facts made vivid by the use of metaphors and imagery. Luckily gifted with a strong visual memory and an aesthetic delight in the diversity of organisms, he transformed simple matters into colourful dramatic concrete mental pictures. Just as, in his *Deliciae Naturae* (1772), Linnaeus conceived the vegetable kingdom as the temple of the goddess Flora, her head crowned with a floral wreath, the walls of her chamber green but adorned with painted flowers and enamelled fruits, most of the side rooms awaiting the hand of Linnaeus to unlock them and reveal their treasures and secrets, and saw a little pink-flowered Lapland ericaceous plant on a rock by a pool with a newt as representing the blushing naked princess Andromeda, lovable and beautiful, chained to a sea rock and exposed to a horrible dragon, so he portrayed the world of flowers as acting, in Croizat's phrase, 'like husbands and wives in unconcerned freedom'. Thus, in his exposition of the classes, he described the *Monandria* as like 'One husband in a marriage', *Diandria* as 'Two husbands in the same marriage', and so on to the *Polyandria* with 'Twenty males or more in the same bed with the female', a state of affairs enjoyed by the poppy (*Papaver*) and the linden (*Tilia*). An even more remarkable arrangement was exemplified by the flower-head of marigold (*Calendula*) with sterile disc florets and fertile ray florets and accordingly placed in the *Syngenesia Polygamia Necessaria* (i.e. Confederate Males with Necessary Polygamy), 'where the beds of the married occupy the disk and those of the concubines the circumference, the married females are barren and the concubines fertile'. This system was attractively but also deceptively simple. To place a plant in its class and order it was necessary only to count the stamens and pistil; after which, by studying the characters of the genera within that group, a much more exacting task, it could be placed in its genus. There were two major drawbacks. Some species may vary in the number of floral parts, one flower, for example belonging to the *Tetrandria* (with four stamens) and others on the same individual to the *Hexandria* (with six stamens). Also Linnaeus sometimes placed in the same genus one or more species which, since they differed in their number of stamens, should have gone into different classes, his sense of affinity triumphing over logical consistency. Thus his genus *Verbena*, which he placed in the class *Diandria*, comprised species with two stamens and others with four stamens; consequently an inquirer confronted for the first time with vervain (*Verbena officinalis*, lectotype of the genus *Verbena*) would naturally look for this four-stamened plant in the *Tetrandria* and would never guess that Linnaeus had enumerated it in the *Diandria*. Such difficulties could have been overcome by double entries and cross-references but unfortunately Linnaeus never thought of providing them. They gave his critics, notably the sarcastic Medicus, abundant material.

Nevertheless, the Linnaean classification commended itself to many of Linnaeus's contemporaries as more practical than any other then available and between 1737 and 1810 it became the most widely used system in botanical works, since the information necessary for the construction of more natural systems had not yet been obtained and assembled for synthesis. It certainly helped to popularize the study of botany.

The German botanical artist Georg Dionys Ehret (see p. 106) contributed to its popularity by printing at Leyden in 1736 a personally designed, engraved and coloured illustration entitled *Linnaei Methodus Plantarum Sexualis* which, according to Ehret himself, almost all the botanists in Holland bought but of which apparently only two prints, one in London, the other in Uppsala, besides Ehret's original drawing in the British Museum (Natural History), London, have survived. Linnaeus, however, published a version of Ehret's print without acknowledgment in his *Genera Plantarum*, and this was copied in later works (cf. Stearn, 1959 a: 63). The period 1805 to 1830 saw the Linnaean sexual system replaced in major botanical works by systems derived from the later one of A. L. Jussieu, but it can still be used as the basis of an artificial key to the plants of a limited area. David Prain published such a key in his *Bengal Plants* (1900). Since a knowledge of the Linnaean system of arrangement is needed when consulting Linnaeus's botanical works, Prain's version is here reprinted.

KEY TO THE CLASSES OF THE LINNAEAN SYSTEM

Plants with conspicuous flowers (PHANEROGAMIA):
 Stamens and pistils in the same flower:
  Male and female organs distinct:
   Stamens not united either above or below:
    Stamens solitary   I. MONANDRIA
    Stamens 2   II. DIANDRIA
    Stamens 3   III. TRIANDRIA
    Stamens 4   IV. TETRANDRIA
    Stamens 5   V. PENTANDRIA
    Stamens 6 equal, or if unequal then 3 long and 3 short
           VI. HEXANDRIA
    Stamens 7   VII. HEPTANDRIA
    Stamens 8   VIII. OCTANDRIA
    Stamens 9   IX. ENNEANDRIA
    Stamens 10 or 11   X. DECANDRIA
    Stamens 12 or any number between 12 and 19
           XI. DODECANDRIA
    Stamens 20 or more than 20:
     Filaments attached to calyx   XII. ICOSANDRIA
     Filaments not attached to calyx
            XIII. POLYANDRIA
    Stamens of markedly unequal length:
     Stamens 2 long and 2 short   XIV. DIDYNAMIA
     Stamens 4 long and 2 short
            XV. TETRADYNAMIA
   Stamens united
   Union of stamens occurring in the filaments:
    Stamens in one phalanx or bundle
           XVI. MONADELPHIA
    Stamens in two phalanges   XVII. DIADELPHIA
    Stamens in three or more phalanges
           XVIII. POLYADELPHIA
   Union of stamens confined to anthers
          XIX. SYNGENESIA
   Male organs attached to and standing upon the female
          XX. GYNANDRIA
 Stamens and pistils in different flowers:
  Male and female flowers not mixed with
   hermaphrodite flowers:
    Male and female flowers on the same plant
           XXI. MONOECIA
    Male and female flowers on different plants
           XXII. DIOECIA
  Male and female flowers mixed with hermaphrodite flowers, the unisexual flowers sometimes on the same, sometimes on different plants XXIII. POLYGAMIA
 Plants without proper flowers
        XXIV. CRYPTOGAMIA

Erasmus Darwin, the grandfather of Charles, in his long versification of the Linnaean system, *The Loves of the Plants* (1789), reduced Linnaeus's metaphorical concept to charming absurdity by personifying the genera and treating the stamens as youths, brothers, swains, husbands, and knights, the pistils as virgins, wives and nymphs. Thus he writes of *Colchicum*:

Three blushing maids the intrepid nymph attend
And *six* gay youths, enamour'd train! defend

while

With charms despotic fair Chondrilla reigns
O'er the soft hearts of *five* fraternal swains.

In Turmeric (*Curcuma*), which has one fertile stamen, the four staminodes or petal-like sterile stamens, called 'eunuchs' by Linnaeus because lacking anthers, become 'beardless youths':

Woo'd with long care, Curcuma cold and shy
Meets her fond husband with averted eye:
Four beardless youths the obdurate beauty move
With soft attentions of Platonic love.

Linnaeus's exposition amused some of his contemporaries but scandalized others, notably Siegesbeck and Alston, and had the same effect long after his death. 'To tell you that nothing could equal the gross prurience of Linnaeus's mind is perfectly needless,' wrote the Rev. Samuel Goodenough, later Bishop of Carlisle, to that devoted Linnaean scholar J. E. Smith in January 1808. 'A literal translation of the first principles of Linnaean botany is enough to shock female modesty. It is possible that many virtuous students might not be able to make out the similitude of *Clitoria*.' Goethe as late as 1820 was anxious that the chaste souls of women and young people should not be embarrassed by botanical textbooks expounding the 'dogma of sexuality'.

LINNAEUS'S ZOOLOGICAL CLASSIFICATION

Animals can be recognized more easily than plants as divisible into main groups, a number of which were distinguished by Aristotle. The most important pre-Linnaean contributions to their classification were by the English naturalist John Ray (1628–1705) and, although Linnaeus departed from Ray in basing, for example, his classification of quadrupeds primarily upon teeth instead of feet, he was much indebted to him. The main division in the first edition (1735) of his *Systema Naturae* were 1. *Quadrupedia*, 2. *Aves*, 3. *Amphibia*, 4. *Pisces*, 5. *Insecta*, 6. *Vermes*. His account here covers two large folio pages. The account in the tenth edition (1758) of the *Systema Naturae* occupies a volume of 824 octavo pages and, because here Linnaeus first gave binomials to all the known animal species, this is internationally accepted as the starting point for modern zoological nomenclature.

In outline Linnaeus's 1758 classification is as follows:

I. MAMMALIA (Mammals)
   i. Primates: including man (*Homo*), apes and monkeys (*Simia*), lemurs (*Lemur*), bats (*Vespertilio*).
   ii. Bruta: including elephants (*Elephas*), manatee (*Trichechus*), ai (*Bradypus*), anteaters (*Myrmecophaga*), pangolin (*Manis*).
   iii. Ferae: including seals, dogs, wolves, hyaena, foxes, cats, ferrets, otter, skunk, bears, etc.
   iv. Bestiae: including pigs, armadillos, hedgehog, moles, shrews, etc.
   v. Glires: including rhinoceros, porcupines, hares, rabbit, beavers, mice, lemming, rats, squirrels.

   vi. Pecora: including camel, llama, musk-deer, giraffe, deer, goats, gazelles, sheep, cattle.
   vii. Bellua: including horse, donkey, zebra, hippopotamus.
   viii. Cetae: including narwhal, whales, porpoise, dolphins.

II. AVES (Birds)
   i. Accipiters: including vultures, falcons, hawks, kites, eagles, buzzards, owls, shrikes.
   ii. Picae: including parrots, toucans, crows, rollers, birds-of-paradise, cuckoos, kingfishers, bee-eaters, tree-creepers, etc.
   iii. Anseres: including ducks, swans, geese, auks, petrels, pelicans, albatross, tropic-bird, divers, grebes, gulls, terns, etc.
   iv. Grallae: including flamingo, spoonbill, herons, cranes, snipe, woodcock, avocet, coots, rails, bustards, ostrich, etc.
   v. Gallinae: including gamebirds in general, peacock, pheasants, grouse.
   vi. Passeres: including pigeons and doves, larks, starlings, thrushes, finches, titmice, swallows, nightjars, etc.

III. AMPHIBIA (Amphibians)
   Reptilia: including turtles and tortoises, lizards, frogs, etc.
   ii. Serpentes: snakes.
   iii. Nantes: including rays, sturgeon, etc.

IV. PISCES (Fish)
   i. Apodes: including eels, barbels, etc.
   ii. Jugulares: including cod, blennies, gurnards, etc.
   iii. Thoracici: including flatfish, stickleback, gobies, butterfly-fishes, etc.
   iv. Abdominales: including catfish, salmon, trout, pike, herring, carp, etc.
   v. Branchiostegi: including puffer-fish, trigger-fish, sea-dragons, etc.

V. INSECTA (Insects)
   i. Coleoptera: including beetles, earwigs, grasshoppers, cockroaches, praying mantis, stick- and leaf-insects, etc.
   ii. Hemiptera: bugs, thrips.
   iii. Lepidoptera: butterflies and moths.
   iv. Neuroptera: including dragonflies, mayflies, caddisflies, scorpionflies, etc.
   v. Hymenoptera: including ants, bees, wasps, sawflies, woodwasps, etc.
   vi. Diptera: flies.
   vii. Aptera: including silverfish, springtails, biting lice, pseudoscorpions, fleas, harvestmen, spiders, mites and ticks, king-crab, woodlice, etc.

VI. VERMES ('Worms', Invertebrates)
   i. Intestina: including earthworms, bristleworms, leeches, flukes, tapeworms, etc.
   ii. Mollusca: including slugs, sea-slugs, cephalopods, sea-cucumbers, squids, starfish, octopus, sea-urchins, etc.
   iii. Testacea: shellfish in general, mussels, sedentary polychaetes, oysters, nautilus, limpets, snails, goose-barnacles, etc.

iv. Lithophyta: including millepores, corals, bryozoons.
v. Zoophyta: including horny corals, sea‑pens, hydroids, bryozoons, etc.

In this edition Linnaeus recognized the importance of the mammary glands and suckling of young for the distinction of the group formerly called *Quadrupedia* and he coined the term *Mammalia* (from *mammalis*, relating to the breasts) by analogy with *Animalia*.

GENERA OF PLANTS

For Linnaeus, as stated in his *Philosophia botanica*, no. 159 (1751), a *genus* of plants was a group of species possessing similarly constructed organs of fructification, i.e. flowers and fruits, and hence distinguishable by these from other genera. He regarded genera and species as units formed by Nature (*Phil. bot.* no. 162), whereas classes and orders were categories devised in the mind though based upon fact, i.e. the work of Nature and Art, and hence possibly natural. His predecessor Tournefort was the first to define genera by providing descriptions of what were regarded as essential features listed in a set order facilitating comparison. As Tournefort himself stated, he recognized two grades of genera, those founded on the form of the flower and fruit alone and those for which vegetative differences were needed. Linnaeus, with his emphasis on fructification characters, recognized only the first‑grade genera of Tournefort and united Tournefort's second‑grade genera with them. Linnaeus's generic concept was thus narrower by definition and wider by applica‑ tion than Tournefort's. Experience has shown that groups of species most easily distinguished by vegetative characters may nevertheless have less obvious distinctive floral or fruiting characters associated with these. Many of the Tournefortian genera suppressed by Linnaeus in 1753 have accordingly been restored to recognition.

Increased knowledge and a different viewpoint often necessi‑ tate division of genera as accepted by Linnaeus and since the name he used must be retained for one of the divisions it is necessary to choose a species with which that name will be constantly associated. Such a species is called the *type of the generic name*. When the Linnaean genus contained only one species, that one is the *type by monotypy*, e.g. *Linnaea borealis*. When Linnaeus stated that he had based his account on a particular species, e.g. *Bauhinia divaricata*, that one is the *type by original designation*. A species chosen by a later author from among several species included by Linnaeus is a *lectotype* or *standard species*, e.g. *Chrysanthemum coronarium* accepted by Britton & Brown in 1913, Hitchcock & Green in 1929, Rehder in 1949 and Phillips in 1951 as the lectotype of *Chrysanthemum* out of the fourteen species included in the genus by Linnaeus.

Tournefort's *Institutiones Rei Herbariae* (1700), profusely illustrated with excellent engravings by Aubriet, provided Linnaeus with fundamental information, but the descriptions in Linnaeus's *Genera Plantarum* (1737; 5th ed., 1754) were original, methodically and tersely drafted according to his own plan, with an asterisk * following the generic name to indicate that he had studied living material, a dagger † to indicate that

he had seen only herbarium material, and the absence of these signs to indicate he had seen no material himself and hence depended upon the literature or correspondence.

In preparing his generic description Linnaeus's procedure was to make a description of the flower and fruit of the chief species, i.e. the one known to him by the most complete material, compare this species with the other species of the genus, and then remove from the description all features found not to agree throughout the genus (cf. Stearn, 1959, 1960). When he later referred other species to the genus, Linnaeus should have revised his generic description to ensure agreement between them and it. In fact he was too busy to do so. Hence it may be found that, of the species listed under a given generic name in the *Species Plantarum* (1753), not all fit the generic description in the *Genera Plantarum* (5th ed., 1754). Such non‑conforming species must have been added after the generic description was drafted and should be ignored when selecting a lectotype. Species already chosen by various authors are indicated by the use of *italic* type and various signs, e.g. * ‖ † § $, in the index to volume 2 (1959) of the Ray Society's facsimile of Linnaeus's *Species Plantarum*.

GENERIC NAMES

In his *Critica botanica* (1737) Linnaeus published a series of rules for the acceptance and formation of generic names (cf. Hort, 1938; Stearn, 1966: 283–6). He accordingly discarded many names used by his predecessors and contemporaries, for the latter a procedure neither necessary nor pleasing! His aim was to make generic names as short, euphonious, distinctive and memorable as possible. He accordingly rejected names such as *Chenopodio‑Morus*, *Narcisso‑Leucojum*, *Cornucopioides*, *Hypo‑ phyllocarpodendron*, *Percepier*, *Auricula Ursi*, *Hyacinthus stellaris*. Other botanists, Plumier in particular, had named genera after their fellow botanists. Linnaeus followed their example on a grand scale and by means of such names as *Artedia*, *Burmannia*, *Celsia*, *Cliffortia*, *Dillenia*, *Gronovia*, *Halleria*, *Lawsonia*, *Milleria*, *Royena*, *Rudbeckia* and *Sauvagesia* he commemorated his patrons and friends. He also took many names from Greek and Roman mythology.

DIFFERENTIATION OF SPECIES

A plant or animal having been referred to a genus, the next task in identification is to allocate it to a species or a hybrid group within the genus. Linnaeus in his *Critica botanica*, no. 237 (1737) ruled that 'The specific name should distinguish the plant from all others of the genus.' By 'specific name' (*nomen specificum*) he then meant a diagnostic phrase. Hence when a genus had only one species, the generic name by itself was enough, e.g. *Costus*, *Maranta*, *Hippuris*, *Ligustrum*: 'a specific name is nothing but a mark by which I may distinguish species from others of the same genus; therefore, where there is only one species there is no distinction to be made, and hence no diagnostic character'. When a species differed from all others in one striking charac‑ teristic, it could receive an 'essential' name recording that unique feature, e.g. *Plantago scapo unifloro* (plantain with a one-flowered scape). Usually, however, species had to be distinguished by a combination of features. Thus the plantain which in 1753 he designated *Plantago media* he had named in 1738 *Plantago foliis ovato-lanceolatis pubescentibus, spica cylindrica, scapo tereti* (plantain with pubescent ovate-lanceolate leaves, a cylindric spike and a terete scape), thereby distinguishing it from his *Plantago foliis ovatis glabris* (plantain with glabrous ovate leaves, i.e. *P. major*) and his *Plantago foliis lanceolatis, spica subovata nuda, scapo angulato* (plantain with lanceolate leaves, an almost ovate naked spike and angled scape, i.e. *P. lanceolata*). These descriptive phrase-names functioned like the divisions of a modern key (cf. Stearn, 1957: 86; Stearn, 1961: lxxi). They formed the most important part of his method of distinguishing species. 'The specific name,' he wrote, 'will identify the plant which bears it at the first glance, since it expresses the "differentia" which is imprinted on the plant itself' (*Critica botanica*, no. 258). Hence he devised very sensible rules for their formation, i.e. the characters used should not be inconstant, purely quantitative, ecological or geographical, but should be based on the number, shape, position and proportion of parts of the plant, especially the leaves. He banned as misleading, indefinite or unhelpful characteristics those of size, resemblance to other genera, locality, time of development, colour, smell, taste, uses, sex, monstrosities, hairiness, duration and increase in a number of parts. He himself took great care over drafting these diagnostic names, which were the basis of his system of specific distinction, and he endeavoured to make them as brief as possible, regarding twelve words as the maximum permissible. Unfortunately, since such names were comparative, the naming of a new species often necessitated also emendation of the names of the allied species, in order that all the names should be adequate. Thus the *Plantago foliis ovatis glabris* of 1738 had to be renamed in 1753 as *Plantago foliis ovatis glabris, nudo scapo tereti, spica flosculis imbricatis* so as to distinguish it from a new species (*P. asiatica*) likewise possessing ovate glabrous leaves but with an angled scape and separated flowers which he named *Plantago foliis ovatis glabris, scapo angulato, spica flosculis distinctis*.

To stabilize the application of names, systematic biologists associate names with a definite element, e.g. a specimen or an illustration, to which the name is permanently attached for reference purposes. Such an element is called a 'type'. The process of selecting a type is called *typification* and the selected type a *lectotype*. The typification of a Linnaean name is essentially the selection of the specimen or illustration from which Linnaeus obtained the information embodied in his diagnostic phrase-name. Sometimes the type is a published illustration, because Linnaeus himself possessed no specimen, e.g. *Sagittaria trifolia* based on an illustration in Petiver's *Gazophylacium* (1702). Often it is a specimen in Linnaeus's own herbarium, now in the keeping of the Linnean Society of London (cf. Savage, 1945; Stearn, 1952: 105; Stearn, 1961). It may, however, be a specimen elsewhere, e.g. in Gronovius's herbarium or Clifford's herbarium or Hermann's herbarium, all three in the British Museum (Natural History), London (cf. Stearn, 1957: 119), Burser's herbarium in Uppsala (cf. Juel, 1936), or Alströmer's herbarium in Stockholm (cf. Lindman, 1908–10).

Linnaeus employed the same methods when distinguishing species of animals but made much use of colour, particularly in birds and insects, and also of habitats and hosts in insects. Thus he distinguished the species of *Aphis*, *Chermes* and *Coccus* by their host plants, e.g. *Aphis Ribis rubri*, *A. Ulmi campestris*, *A. Pastinacae sativae*, *A. Rumicis Lapathi*. For shells he used morphological characters expressed in a manner which disgusted Goodenough and Gray: *Venus testa cordata transversim parallele sulcata, sulcis obtussimis, vulva glabra, ano ovato*, *V. testa cordata glabra, vulva fusca gibba, nymphis hiantibus*, etc. Linnaeus's definition of Man (his *Homo sapiens*) as a species is, however, not morphological but psychological and indeed profound: *Homo nosce Te ipsum* (Man, know yourself). Since for nomenclatural purposes the specimen of a species most carefully studied and recorded by the author must be chosen as the lectotype and since Linnaeus studied Linnaeus to the extent of writing his autobiography five times, it follows that the lectotype of *Homo sapiens* lies in Uppsala Cathedral beneath a stone slab inscribed 'Ossa Caroli a Linne'!

BOTANICAL LATIN AND TERMINOLOGY

By writing in Latin, Linnaeus made his work immediately available to the whole learned world of his day. Had he written it in his native Swedish, he and it would long have passed unnoticed. His Latin was not, however, classical Latin but a technical language derived from renaissance and medieval Latin in which Latin words had been given specialized meanings sometimes very remote from their original application (cf. Stearn 1955, 1966). Botanical Latin, still an important means of international communication in systematic botany, was largely his creation. He standardized terminology in his *Fundamenta botanica* (1736), *Hortus Cliffortianus* (1738), *Philosophia botanica* (1751), and *Termini botanici* (1762), and established the standard general style of technical descriptions, with each organ described in a set order, as concisely and precisely as possible, verbs being mostly omitted. He introduced the term *corolla* and by adopting such terms as *petalum*, *stamen*, *filamentum* and *anthera* made their use general, thereby leading to the introduction of words based upon them into English and modern Romance languages, e.g. 'petal', 'pétale', 'pétalo', 'pétala'.

BINOMIAL NOMENCLATURE

Before Linnaeus's introduction of consistent binomial nomenclature for species in 1753 and its general adoption during the next twenty-five years, there existed no single accepted method of naming species. Hence pre-1753 nomenclature, though by no means as chaotic as sometimes stated, tended to be awkward, unstable, and inconsistent. Linnaeus's predecessors used names of varying length, as did Linnaeus himself, which were intended both to designate the species and to give some information about it. As more and more species became known, so their names lengthened. Thus the species which Clusius named *Convolvulus folio Altheae* in 1576 was named *Convolvulus argenteus Altheae folio* by Caspar Bauhin in 1623 and *Convolvulus foliis ovatis divisis basi truncatis: laciniis intermediis duplo longioribus* by Linnaeus in 1738. By 1753 Linnaeus had found it necessary to devise an even more unwieldy name in order to distinguish this from its allies, *Convolvulus foliis palmatis cordatis sericeis: lobis repandis, pedunculis bifloris*. Such diagnostic names were quite unsuited for use outside learned books. Indeed Linnaeus himself said that 'generic names have to be committed to the memory, but few need remember specific names'. His students on excursions did not use a lengthy name such as *Achillea foliis duplicato-pinnatis glabris, laciniis linearibus acute laciniatis* for milfoil. They simply recorded it in their notes as 'Achillea no. 5', the numeral referring to the entry under *Achillea* thus numbered in Linnaeus's *Flora Suecica* (1745). Haller used the same method when labelling herbarium specimens of species listed in his *Enumeratio methodica Stirpium Helvetiae* (1742). Substitute a catch-word, a one-word specific epithet, for the numeral, as Linnaeus did later, and this system of designating species becomes binomial nomenclature (cf. Stearn, 1959; Heller, 1964).

Thus before 1753 a specific name drafted according to Linnaeus's rules, as set out in his *Critica botanica* (1737) and exemplified in his other publications, such as the *Hortus Cliffortianus* (1738), *Flora Lapponica* (1737), *Flora Suecica* (1746) and *Fauna Suecica* (1746), had two functions which were ultimately incompatible, (1) to serve as a label, (2) to serve as a diagnosis of the species. His major contribution to science was to separate these designatory and diagnostic functions by using for a time two sets of names concurrently. The generic name was the same in both, e.g. *Iris*. For everyday use he added to this a one-word or rarely a two-word specific epithet or trivial name (*nomen triviale*), e.g. *pumila*, thus creating a deliberate binomial (two-word specific name), e.g. *Iris pumila*. For diagnostic purposes, in order to distinguish this species from its allies, he used the diagnostic phrase, thus retaining polynomials (several-word specific names) or phrase-names, e.g. *Iris corollis barbatis, caule foliis breviore unifloro*. Such a polynomial determined the application of the binomial, hence its importance in the typification of Linnaean names (cf. Stearn, 1957: 125).

Linnaeus used binomial names for a limited number of plants in his *Öländska och Gothländska Resa* (1745), *Gemmae Arborum* (1749), *Pan Suecicus* (1749), *Splachnum* (1750), and *Plantae esculentae Patriae* (1752) and for a limited number of animals in *Hospita Insectorum Flora* (1752) and *Museum Tessinianum* (1753) before applying it to the whole vegetable kingdom in his *Species Plantarum* (1753) and to the whole animate world in his *Systema Naturae* (10th ed., 1758–59). The object of the *Species Plantarum* was not to introduce binomial nomenclature; it was to provide a concise usable survey of all known plants with brief diagnoses, references to earlier literature, and statements of geographical range. He had such a work in mind in 1733 and then made a preliminary draft, but did not begin intensive labour on this until 1746. His manuscript draft of 1746–8, now in the possession of the Linnean Society of London, reveals that he had not then adopted specific epithets (*nomina trivialia*) for the whole vegetable kingdom, although he had already used them for Swedish plants in the index to his *Öländska och Gothländska Resa* (1745). Presumably he began to add specific epithets to the manuscript of the *Species Plantarum* when he resumed work on it in June 1751; he finished it in June 1752, thus in twelve months dealing with the characters and synonymy of some 5,900 species.

Working with such intensity against time, Linnaeus could not give much attention to the choice of specific epithets, then for him relatively unimportant, and presumably he adopted whatever came quickly to mind, which might be a descriptive word such as *procumbens*, suggested by his diagnostic phrase *ramis procumbentibus*, a geographical epithet such as *lapponica*, suggested by the statement 'Habitat in Alpibus Lapponiae', a habitat epithet such as *sepium*, from 'Habitat in Europae sepibus', an old generic name such as *Rapunculus*, extracted from the synonymy, a vernacular name such as *Phu*, or a commemorative epithet such as *Osbeckii*, referring to a previous author or the discoverer. Epithets indicating a resemblance to a species of another genus were mostly prompted by the synonymy; thus Clusius's *Convolvulus Altheae folio* became in 1753 Linnaeus's *Convolvulus althaeoides*; Plukenet's *Jacea peregrina napifolia* became Linnaeus's *Centaurea napifolia*, and so on. Linnaeus objected strongly to two-word names for genera but adopted some such pharmaceutical or discarded generic names as specific epithets, as in *Thlaspi Bursa pastoris*, *Impatiens noli tangere*, *Strychnos Nux vomica* (cf. Hylander, 1954).

Linnaeus's epithets for animals are mostly of the same kind, with those for insects often referring to their host plants, e.g. *Populi*, *Ulmi*, *Abietis*, sometimes commemorating persons, e.g. *Kalmii*, *Loeflingianus*, *Rolandri*, sometimes descriptive, e.g. *bicolor* (two-coloured), *caeruleus* (blue), *melanocephalus* (black-headed), sometimes geographical, e.g. *algiricus* (Algerian), *capensis* (of the Cape of Good Hope), *pensylvanicus* (Pennsylvanian), sometimes ecological, e.g. *campestris* (of plains), *littoralis* (of shores), *pelagicus* (marine). In dealing with the genus *Papilio* (Lepidoptera), as pointed out by Heller (1945) and Langer (1959), he adopted a different procedure, which in the first place was to honour the butterflies with names which nearly all recall persons of classical mythology, and in the second place, to distribute these names in certain categories, in such a way that the trivial name should immediately suggest one of the several natural groups into which he chose to divide this unwieldy genus (cf. Heller, 1945). Thus his group *Equites Trojani* includes species of *Papilio* with the epithets *Priamus*, *Hector*, *Paris*, *Helenus*, *Troilus*, *Anchises*, *Aeneas*, etc.; his *Equites Achivi* include *Helena*, *Menelaus*, *Ulysses*, *Agamemnon*, *Patroclus*, *Ajax*, *Nestor*, *Telemachus*, *Achilles*, etc.; his *Heliconii* include *Apollo*, *Mnemosyne*, *Terpsichore*, *Calliope*, *Clio*, etc. Some of these refer to very obscure figures indeed. A number came from his general reading of Virgil and Ovid; other sources, according to a very scholarly investigation by Heller (1945), include the *Fabulae* of Hyginus (available to him in 1681 and 1742 editions), the *Syntagmata* of Giraldi (available in 1548, 1696, and other editions), the *Historia naturalis* of Pliny (available in many editions), and the *Gründliches mythologisches Lexikon* of Hedrich (1724). Comparison of these with Linnaeus's work provides, Heller regretfully concludes, 'ample evidence of his carelessness ... working here, as always, in great haste'.

Whenever possible Linnaeus chose epithets which preserved an association with earlier literature. Thus when he placed the lion, the tiger, the leopard, the jaguar, the ocelot, the cat and the lynx in the one genus, *Felis*, he adopted their customary names as epithets, *Leo*, *Tigris*, *Pardus*, *Orca*, *Pardalis*, *Catus* and *Lynx*, these being nouns in apposition.

The term *protologue* (introduced by A. J. Wilmott in *J. Bot.* (*London*) 77: 206; 1939) covers 'the printed matter accompanying the first publication of a name', 'everything associated with a name at its first publication, i.e. diagnosis, description, illustrations, references, synonymy, geographical data, citation of specimens, discussion and comments' (cf. Stearn, 1957: 126). To check the application of a Linnaean name, all the elements in the protologue should be studied. The following protologue [with roman numerals added for reference] from the *Species Plantarum* 2: 860 (1753) exemplifies them:

[iii] *tenuifolia*. 2: BACCHARIS [i] foliis ovato-lanceolatis serratis, caule suffruticoso [ii] *Hort. Cliff.* 404*. [iv]

Conyza africana tenuifolia subfrutescens, flore aureo. *Dill elth.* 104, *t.* 88. *f.* 103. [v]
Habitat in Africa. [vi], ♃ [vii].

This account has several parts: [i] the generic name *Baccharis* to be associated with the generic description in the *Genera Plantarum*, 5th ed., 370 (1753); [ii] the diagnosis or nomen specificum legitimum setting out the leaf character distinguishing this from the five other species placed by Linnaeus in *Baccharis*; [iii] the specific epithet or *nomen triviale*, put in the margin, this with the generic name making the binomial specific name *Baccharis tenuifolia*; [iv] reference to earlier publication of the diagnosis in the *Hortus Cliffortianus* (1738) where, as the asterisk indicates, a more detailed account will be found; [v] reference to a synonym used in Dillenius's *Hortus Elthamensis* (1732), including an illustration (plate 88, fig. 103); [vi] statement of range; [vii] sign indicating perennial habit.

This protologue refers to a species already known although not previously given a binomial. The following exemplifies Linnaeus's treatment of a new species brought from China:

hirsuta [iii]. 11: CONYZA [i] foliis ovalibus integerrimis scabris subtus hirsutis. [ii]
Habitat in China. [vi]
Caulis *subvillosus*. Folia *oblonga s. ovalia, integerrima, scabra, subtus valde hirsuta pallida.* Flores Flores *in racemis conferti.* Calyces *Asteris.* [viii].

Here there are [i] the generic name, [ii] the diagnosis, [iii] the specific epithet, [vi] the geographical statement, as above, but also [viii] a short description based on the specimen seen by Linnaeus and now in the Linnaean Herbarium (sheet 993.26).

Since Linnaeus's protologues were deliberately as economical of space as possible, written in a kind of telegram style, they often fail to provide information needed for modern purposes. Hence, whenever possible, the original or authentic Linnaean material should be consulted. This is scattered through a number of institutions.

Linnaeus presented the herbarium specimens collected on his celebrated Lapland journey and used when writing his *Flora Lapponica* (1737) to his Amsterdam friend Johannes Burman. These are now at the Institut de France, Paris (cf. Fries, 1861; Stearn, 1957:115).

The specimens used when writing his *Hortus Cliffortianus* (1738) which belonged to George Clifford (1685-1760) are now in the British Museum (Natural History), London (cf. Stearn, 1957; 46, 118; Heller, 1968; Stearn, 1970a).

The herbarium and drawings of Paul Hermann (1646-95), used by Linnaeus when writing his *Flora Zeylanica* (1747), are now in the British Museum (Natural History), London (cf. Stearn, 1957:119; Trimen, 1887).

At Uppsala he often consulted the herbarium of Joachim Burser (1583-1639), which exemplifies the entries in Caspar Bauhin's *Pinax* (1623). It is now in the Botanical Museum, Uppsala (cf. Juel, 1936; Stearn, 1957:116). Duplicates of specimens collected by Hasselqvist and by Kalm are also in Uppsala (cf. Juel, 1918, 1921).

During his professorship Linnaeus gave herbarium specimens to his son, his students and his friends. Many of these, about 2,000 in all, are now assembled in the Natural History Museum, Stockholm (cf. Lindman, 1908-10; Stearn, 1957: 113; Lundevall, 1969).

Linnaeus's main collections were sold by his widow in 1784 to James E. Smith and were purchased from the latter's widow in 1829 by the Linnean Society of London, in whose keeping they have remained. They include Linnaeus's botanical and zoological library, with manuscripts, correspondence and annotated copies, his herbarium, his dried fishes (cf. Gunther, 1899), insects (cf. Jackson, 1913) and shells (cf. Dance, 1967; Kennard & Woodward, 1920; Kohn, 1963). Accounts of the herbarium have been published by Jackson (1912, 1923), Savage (1945), and Stearn (1957:105; 1961 a). Smith had, however, himself sold by auction in 1796 Linnaeus's collection of minerals.

Many authentic Linnaean specimens of birds, reptiles, batrachians and fishes are in the Zoological Museum, Uppsala (cf. Holm, 1957; Lönnberg, 1896). There are also Linnaean specimens of snakes in the Natural History Museum, Stockholm (cf. Anderson, 1899).

A catalogue of the fishes in the keeping of the Linnean Society of London was published by Gunther in 1899, of the Amphibia, Insecta and Testacea by Jackson in 1913.

SOME SOURCES OF FURTHER INFORMATION

ANDERSON, L. A. 1899. Catalogue of Linnean type-specimens of snakes in the Royal Museum in Stockholm. *Bihang till K. Svenska Vet.-Akad. Handl.* 24 Afd. iv. n.6.

AURIVILLIUS, P. O. C. 1884. Revisio critica Lepidopterorum Musei Ludovicae Ulricae quae descripsit Carolus a Linné. *K. Svenska Vet.-Akad. Handl.* 19 n.5.

BATHER, F. A. 1927. Biological classification, past and future. *Quart. J. Geol. Soc. London* 83: Proc. lxii–civ.

BERG, A. & UGGLA, A. Hj. 1951. Herbationes Upsalienses; protokoll över Linnés exkursioneri Uppsalatrakten, 1747. *Svenska Linné-Sällskap. Årsskr.* 33–34 (1950–51): 95–162.

BREMEKAMP, C. E. B. 1962. The various aspects of biology. *Verhandl. Koninkl. Nederl. Akad. Wet. Natuurk.* II. 54 no. 2.

BRYK, F. 1924. *Linné als praktischer Entomolog.* Stockholm.

CAIN, A. J. 1958. Logic and memory in Linnaeus's system of taxonomy. *Proc. Linnean Soc. London* 169: 144–163.

—— 1963. The natural classification. *Proc. Linnean Soc. London* 174:115–121.

DANCE, S. P. 1967. Report on the Linnaean shell collection. *Proc. Linnean Soc. London* 178:1–24, tt. 1–10.

DRAKE of Hagelrum, C. 1939. *Linnés Disputationer.* Nässjö.

Du RIETZ, G. E. 1957. Linné som myrforskare. *Uppsala Univ. Årsskr.* 1957 n.5.

FRIES, Th. M. 1861. Anteckningar rörande en i Paris befintlig Linneanska herbarium. *Öfversigt Kongl. Vet.-Akad. Förh.* 18:255–272.

GUNTHER, A. C. L. G. 1899. President's Anniversary address [Fishes from Linné's private collection]. *Proc. Linnean Soc. London, Sess.* III (1898–99): 15–38.

HELLER, J. L. 1945. Classical mythology in the *Systema Naturae* of Linnaeus. *Trans. Amer. Philol. Assoc.* 76:333–.

—— 1962. 'List loqu.' and 'List mut.', two puzzling Linnaean abbreviations. *Proc. Linnean Soc. London* 173:61–64.

—— 1964. The early history of binomial nomenclature. *Huntia* 1:33–70.

—— 1968. Linnaeus's *Hortus Cliffortianus. Taxon* 17:663–719.

HOFSTEN, N. von 1958. Linnaeus's conception of Nature. *Kungl. Veten.-Soc. Uppsala, Årsbok* 1957: 65–105.

—— 1960. Linnés djursystem [Linnaeus's classification of animals]. *Svenska Linné-Sällskap. Årsskr.* 42 (1959): 9–49.

—— 1963. A system of 'double entries' in the zoological classification of Linnaeus. *Zool. Bidrag från Uppsala* 35:603–631.

HOLM, A. 1957. Specimina Linnaeana i Uppsala bevarade zoologiska samlingar från Linnés tid. *Uppsala Univ. Årsskr.* 1957 n.6.

HOPWOOD, A. T. 1950. Animal classification from Linnaeus to Darwin. *Linnean Soc. London, Lect. Developm. Taxon.* 46–59.

HYLANDER, N. 1954. Apans stege och Pyrrhas hår. *Svenska Bot. Tidskr.* 48:521–549.

ISOVIITA, P. 1970. Dillenius's *Historia Muscorum* as the basis of Hepatic nomenclature. *Acta Bot. Fennica* 89.

JACKSON, B.D. 1912. Index to the Linnean Herbarium. *Proc. Linnean Soc. London,* Sess. 124 (1911–12), Suppl.

—— 1913. Catalogue of the Linnean specimens of Amphibia, Insecta, and Testacea, noted by Carl von Linné. *Proc. Linnean Soc. London,* Sess. 125 (1912–13), Suppl.

—— 1922. Notes on a catalogue of the Linnean Herbarium. *Proc. Linnean Soc. London,* Sess. 134 (1921–22), Suppl.

JUEL, H. O. 1921. A revision of Kalm's herbarium in Uppsala. *Svenska Linné-Sällskap. Årsskr.* 4:16–23.

—— 1936. Joachim Burser's Hortus siccus. *Symbolae Bot. Upsal.* 2 no.1.

KENNARD, A. S. & WOODWARD, B. B. 1920. On the Linnean species of non-marine Mollusca. *J. Linnean Soc. London, Zool.* 34:203–215.

KOHN, A. J. 1963. Type specimens and identity of the described species of Conus. The species described by Linnaeus, 1758–1767. *J. Linnean Soc. London, Zool.* 44:740–768.

LANGER, T. W. 1959. De linnéánske sommerfuglenamne of 1758 [The Linnaean names of butterflies of 1758]. *Svenska Linné-Sällskap. Årsskr.* 41 (1958): 50–60.

LINDMAN, C. A. M. 1908–10. A Linnaean Herbarium in the Natural History Museum in Stockholm. *Arkiv for Bot.* 7 no. 3 (1908), 9 no. 6 (1910).

LINDROTH, S. 1966. Two centuries of Linnean studies. T. R. Buckman (Ed.), *Bibliography & Natural History (Univ. Kansas Publ., Library Ser. 27)* 27–45.

—— 1967. Linné, legend och verklighet. *Lychnos* 1965–66: 57–122 (with English summary. The two faces of Linnaeus on pp. 118–122).

LÖNNBERG, L. G. 1896. Linnean type-specimens of birds, reptiles, batrachians and fishes in the zoological Museum of the R. University in Uppsala. *Bihang till K. Svenska Vet.-Akad. Handl.* 22. Afd. iv. n.1.

LOVEN, S. 1888. On the species of Echinoidea described by Linnaeus in his work: *Museum Ludovicae Ulricae. Bihang till K. Svenska Vet.-Akad. Handl.* 13. Afd. iv. n.5.

LUNDEVALL, C. F. 1969. Carl von Linnés Växtsamling. *Fauna och Flora (Stockholm)* 1969:291–295.

McATEE, W. L. 1957. The American birds of Linnaeus. *J. Soc. Bibl. Nat. Hist.* 3:291–306.

SAVAGE, S. 1945. *A Catalogue of the Linnaean Herbarium.* London (Linnean Soc. of London).

STAFLEU, F. A. 1969. A historical survey of systematic biology. *Systematic Biology (Proc. Int. Conf., Nat. Acad. Sci. Washington, DC)* 16–44.

STAUFFER, R. C. 1960. Ecology in the long manuscript

version of Darwin's *Origin of Species* and Linnaeus' *Oeconomy of Nature*. *Proc. Amer. Philos. Soc.* 104:235–241.

STEARN, W. T. 1955. Linnaeus and the language of botany. *Proc. Linnean Soc. London* 165:158–164.

—— 1957. *An Introduction to the 'Species Plantarum' and cognate botanical Works of Carl Linnaeus*. Prefixed to C. Linnaeus *Species Plantarum*, 1753, Ray Society facsimile, vol. 1.

—— 1958 a. Carl Linnaeus, classifier and namer of living things. *New Scientist* 4:401–403.

—— 1958 b. Botanical exploration to the time of Linnaeus. *Proc. Linnean Soc. London* 169:173–196.

—— 1959 a. (with J. L. Heller) *An Appendix to the 'Species Plantarum' of Carl Linnaeus*. Appended to C. Linnaeus, *Species Plantarum*, 1753, Ray Society facsimile, vol. 2.

—— 1959 b. Museums and the eighteenth century: Natural History. *Museums J.* 59:44–48.

—— 1959 c. The background of Linnaeus's contributions to the methods and nomenclature of systematic biology. *Systematic Zoology* 8:4–22.

—— 1960. *Notes on Linnaeus's 'Genera Plantarum'.* Prefixed to C. Linnaeus, *Genera Plantarum*, 1754, Historiae Naturalis Classica facsimile.

—— 1960. *Notes on Linnaeus's 'Genera Plantarum'.* Prefixed to Herbarium. *Taxon* 10:16–19.

—— 1961 b. *Notes on Linnaeus's 'Mantissa Plantarum'.* pp.

v–xxiv. Prefixed to C. Linnaeus, *Mantissa Plantarum*, 1767–71, Historiae Naturalis Classica facsimile.

—— 1961 c. Linnaeus, Carl (1707–78). Peter Gray (Ed.), *Encyclopedia of the Biological Sciences*, 568–570.

—— 1961 d. Botanical gardens and botanical literature in the eighteenth century. *Catalogue of Botanical Books in the Collection of Rachel McMasters Miller Hunt* 2:xlii–cxi.

—— 1962. The origin of the male and female symbols of biology. *Taxon* 11:109–113.

—— 1963. The influence of Leiden on botany in the seventeenth and eighteenth centuries. *Brit. J. Hist. Sci.* 1:137–158.

—— 1966. *Botanical Latin*. London (Nelson); New York (Hafner Publishing Co.).

—— 1970a. The enigmatic *Cyclamen indicum* of Linnaeus. *Israel J. Bot.* 19:266–270.

—— 1970b. Boerhaave as a botanist. G. A. Lindeboom (Ed.) *Boerhaave and his Time*, 114–122.

SVENSON, H. K. 1945. On the descriptive method of Linnaeus. *Rhodora* 47:273–302, 363–388.

TRIMEN, H. 1887. Hermann's Ceylon herbarium and Linnaeus's *Flora Zeylanica. J. Linnean Soc. London, Bot.* 24:129–155.

VERITY, R. 1913. Revision of the Linnean types of Palaearctic Rhopalocera. *J. Linnean Soc. London, Zool.* 32:173–191.

WASTENSON, A. 1927. Linné als Biochronolog. *Svenska Linné-Sällskap. Årsskr.* 10:150–153.

THE PRINCIPAL WORKS OF LINNAEUS PUBLISHED IN HIS LIFETIME

First editions only are listed except for certain works of special nomenclatural importance.

Systema Naturae [System of Nature], Leyden 1735 (facsimile, Stockholm 1960); 10th ed., Stockholm 1758–9 (facsimile, Vol. 1, London 1956; Vol. 2, Weinheim 1964); 12th ed., Stockholm 1766–8.

Bibliotheca Botanica [The Botanical Library], Amsterdam 1736.

Fundamenta Botanica [Foundations of Botany], Amsterdam 1736.

Musa Cliffortiana [Clifford's Banana], Leyden 1736 (facsimile, Lehre 1967).

Critica Botanica [Rules for Botanical Naming], Leyden 1737.

Flora Lapponica [Lapland Flora], Amsterdam 1737.

Genera Plantarum [Genera of Plants], Leyden 1737; 5th ed., Stockholm 1754 (facsimile, Weinheim 1960); 6th ed., Stockholm 1964.

Hortus Cliffortianus [Clifford's Garden], Amsterdam 1738 (dated '1737') (facsimile, Lehre 1968).

Viridiarum Cliffortianum [Clifford's Pleasure-garden], Amsterdam 1737.

Classes Plantarum seu Systemata Plantarum omnia a Fructificatione desumpta [The Classes of Plants or Systems of Plants all taken from the Fructification], Leyden 1738.

Flora Suecica [Swedish Flora], Stockholm 1745; 2nd ed., Stockholm 1755.

Öländska och Gothländska Resa [Öland and Gotland Journey], Stockholm and Uppsala 1745 (facsimile, Malmö 1957).

Fauna Suecica [Swedish Fauna], Stockholm 1746; 2nd ed., Stockholm 1761.

Wästgöta-resa [Wästergötland Journey], Stockholm 1747.

Flora Zeylanica [Ceylon Flora], Stockholm 1747.

Hortus Upsaliensis [The Uppsala Garden], Stockholm 1748.

Materia Medica, Liber I [Materia Medica, Book 1], Stockholm 1749.

Amoenitates Academicae [Academic Delights], Vols I–VII, Stockholm and Leipzig, 1749–69.

Specimen academicum de Oeconomia Naturae submittit I. J. Biberg [Academic Essay concerning the Economy of Nature submitted by I. J. Biberg], Uppsala 1749.

Philosophia botanica [Botanical Philosophy], Stockholm 1751 (facsimile, Lehre 1966).

Skånska Resa [Skåne Journey], Stockholm 1751.

Species Plantarum [Species of Plants], Stockholm 1753 (facsimiles, Berlin 1907, Tokyo 1934, London 1957–60); 2nd ed., Stockholm 1762–3.

Museum Tessinianum [Tessin's Museum], Stockholm 1753.

Museum S:ae R:ae M:tis Adolphi Friderici [Museum of His Royal Majesty Adolf Frederic], Stockholm 1754.

Museum S:ae R:ae M:tis Ludovicae Ulricae Reginae [Museum of Her Royal Majesty Queen Lovisa Ulrika], Stockholm 1764.

Mantissa Plantarum [Supplement of Plants], Stockholm 1767 (facsimile, Weinheim 1961).

Mantissa Plantarum altera [Second Supplement of Plants], Stockholm 1771 (facsimile, Weinheim 1961).

Systema Vegetabilium [System of the Vegetable Kingdom], Göttingen & Gotha 1774.

PICTURE ACKNOWLEDGMENTS

COLOUR

Frontispiece reverse: Linnaea borealis: herbarium specimen collected by Linnaeus. Reproduced by permission of the Council of the Linnean Society, London.

Frontispiece: Linnaeus, engraved by J. Meyer after Hofmann and Bartolozzi, from the Temple of Flora, by R. J. Thornton. Reproduced by permission of the Council of the Linnean Society, London.

Page 19: reproduced by courtesy of the Muséum National d'Histoire Naturelle, Paris.

Page 20: from Uppsala Museum.

Page 45: reproduced by courtesy of the Trustees, the National Gallery, London.

Pages 46–7: from Uppsala University.

Page 81: reproduced by permission of the Council of the Linnean Society, London.

Pages 82–3: reproduced by courtesy of the Trustees of the British Museum (Natural History).

Page 84: reproduced by permission of the Council of the Linnean Society, London.

Page 109: from the Victoria and Albert Museum.

Page 110: from the Victoria and Albert Museum.

Page 127: from Hammarby.

Page 127 below: from the Orangery, Uppsala.

Page 128: from the Ashmolean Museum, Oxford.

Page 137: reproduced by permission of the Council of the Linnean Society, London.

Pages 138 and 139: from Hammarby.

Page 181: reproduced by permission of the Council of the Linnean Society, London.

Page 182: reproduced by permission of the Council of the Linnean Society, London.

Page 199: reproduced by permission of the Council of the Linnean Society, London.

Page 200: reproduced by permission of the Council of the Linnean Society, London.

Page 209: from the Victoria and Albert Museum.

Pages 210–11: reproduced by courtesy of the Trustees of the British Museum (Natural History).

Page 212: reproduced by courtesy of the Muséum National d'Histoire Naturelle, Paris.

Page 239: from Uppsala.

All the colour photographs except those on pages 19, 48, 128 and 212 were taken by Gordon Roberton of A. C. Cooper.

The picture on the jacket is reproduced by courtesy of Lord Faringdon.

MONOCHROME

Page 28: photographed by Bertil Gullander.

Page 33: reproduced by courtesy of the Zoological Museum, Amsterdam.

Page 34 top: from the Hunt Botanical Library Collection, Carnegie-Mellon University, Pa.

Pages 36, 37: from the Tekniska Museet, Stockholm.

Page 50: from the Victoria and Albert Museum, photographed by Gordon Roberton.

Page 51: property of the author, photographed by Gordon Roberton.

Page 69: from the Victoria and Albert Museum, photographed by Gordon Roberton.

Page 77: from the Victoria and Albert Museum, photographed by Gordon Roberton.

Page 78: from the National Museum of Finland, Helsinki.

Page 91: photograph from Bavaria-Verlag.

Page 93: reproduced by courtesy of the Trustees of the Pierpoint Morgan Library.

Page 96: supplied by Uniboek from Gem. Archiefdienst, Amsterdam.

Page 97 left: reproduced by courtesy of the Trustees of the British Museum (Natural History), photographed by Gordon Roberton.

Page 97 right: from the Hunt Botanical Library Collection, Carnegie-Mellon University, Pa.

Page 98: reproduced from the S.L.Å.

Page 99: from the Mauritshuis, photographed by A. Dingjan.

INDEX

Page numbers in italics refer to illustrations